QUEER THEOLOGIES

Queer Theologies: The Basics is a concise and illuminating introduction to the study of this controversial and discursive subject area. As an updated Second Edition, this popular book provides an accessible exploration into the major themes within queer studies, queer and trans theologies, and themes of gender and sexuality in Christianity. Topics covered include:

- The development of queer theologies;
- Queering 'traditional' theology;
- Queer theologies in global contexts;
- Queer Bible;
- Queer theologies from queer lives; and
- Trans theologies (new for the Second Edition).

With a glossary of key terms and suggestions for further reading throughout, this book is an ideal starting point for anyone seeking a full introduction to Christian queer theologies as well as broader themes in theology, gender, and sexuality.

Chris Greenough is Professor of Social Sciences at Edge Hill University, UK.

THE BASICS

THE QUR'AN (SECOND EDITION)
MASSIMO CAMPANINI

RELIGION IN AMERICA
MICHAEL PASQUIER

MORMONISM
DAVID J. HOWLETT AND JOHN-CHARLES DUFFY

RELIGION AND SCIENCE (SECOND EDITION)
PHILIP CLAYTON

THE BIBLE (SECOND EDITION)
JOHN BARTON

CHRISTIAN ETHICS
ROBIN GILL

BAHA'I FAITH
CHRISTOPHER BUCK

THOMAS AQUINAS
FRANKLIN T. HARKINS

BIBLE AND FILM
MATTHEW S. RINDGE

RELIGION AND FILM
JEANETTE REEDY SOLANO

SECULARISM
JACQUES BERLINERBLAU

NEW RELIGIOUS MOVEMENTS
JOSEPH LAYCOCK

FILM MUSIC
KENNETH LAMPL

JEWISH ETHICS
GEOFFREY D. CLAUSSEN

QUAKERISM (SECOND EDITION)
MARGERY POST ABBOTT AND CARL ABBOTT

SIKHISM
NIKKY-GUNINDER KAUR SINGH AND ELEANOR NESBITT

ORTHODOX CHRISTIANITY
NICHOLAS E. DENYSENKO

FEMINIST THEOLOGIES
SUSAN M. SHAW AND GRACE JI-SUN KIM

QUEER THEOLOGIES (SECOND EDITION)
CHRIS GREENOUGH

For more information about this series, please visit: www.routledge.com/The-Basics/book-series/B

QUEER THEOLOGIES

THE BASICS

SECOND EDITION

CHRIS GREENOUGH

LONDON AND NEW YORK

Designed cover image: Getty Images

Second edition published 2027
by Routledge
4 Park Square, Milton Park, Abingdon, Oxon, OX14 4RN

and by Routledge
605 Third Avenue, New York, NY 10158

Routledge is an imprint of the Taylor & Francis Group, an informa business

First edition published by Routledge 2019

British Library Cataloguing-in-Publication Data
A catalogue record for this book is available from the British Library

Library of Congress Cataloging-in-Publication Data
Names: Greenough, Chris, 1979– author
Title: Queer theologies: the basics / Chris Greenough.
Description: Second edition. | Abingdon, Oxon; New York, NY: Routledge, 2026. |
Includes bibliographical references and index.
Identifiers: LCCN 2026008960 (print) | LCCN 2026008961 (ebook) |
ISBN 9781032563343 hardback | ISBN 9781032563350 paperback | ISBN 9781003434993 ebook
Subjects: LCSH: Gender identity–Religious aspects–Christianity | Queer theory |
Sex role–Religious aspects–Christianity
Classification: LCC BT708 .G69 2026 (print) | LCC BT708 (ebook)
LC record available at https://lccn.loc.gov/2026008960
LC ebook record available at https://lccn.loc.gov/2026008961

ISBN: 9781032563343 (hbk)
ISBN: 9781032563350 (pbk)
ISBN: 9781003434993 (ebk)

DOI: 10.4324/9781003434993

Typeset in Bembo
by Newgen Publishing UK

To Mark Edward, forever fabulous.

CONTENTS

Acknowledgements ix

Introduction 1

1 **The development of queer theologies** 11

2 **Queering 'traditional' theology** 38

3 **Queer theologies in global contexts** 67

4 **Queer Bible** 101

5 **Queer theologies from queer lives** 135

6 **Trans theologies** 160

Afterword: Beyond the basics 191
Glossary 194
Biblical references index 203
Author index 205

ACKNOWLEDGEMENTS

I am grateful to Rebecca Clintworth and Katie Beaumont at Routledge, for commissioning and working with me on this Second Edition.

I want to give some special mentions of gratitude.

To Deryn Guest for her faith, support, critical eye, and offering such a priceless supportive space to me over the years. I am very grateful for Deryn's review of the first manuscript and her feedback on sections in this updated edition. Any mistakes are entirely my own, of course.

To Barbara Thiede, for her voice messages of love, support, encouragement, and wisdom.

To Caroline Blyth, for our chats and for being the most marvellous co-editor on *T&T Clark Handbook of Sexualities in the Bible and Its Reception*.

To Yoshiko Usui, who worked diligently on the translation of the First Edition into Japanese. I enjoyed our dialogue where points of clarification on the original were made. This has helped refine some areas in this Second Edition.

I thank my supportive and caring family. There are a number of friends who I thank for checking in: Cathy Butterworth, Nikki Craske, and Helen Thomas. My colleagues' valued support is beyond words, especially:

At Edge Hill: Vicky Bosward, Seán Henry, and Allison Moore for their friendship and encouragement.

Across the globe: Emily Colgan, Joseph Goh, Johnathan Jodamus, Mmapula Kebaneilwe, Sarojini Nadar, Ralf Thiede, and David Tombs.

In the UK: Hannah Bacon, Alberto Fernández-Carbajal, Lisa Isherwood, Sarah-Jane Page, and Johanna Stiebert.

I would like to recognise my LGBTQ+ Christian friends and contacts who read and gave feedback on a number of chapters in this book.

Thanks to Mr Rajaganeshan for your care. And to Hylda, who often perched her Shih Tzu head on my laptop or leg as I wrote and forced me outside on our walks.

Final thanks go to my fabulous partner, Mark Edward, who makes me laugh daily and shares his wisdom.

INTRODUCTION

INTRODUCTION

This is a book that would have been banned in many historical contexts, and in some contemporary contexts, it would still be banned or deemed heretical. It is a text that some may hide and read only in secret, with the cover and title disguised. Alternatively, readers may be LGBTQ+ activists in digital or public spaces, perhaps taking part in Pride events or challenging hateful preaching from conservative Christians. As LGBTQ+ Christians or allies, readers may pray with and affirm others or organise community gatherings where faith and sexuality can be brought together. It may appeal to people returning to a church for the first time after years of exclusion. While the church building may be familiar, they might find themselves surrounded by an unfamiliar congregation or feel the weight of eyes that recognise and judge them. Some may be unable to return, or decide not to, knowing that some churches remain closed to them. As well as churches, the relationship with scripture is similarly complicated: verses memorised in childhood now sit alongside doctrines that discriminate. The search for affirming interpretations is deeply personal.

Queer theologies refuse to separate faith from flesh. As will become clear throughout the chapters of this volume, queer

DOI: 10.4324/9781003434993-1

theologies are not only about the inclusion of LGBTQ+ people who find themselves positioned as guests at a table, as long as they are quiet and well-behaved. Queer theologies notice that the table itself is unstable, and what is considered 'tradition' is held together by stories rather than certainties. Queer lives have their own stories to offer. If readers are looking for a theology that behaves itself, queer theologies are not it!

For all readers, including clergy, lay people, students, scholars, people of faith, or none, this book offers a deeper insight into how queer people construct faith, and how faith is queer. It begins from the recognition that queer theologies are lived realities as well as academic conversations. They are not abstract 'issues' to be debated on media platforms, but embodied and real experiences, often sites of personal and spiritual struggle, yet also stories of flourishing. Queer theologies hold stories of exclusion and inclusion, silence and speech. Above all, queer theologies speak to how faith persists in marginalised people's lives, offering possibilities for transformation within Christianity itself.

OVERVIEW OF THE BOOK

The focus of this book is Christian queer theologies, an area which has garnered much attention in the field of theology and religious studies. Queer theory has become a growing area of critical studies within the academy. Universities are offering courses on gender, sexuality, and queer studies. Such courses may be taught by queer-identifying individuals, while some may not. Queer theory has been applied across academic subjects, such as the arts, humanities, and social sciences. One of my aims with this book is to introduce readers in an accessible way to the authors, themes, histories, movements, and texts which have shaped queer theologies.

This book is an introductory text, aimed at non-specialists or those coming to the area for the first time. Each chapter is designed to stand alone, and this allows immediate access to different themes in order to suit the interests of a wide range of readers. In this book, I have attempted to give some organisation and structure in the form of chapters and sections, yet structure and order are both unqueer. Where themes and structures overlap, I have assigned them to the most suitable chapter and heading for discussion. Additionally, a glossary provides working definitions for a number of terms used in the text.

In Chapter 1, I offer an overview of the development of queer theologies. Chapter 2 looks at the development of queer theologies specifically, and their relationship with tradition and authority. Chapter 3 details queer theologies in global contexts. The Bible has also been used to attempt to justify religious positions which are against the inclusion of non-normative gender and sexuality. Accordingly, Chapter 4 looks more closely at the so-called 'clobber texts' in the Bible and details strategies of re-reading and resistance. Chapter 5 examines the lived experiences of queer people of faith. Finally, Chapter 6 examines trans theologies specifically, and their relationship as siblings to queer theologies, given they share characteristics but remain distinct.

Of course, all of the ideas contained in this book are not mine! Therefore, I engage with scholarship and ideas from others, so there are a number of academic references throughout. This assessment and appraisal of a vast range of scholarship is what makes this book unique. It provides expertise that underpins this overview of queer theologies that cannot be generated by artificial intelligence or internet search engines! Some of these references are from sources located in historical contexts and may use language that reflects the cultural understandings of gender and sexuality at the time. These sources are used to reflect the development of thinking around gender and sexuality, or because the concepts are still relevant today.

It is important to emphasise that this is a 'basics' book. Condensing the field of queer theologies into a beginner's guide is no easy task. This is particularly difficult as a number of texts within queer theory and queer theologies are known for being very challenging in terms of the academic language used. In the hope that the reader will share the same passions and motivations for such an exciting field of study, my intention is to ensure that the language used throughout this text is purposefully accessible. Due to this fact, I am aware of concerns that this pursuit of accessibility means the depth of material has been compromised in some way. To address this concern, at the end of each chapter, I provide a brief list of suggested further reading and resources. A comprehensive reference list for each chapter also directs readers to further study. That said, much of the scholarship engaged in this book is produced within academic publishing systems that rely on costly books and subscription-based journals, which are not equally accessible to all readers. Where readers are able to access these resources, through libraries, rights, or other means, I strongly encourage further exploration. Where this is not possible, this book aims to provide a meaningful point of engagement in its own right.

UPDATES TO THE SECOND EDITION

The First Edition has been met with positive appraisal. I have received emails and messages from LGBTQ+ Christians across the globe, thanking me for the work. The book has been translated into Japanese. These responses have been humbling, yet they also serve as fuel to continue such important research. In this Second Edition, I have refocussed and expanded the content relating to trans theologies specifically, as a necessary development that sits alongside queer, feminist, liberation, and contextual theologies. Trans theologies' relationship with queer theologies is one I describe as 'siblings' rather than 'twins'. The first major update is that I have included a brand-new chapter that engages specifically with trans theologies, their relationship with queer theologies, and how trans readings both correct theology as well as construct theology. This, in turn, helps to hold all theology to account. I considered the placement of this chapter carefully. I did not want it to seem an afterthought, or an add-on; however, the existing structure leads coherently into this discussion. It is therefore Chapter 6 of the new edition. Its conclusions demonstrate how trans approaches can unqueer queer approaches! Second, in Chapter 3, I include a short section on contextual queer theologies from Aotearoa New Zealand. And finally, I have updated a number of specific areas of the original manuscript in order to address current thinking, language, and research across all the chapters.

THE QUEER THEOLOGIAN

There is a common practice among feminist and queer writers that they will offer some detail about themselves as part of their writing. This is to provide some context about the author: their location, position, and some aspects of their identity which may be considered important to the text. Following this custom, I offer my own position as a cisgender, gay, queer scholar. Nevertheless, each of these markers of identification – 'cisgender', 'gay', 'queer' – does not accurately represent who I am. They may give some clues, but they leave additional questions. With 'gay', for example, the reader may wonder if I am celibate, married, have a partner? How does being gay coexist with writing theology? There are also aspects of my identification which I did not include, such as those relating to race, dis/ability, class, and so on. The reader may also wonder whether I am placed to write on trans theologies, given I am not trans. In response to this, I engage with scholarship from trans people directly in order to attend to and amplify their voices. As will be seen, queer is a term which does not adequately describe those who use it. It is an ambiguous word, which cannot be pinned down satisfactorily.

To give a small taster for the contents of the book, here I offer a very brief sketch of three important questions: (1) What is queer? (2) What is theology? (3) What are queer theologies? And (4) Why are they important?

WHAT IS QUEER?

One of the earlier definitions of 'queer' meant 'strange' or 'odd'. But the term was also later used in the form of homophobic, verbal abuse. This insult was later reclaimed, and was used to describe lesbian, gay, bisexual, transgender, and other individuals who identify as non-normative in terms of their gender or sexuality. 'Non-normative' does not mean 'non-normal'. 'Non-normative' is an important catch-all term used to refer to people whose self-identifications and/or sexualities do not align with traditional, dominant, and binary ideas of gender and sex. The traditional understanding of gender has, until very recently, been based on biological sex: male or female. A binary is a system of two opposites. Therefore, the dominant understanding of gender has been determined through the sex binary: either male or female. Similarly, heterosexuality has been privileged as the dominant sexuality.

Thankfully, life in the 20th and 21st centuries witnessed radical and significant shifts in human understandings of gender and sexualities. Such shifts are down to the work of gender theorists and of activists. Gender theorists saw how traditional views on binary gender (male/female) were restrictive. Important critical thinking in gender studies revealed how biological sex does not automatically determine gender, and that gender is a construct. Intersex, transgender, non-binary, gender-fluid and queer widen the scope of our understanding of sex and gender. In addition to heterosexuality, homosexuality, bisexuality, pansexuality, polysexuality, asexuality are all legitimate forms of sexual identification. See the Glossary for a definition of each of these terms.

The work of gender theorists ran parallel to the work of activists, who wanted to promote equality for all identifications of gender and sexuality. In time, the activist movement led to changes in how non-normative identities are viewed, particularly in terms of psychology. Previously, for example, to be gay was considered a psychological illness. Moreover, in large parts of the world there have been significant changes in laws which now protect the rights of individuals in relation to their gender and sexuality.

In addition to the definition of 'queer' as 'odd', and as a collective grouping for non-normative identifications of gender/sexuality, there is a third, critical, usage of the word 'queer' which emerges from its use as an academic term. In this context, 'queer' means to 'disturb' or 'disrupt'. It is this definition that was later applied to theory, and theology, as a critical lens. It calls for the uncovering and dismantling of power structures. Further discussion on this use of queer is found in Chapter 1.

WHAT IS THEOLOGY?

Theology is a word made up from two Greek compounds: *Theos* (God) and *logos* (word). Theology therefore means 'words about God' or 'speaking of God'. There are four main sources of authority in the development of theology: scripture, tradition, reason, and experience (McGrath, 2011). Christian theologians talk about God and use sources such as the Bible, the writings from early saints, Church history, and human reason. Theology also examines human experience of faith and religion, what people believe and how they practise their beliefs, as well as the relationship between religion to society and culture. As will become clear, power dynamics and monopolies over various interpretations of scripture have shaped tradition, determined which reasoning has dominated theological discourse, and prioritised certain experiences over others.

Contextual theologians examine particular communities and experiences – contexts – to shape talk about God. Contextual theologies include feminist theology, Black theology, Asian American theology, liberation theology, disability theology, and LGBTQ+ theology to name just a few representative examples.

WHAT ARE QUEER THEOLOGIES?

Queer theologies disrupt the tradition of Christianity, including the Bible, and demonstrate how it has treated some groups unfavourably. Some queer theologians have re-examined theology and the history of Christian thought, beliefs, and practices, and hold the view that it has, in some way, always been queer (e.g., Loughlin, 2007). At the same time, queer theologies have referenced non-normative gender and sexuality, and this has been one of the major concerns with theologians in the area of study. Evidently, important theologies emerging from LGBTQ+ contexts have had a major impact on its development and on individuals and communities. In this sense, queer theologies are radical as they work for change. They ask important questions, they challenge accepted ideas, and they allow new, more inclusive, theologies to emerge from queer contexts. In many respects, rather than talking about 'queer theology' in the singular, as has often been done by those in the field, it is more appropriate to talk about 'queer theologies' as a plural term. It is misleading to suggest that all queer theologians are talking about the same thing! There is no universal 'queer theology', and queer theologians are rarely neutral in the approaches they adopt.

WHY ARE QUEER THEOLOGIES IMPORTANT?

Queer theologies examine how Christianity has been constructed throughout history and ask questions about whose voices and experiences have been excluded. These efforts destabilise the structures of power in the religion. Equally, theology is tied up with power, as there are authority structures within church organisations that have developed teachings or biblical interpretations which have had enormous influence in society and culture. Queer theologies interrogate this power.

In some parts of the world, to identify publicly as LGBTQ+ is a criminal offence and can be punishable by death. In relation to sexuality, research by the International Lesbian, Gay, Bisexual, Trans, and Intersex Association (ILGA) shows that consensual same-sex sexual acts continue to be criminalised in numerous United Nations member states. Such laws impose penalties ranging from imprisonment to, in a small number of jurisdictions, the death penalty. Religion is often used as a justification to discriminate against those who identify as LGBTQ+ within these contexts. So, there is much-needed work to be done on an activist level to continue to fight against prejudice and injustice. It is also significant to note that while protection by law exists in a number of countries, this does not eradicate biphobic, homophobic, or transphobic attacks or discrimination.

Church organisations have often been thought of as hostile to non-normative individuals, and this is reflected in the positional statements from church organisations about LGBTQ+ people. It is hoped that engagement with living experiences of queer identified people will allow others to learn, to empathise, and to effect change – whether on an individual or an institutional level.

Queer theologies push boundaries. The relevance and impact of queer theologies for contemporary Christianity raise questions and disturb long-held ideas in relation to debates on homosexuality, transgender, what constitutes marriage, and ideas of 'family'. Just as the insult 'queer' was offensive, there are many individuals who have experienced hostility or rejection from their churches and turned away from faith. Queer theologies remind them of the radical love which must be central to Christianity (Cheng, 2011). Queer theologies matter on a personal and individual level.

QUEER RELIGIOUS LITERACY

There can be an unease around the term 'queer' or when engaging in discussions of gender and sexuality. The language surrounding gender or sexual identification can often be perplexing, especially as the LGBTQ+ acronym continues to grow; for example, LGBTQIAA (lesbian, gay, bisexual, transgender, queer/questioning, intersex, asexual, ally). Where there is a lack of understanding or a fear of making mistakes and upsetting others, people can shy away from important discussions and conversations. Or, where conversations do take place, they may be heated or based on misguided assumptions. This is why it is important to be 'literate' when engaging with queer studies. Queer literacy in this regard does not simply mean knowing each of the terms for gender and sexual identity, but it means having the capacity and openness to engage and learn more (Edward & Greenough, 2020).

The idea of queer literacy can be coupled with the idea of religious literacy. Adam Dinham and Matthew Francis advocate the promotion of 'religious literacy' which serves to 'move religion away from anxiety and tension, and look at it instead as something far too pervasive, far too interesting, and far too nuanced to write off as too risky to talk about' (Dinham & Francis, 2016: 3). For Dinham and Francis, religious literacy takes the heat out of controversial topics and seeks to shed more light on such issues. Religion is relevant to all aspects of society, settings, and sectors, irrespective of an individual's personal beliefs. More significantly, Dinham and Francis highlight its importance on a personal, practical level, stating how religious literacy allows for 'deeper and richer relationships between people involved – deeper understanding of each other's positions and practices of argument' (2016: 45). This is an essential element when engaging with queer theologies.

Engaging in religious literacy does not require an individual to be religious, nor does it aim to promote religion in public life. It allows people (religious or non-religious) to engage in informed conversations with openness, especially when some of the issues may appear to be controversial. Queer religious literacy tackles such issues head on, and rather than focusing on traditional theology, it recognises that there is no common fixed representation of the identities 'Christian' or 'queer'. Engaging with queer lives demonstrates how religion is significant on an individual level, rather than on an institutional level.

REFERENCES

Cheng, P. S. (2011) *Radical Love: An Introduction to Queer Theology*. New York: Seabury Books.

Dinham, A. and Francis, M. (2016) *Religious Literacy in Policy and Practice*. Bristol: Policy Press.

Edward, M. and Greenough, C. (2020) 'Queer Literacy', In Iphofen, R. (Ed.), *Handbook of Research Ethics and Scientific Integrity*, pp. 707–718. Cham: Springer.

Loughlin, G. (Ed.) (2007) *Queer Theology: Rethinking the Western Body*. London: Blackwell.

McGrath, A. E. (2011) *Christian Theology: An Introduction*. London: Wiley.

THE DEVELOPMENT OF QUEER THEOLOGIES

INTRODUCTION

This chapter traces, briefly and in broad strokes, the development of queer theologies, which chronologically followed on from modern liberation theologies and queer theory. It looks at insights from three major theological movements in the development of queer theologies: liberation theology, feminist theology, and gay and lesbian theologies. There are overlaps between each movement not only in terms of the time frames in which they were developed, but also in the fact that each movement was mobilised by activism and the pursuit of social justice. Before queer theologies came to be known as such, liberation theology and feminist theology were concerned with issues around equality, justice, and inclusion. From the late 1960s, gay and lesbian activism highlighted and responded to injustice and mistreatment from authorities towards non-heterosexual people. At a similar time, early gay and lesbian theologies began to emerge. They reflected on the liberation movement and sought to find an inclusive space within Christianity for lesbian and gay people. In the 1990s, the term 'queer theory' was coined, informed by feminist, womanist, and post-structuralist thought. This chapter therefore provides a brief overview of the rise and agenda of those who came to be known

DOI: 10.4324/9781003434993-2

as queer theorists, as well as the function of queer theory. Insights from these areas provided fertile ground from which queer theologies began to flourish. In offering a brief overview of the predecessors and rise of queer theologies, there is not enough space to give a more detailed narrative than the one traced below. Readers should be drawn to the suggestions for further reading at the end of this chapter in order to plug some of the omissions.

LIBERATION THEOLOGY

Liberation theology developed in Latin America during the 1960s, in a period characterised by dictatorships and regimes which required complete obedience from the people to the state. The primary concern of liberation theology was the poor and the oppressed. In sharp contrast to the dominant theologies of the West, liberation theology took Jesus's message of liberation in the gospels as real. The notion of Jesus as liberator was an important message to those who lived in poverty and oppression. Liberation theology, therefore, exposes how traditional theology was produced in privileged or wealthy contexts, yet hunger and persecution characterised the social and economic locations of the majority of the world.

In 1971, Gustavo Gutiérrez (1971), a Peruvian theologian, released *A Theology of Liberation*. He popularised the phrase that became a central motif of liberation theology, that God had a 'preferential option for the poor'. In the fight for economic justice, human rights, and an end to poverty, liberation theology looks at biblical narratives which show how God sided with the oppressed and marginalised. Ivan Petrella comments how Gutiérrez's theology was practical: 'Theology is a second step, commitment and participation in the struggles of marginalised communities is the first step' (Petrella, 2007: 162).

The liberation theology movement was criticised by the Roman Catholic Church. In the early 1980s, the Vatican stated how it was too close to secular Marxism. Marxism, from the economic and philosophical writings of Karl Marx (1818–1883), revealed how social class and conflict were a result of wealth and the powerful systems which produced wealth. The idea of liberation for the oppressed and marginalised became a lens used in feminist, and gay and lesbian theologies. These are known as contextual theologies – theologies that are grounded in particular social contexts and experiences.

FEMINIST THEOLOGY

In the late 19th and early 20th centuries, the first wave of feminism advanced issues of women's equality in the Western world. Its focus was on allowing women the right to vote (suffrage) and on legal inequalities which favoured and were biased towards men. An example of this included the fight for married women's right to own property, which was granted in the UK in 1882. Yet, it was in the 1960s that a second wave of feminism drew attention to further important and timely issues including sexuality, workplace rights, reproductive rights, and the role of women in the family. It was during this period of second-wave feminism, which lasted approximately 20 years, that feminist concerns in relation to Christianity were voiced. Thus, the idea of feminist theology developed.

Feminist theology exposes and challenges the role of women within the Christian churches. Traditionally, the fact that Jesus and his disciples were male was used to justify the subordination of women within the churches; for example, it is cited as the rationale for why women could not become priests. Throughout, feminist theology has also re-examined the role of women in the Bible through feminist biblical interpretations. Scholars have examined women across the biblical canon, as well as women's roles in the development of the early church. Feminist theology exposes how theology is soaked in assumptions and practices based on male experiences, and how theology is overwhelmingly authored by men. Patriarchy is a system by which men are privileged power holders and women are subjugated. The agenda of feminist theology is to dismantle patriarchal theology. Feminist theology, therefore, developed methodologies which prioritised and promoted women's experiences as a source of theology. Such experiences included discussions of motherhood, childbearing, sexual violence, and lesbianism. The turn to women's experiences highlights how traditional theology had been a source of oppression towards women. At their origins, feminist theologians were also concerned with promoting the rights of women to be ordained. Feminism helped clear a way for later gay and lesbian theologies which also focussed on experience as a source of theology, and to afford space for voices that had been silent in theology, as well as the problematic nature of theologies for LGBTQ+ people.

One of the most prominent voices in feminist theology at the time of its emergence was Mary Daly. In 1968, Daly (1968) published *The Church and the Second Sex*, a critique of the Catholic Church. Daly exposes how a woman's role in Christianity is to be passive and silent, like the Mary revered by the Church. Daly's critique is formed from her observation of how the Church puts women on a pedestal, yet this pedestal renders women invisible at the same time. More radical explorations in feminist theology came from Daly five years later. In 1973, she authored *Beyond God the Father*, a critique of the Christian tradition as a model of patriarchy. Daly's work reveals how the masculine language used to talk about God (God the Father; God the Son) is an obstacle for women. The patriarchy in Christianity was exposed by Daly, who states, 'if God is male then male is God' (Daly, 1973: 19). In a shocking move, Daly claims that the task of feminist theology was to 'castrate' the male God of Christianity.

Daly exposes the problematic nature of the personhood of Jesus as male, referring to Jesus as the God-man. This highlights the problem when the 'image of God' is male, Daly says, as this image is reflected in men's roles in politics and society. In such terms, the idea of Jesus's maleness is in collusion with sexual hierarchy and patriarchy. If idolatry is defined as the worship of false gods or idols, then Daly's 'Christolatry' reveals that worshipping Jesus equates to worshipping the male. According to Daly, women cannot accept the idea of incarnation in the form of a male saviour.

Another pioneering feminist theologian is Rosemary Radford Ruether who offers a different approach to Daly. Ruether seeks to remain within the Christian tradition and sees potential in its renewal by reclaiming its prophetic and liberating roots. While Daly envisions a post-Christian, women-centred spirituality beyond the church, Ruether seeks to reform Christianity itself into an ecofeminist, justice-oriented faith.

In response to the problem of God's maleness, in *Sexism and God-Talk*, Ruether famously asks, 'Can a male saviour save women?'

(Ruether, 1983: 116). She exposes how women's experiences have been virtually excluded from theology and that theology is based on male experience rather than human experience. Ruether states:

> The uniqueness of feminist theology lies not in its use of the criterion of experience but rather in its use of women's experience, which has been almost entirely shut out of theological reflection in the past. The use of women's experience in feminist theology, therefore, explodes as a critical force, exposing classical theology, including its codified traditions, as based on male experience rather than on universal human experience.
>
> (Ruether, 1983: 13)

In responding to her own question – 'can a male saviour save women?' – Ruether's answer is similar to the ideas found in liberation theology, as she envisages Christ as the liberator. In this role as liberator, Christ liberates women from oppression, just as he liberates the poor. The idea of Christian justice can therefore be applied to women. Ruether's work sets out an important agenda for feminist theology, as she states, 'the critical principle of feminist theology is the promotion of the full humanity of women' (1983: 18). Her aim was to recover the contributions and beliefs of women as a neglected aspect of Christianity. Theology can then be constructed with feminist principles and women's experiences. Rather than abandoning the language of God altogether, she works to widen it, reclaiming feminine, maternal, and gender-neutral images that can reshape worship and theological imagination.

Ruether's vision was concerned with both ecology and feminism: an ecofeminist theology. She calls for a transformation in how humans live together, both humans with fellow humans and humans with the natural world. At the heart of her theology is what she calls 'the promotion of the full humanity of women' (1983: 18), a principle she uses as the measure for all theology. By drawing on neglected strands of the Christian tradition, particularly the contributions and experiences of women, Ruether seeks to rebuild theology so that it speaks truthfully to both women's lives and the life of the planet.

The idea of language used to talk about God as being masculine was still problematic for some feminist theologians. Sallie McFague addresses the concern about male-centric language used to describe God and argues that language is a metaphor, stating how 'theology is mostly fiction' (McFague, 1987: xi). She envisages God as mother, lover, and friend, and uses female pronouns (she/her) to refer to God. Feminist theology, therefore, challenges traditional concepts of God.

Other feminist theologians observed how the tensions between feminism and the patriarchal tradition of Christianity were beyond repair. In 1990, Daphne Hampson authored *Theology and Feminism*, in which she concludes that Christian theology and feminism are incompatible. For Hampson, the sexism within Christianity means it is beyond repair, despite the work of feminist theologians. She states: 'an observant friend of mine once remarked that whereas Christian feminists want to change the actors in the play, what I want is a different kind of play' (Hampson, 1990: 162). Because of this incompatibility, she describes her theology as 'post-Christian'. Identifying as post-Christian means that the theologian chooses to distance herself from the language and assumptions of Christianity.

LESBIAN AND GAY LIVES

In the late 1940s and early 1950s, scientific studies in human sexuality revealed pioneering insights into sexual behaviours. Sexologist Alfred Kinsey conducted two major research projects in human sexuality (Kinsey et al., 1948, 1953). It is important to note that his publications were released at a time when sex between men was criminalised in the UK and in many US states. Kinsey's results led to new thinking around sexual variation and behaviours.

Despite this work, in the history of homosexuality, being gay or lesbian was once considered a psychological disorder and was treated like an illness. To be gay was to be sick. Medical interventions attempted to establish cures for such an illness, with the aim of transforming 'sick' gay or lesbian people into 'healthy' heterosexuals. Procedures to 'cure' at this time were very invasive, with lasting physical and psychological damage. In some extreme examples, gay men underwent castration and lesbians suffered genital mutilation, while experimental shock treatments and hypnosis were also used with the aim of offering a 'cure' to non-heterosexual people. This also extends to the practice of so-called 'conversion therapy', an attempt to make a gay-identifying individual convert to heterosexuality using psychological, behavioural, religious, and other spiritual interventions.

Against the social backdrop of feminist activism, lesbian and gay political movements began to stand up against the anti-gay legal system. One major example of such activism took place in a New York bar, the Stonewall Inn. The bar was welcoming towards LGBTQ+ patrons, especially drag queens and gender-nonconforming people who were often excluded from other gay bars at the time. Yet, it was subjected to routine police raids. On 28 June 1969, during one such raid, the patrons fought back against police harassment, and this led to several days of protest and unrest. News of the riots at Stonewall spread, and for many, it was a call to activism. Historians and anthropologists are aware of inconsistencies in attempting to document the events at Stonewall: a generation of those at Stonewall died during the AIDS crisis of the 1980s; the riots were disorganised; people were intoxicated; and lots of people claimed to be there as they were aware of its importance as a major event in LGBTQ+ history (see Carter, 2004). Despite debates about actual facts, Stonewall was undoubtedly a major turning point for LGBTQ+ empowerment. Gay rights groups grew across the country, including the Gay Liberation Front (GLF), comprising activists for sexual liberation. The GLF spread to the UK and Canada, and the first Gay Pride event took place in New York in 1970 to mark the one-year anniversary of the riots. Throughout the 1970s, Pride events took place in numerous states across the USA and within European cities such as London, Paris, and West Berlin. Although gay and lesbian liberation movements organised events labelled 'Pride', there was still, for many, a personal and social shame attached to same-sex orientations. Arguably, the whole point of the Pride events was to counter interior feelings of shame. 'Pride' as an emotion was contrasted against 'shame'. The idea of shame has its own emotional and psychological consequences, as LGBTQ+ people can often lead hidden lives or not be open about their relationships with family, friends, or colleagues. This shame can also be a religious or spiritual shame or inner conflict.

GAY AND LESBIAN THEOLOGIES

Alongside gay and lesbian liberation movements, lesbian and gay voices began to speak in theology. Susannah Cornwall is right to note how those who produced gay and lesbian theologies were activist prophets:

> Lesbian and gay theologies, and those who have produced and inhabited them over the years, continue to stand prophetically themselves as testimony to God's good work in non-heterosexual lives and relationships.
> (Cornwall, 2011: 68)

To a large extent, the lineage of queer theologies can be traced back to pathways paved by liberation, feminist, and gay and lesbian theologies. One of the very earliest examples of gay and lesbian theology was a collection of essays entitled *Is Gay Good? Ethics, Theology and Homosexuality,* edited by W. Dwight Oberholtzer (1971). The essays considered questions of ethics, pastoral responses, Christian positions, the role of the Church, and the theological idea of love. In the volume, Del Martin and Phyllis Lyon wrote a significant essay entitled 'A Lesbian Approach to Theology'. They were a lesbian couple living in the USA who were committed to the feminist and gay rights movements. Their paper offered a reminder that the 'homosexual too is a child of God' (Martin & Lyon, 1971: 219).

Within the decades that followed in the USA, gay male theologians also began to put pen to paper in the spirit of activism. Gary David Comstock wrote *Gay Theology Without Apology* (Comstock, 1993). He used personal narrative to articulate the negative impact of theology and church teaching on gay men. Comstock states that biblical interpretations are saturated in heterosexism and patriarchy and are damaging to gay men and lesbians:

> Within such a patriarchal framework, therefore, lesbians and gay men should not be surprised to find passages that malign us. Our tendency, however, has been to apologize for those biblical passages that appear to condemn homosexuality and attack lesbians and gay men.
> (Comstock, 1993: 38)

The theme of intimate relationships as a source for communion runs through Comstock's text, observing that relationships are orchestrated by God. He states, 'I believe that we are created and destroyed in our relationships. God is the mutuality and reciprocity in our relationships, the compelling and transforming power that brings together, reconciles, and creates us' (1993: 127). The notion of apologising, or apologetics (defending same-sex relationships), became one of several frameworks that emerged in early gay and lesbian theologies.

In the UK, Sean Gill edited a collection of essays, *The Lesbian and Gay Christian Movement* (Gill, 1998). In one essay, USA-based scholar Robert Goss discusses the post-Christian turn for feminist scholars and gay and lesbian Christians who have moved into a form of exile by leaving mainstream denominational groups. Goss argues how this is an example of making superficial or ultimately futile changes in the face of a fundamentally failing system. He writes that this is like 'rearranging deck chairs on the Titanic' (Goss, 1998: 192). He asks, 'can we create a Christianity that escapes from its heritage of violence and from its irrelevancy in addressing the spiritual needs of gays/lesbians?' (1998: 192). This question underpins part of the agenda of gay and lesbian theologies.

In the quest for sexual justice, lesbian and gay activists worked together in union. Although this alliance was helpful in many ways, some remained concerned by the collapse of lesbian and gay experiences. By putting them together, as 'lesbian and gay', identities were diluted or lost. Elizabeth Stuart highlights the tensions between gay and lesbian theologies:

> Gay theology began to emerge in the 1970s as gay Christians started to reflect theologically upon the gay liberation movement. In its early days such reflection was dominated by men who felt able to do theology about and on behalf of lesbians.
>
> (Stuart, 2003: 15)

Indeed, the tensions went beyond a claim to voice. While collectively lesbians and gays shared a common struggle against homophobia and heterosexism, some feminists were aware how gay men remained connected to issues of patriarchy and still enjoyed male privilege. Stuart observes how gay men were 'regarded as implicated in the structures of patriarchy' (Stuart, 2003: 7). Elsewhere, she explains some of the general tensions between gay and lesbian theologies:

> Very broadly speaking, gay men often seemed content to seek a place at the Christian table, using already existent and accepted theological concepts and arguments to gain that place. Lesbian theologies, however, wanted to overturn the whole table. They argued that Christian theology was too rooted in patriarchy, racism, heterosexism and other exclusionary beliefs and practices, and that it would have to be rebuilt if it were to be truly liberating.
>
> (Stuart, 1997: 2–3)

In the gay and lesbian theologies produced around the time of the millennium, it is clear that the influence of queer theory and queer theologies begins to take hold. Robert Goss's *Jesus Acted Up: A Gay and Lesbian Manifesto* (1993), for example, uses the term queer in a political sense, reflecting its use in the activist movement. For Goss, queer was used as an expression of radical activism. Within his manifesto, Goss tackles the themes of homophobia, HIV/AIDS, and sexual justice. In a similar vein to ideas in liberation and feminist theology, Goss sees Christ, formed by patriarchal traditional theology, as an oppressor, but the person of Jesus as a liberator. With a commitment to practical theology, Goss's work examines how Christians can live their faith in queer Christian communities. In the final chapter, he states how 'queer anger is holy anger. It's time to be angry [...] Queer Christians need to follow in the steps of Jesus [...] They need to act up against the churches and stop the hatred' (Goss, 1993: 177).

One of the defining transition periods between gay and lesbian theologies and queer theologies is found in Elizabeth Stuart's *Gay and Lesbian Theologies: Repetitions with Critical Difference* (Stuart, 2003). It serves as an excellent bridging text, revealing how gay and lesbian theologies differ from queer theologies. Stuart explains how gay and lesbian theologies had reached a point of stalemate and that something more radical was required: 'gay and lesbian theology reaches a state of theological breakdown, and this is manifested in its tendency to repeat itself' (2003: 11). She uses the French term *répétition*, which, as well as meaning 'repetition' in English, also means 'rehearsal'. Stuart states how gay and lesbian theologies have served as a rehearsal, 'a preparation for something more theologically radical' (2003: 11). This radical theology is revealed as queer theology, or queer theologies.

THE RISE OF QUEER THEORY

The rise of queer theory must not be viewed solely as a development rooted in the transformative brilliance of the 20th century's critical thinkers. Queer theory developed alongside hard-fought activism from second-wave feminism, civil rights movements, and the gay and lesbian liberation movements discussed above. The theory which began to germinate in academic settings was nourished by the social and political climate of the day.

Queer theory disrupts long-held notions of binary gender and sexual identities. As a theory, it is known for its complex language and ideas. To provide a 'way in' to this philosophical area, I briefly trace the basic developments in philosophical thought that preceded and influenced the emergence of queer theory.

In the middle of the 20th century in Europe, structuralism was a popular method that explored how human life and culture was understood in relation to wider structures. So, instead of looking at 'things' as separate items, structuralism focused on the relationship between things. In one example, the word 'light' exists because of its relationship to 'dark'. So, the word 'light' itself does not just describe what it is, but it also describes what it is not. This relationship helps to place it in the structure of things. In one sense, structuralism claims that naming an object describes both presence and absence. Structuralism, therefore, works to examine the limitations of meaning. Ferdinand de Saussure explained this distinction as 'signifier' and 'signified' (1916 [trans 1966]). The signifier is the word used – for example, 'light' – while the signified is a mental concept that extends beyond the word itself. Another example of the relationship between signifier and signified is how red roses come to signify love. This focus on systems or structures led to an understanding of objects within binary structures; the most obvious example of this was 'male/female'. Structuralism was a method based on systems, stability, order, rules, and discipline.

Following engagement with de Saussure and structuralist thinking, post-structuralism countered these claims of stable, universal truths and highlighted that there were more possibilities than simply those that exist in binary structures. The Algerian-born philosopher Jacques Derrida became one of the major figures associated with post-structuralism in 1960s France. Derrida is often referred to as 'the father of deconstruction', as his methods of deconstruction began to have a significant impact on studies across academic disciplines. Derrida would claim that the method of deconstruction is impossible to define. In post-structuralism, Derrida showed how definitions are dangerous as they do not point to what something means, but how they come to mean it. Deconstruction, therefore, went against normal and accepted readings of texts. Texts in this sense do not just mean literary documents, but include different con*texts* – texts can be events, situations, and forms of media. Context refers to identity, location, and time. With different contexts come different possibilities, so there is never a real structure or a real truth, but there are multiple possibilities of interpreting the text or context. Deconstruction is the method of engaging with how a text gets its meaning and how such meanings are unstable. Derrida is famous for saying 'there is nothing outside the text' (*il n'y a pas de hors-texte*). In very simplified terms, Derrida claims that texts do not have a single, fixed meaning but that meaning is shaped by context. There is no final say on a text; there is no final destination.

Deconstruction is a method associated with post-structuralist thought. The method of deconstruction challenged Western culture and was a major concept within emerging philosophical movements. By focusing on context, deconstruction questioned 'normal', assumed meanings; it removed binary thinking and hierarchies by showing how 'structures' were not really stable. There is no single truth about the meaning of a text, but there are multiple interpretations. Post-structuralist thought is therefore highly critical of claims to truth, including claims from science and religion.

Essentialism is a term used to describe the belief that a set of characteristics serves to denote an identity 'group'. During the 20th century, some French philosophers, particularly Sartre and de Beauvoir, questioned the idea that people's identities are fixed or designated at birth (biological essentialism). They foregrounded the notion that identity is determined by social factors. Deconstruction challenges essentialist categories of identity, such as race, gender, sexuality, and class, by showing that such categories are not universal or 'true'. Post-structuralist thinking therefore understands identity as culturally and socially formed. Rather than identity being essentialised, identities are seen as occupied and negotiated.

Among the French philosophers, Michel Foucault is another thinker credited for his contribution to contemporary thought and philosophy. Foucault was a critical thinker who published on mental illness, history, sexuality, power, and the prison system. He revealed how power and knowledge are inextricably connected in his text *Discipline and Punish* (Foucault, 1977), which is considered by many to be a landmark in post-structuralist thought. According to Foucault, power produces knowledge and vice versa, and he uses the example of a prison to demonstrate how power structures in society reflect those of a prison. This example extends to power structures in other public institutions such as schools, hospitals, and factories. One of his main examples was to use the idea of a panopticon – a tower within a prison which creates the sense that prisoners may always be under surveillance. Prisoners would regulate their own conduct through the perception that they were being seen. Rather than focusing on this as a tool for the corrective services of prisons, the panopticon can be used to illustrate how people modify their own behaviours in society based on the perceived critical gazes from others. Because of an individual's awareness of these constant critical gazes, people self-regulate in their presentation and behaviours as a means to avoid negative responses, humiliation, and disapproval. In brief, the panopticon is a mechanism of surveillance and normalisation. Foucault calls this process 'power-knowledge', as power does not come solely from a top-down hierarchy but is shared subtly, leading people to self-regulate.

In his pivotal work, *The History of Sexuality: Volume 1* (1978), Foucault explores this idea in relation to sex, seeing the connection between sex and knowledge. He extends this idea to the accepted understanding of 'sexuality', as sexuality was produced by power-knowledge relations such as science and religion. Foucault himself was openly gay and was fully aware of the social and legal positions which constrained gay relationships and expressions of sexuality. He notes how social systems construct sexual identity by making it central to an individual's character. Foucault examines the historical shift in which homosexuality came to be understood as an identity, rather than simply as a set of acts related to bodies or pleasure. For heterosexuality to be normalised and dominant, it needs an 'other' to which it can exist, and upon which it relies for its normalised status (Foucault, 1978). Therefore, Foucault was able to demonstrate that homosexuality comes to be understood as profoundly threatening by being positioned as the inherently 'abnormal' 'other'. Because it is considered an identity, it is subjected to interpretation by institutions such as medicine, law, and religion. Thus, ideas of heterosexuality as 'natural' and non-heterosexuality as 'unnatural' come about. Sexuality is therefore regulated by power dynamics, rather than being part of a person's essence.

In post-structuralist thought, the lens of power-knowledge is focused firmly on the human body, so aspects of identity – such as gender, sexuality, race, age, dis/ability, and appearance – are all regulated by self and others, thereby producing the idea of 'normal'. Post-structuralism, therefore, calls attention to the idea of there being no 'truth', as knowledge is produced in contextual systems of multiple power structures. Where there is power, there is resistance. This idea of power-knowledge is mirrored in the task of queering theology and examining the relationship between queer theologies and dominant mainstream theologies.

FEMINIST, WOMANIST, AND 'QUEER' THEORISTS

In addition to critical theories emerging from post-structuralism in France, a number of second-wave feminist and womanist thinkers are credited with contributing to what would later become queer thought, even though it was not identified or labelled as 'queer' at the time. Feminist theorists include Adrienne Rich, Monique Wittig, Gayle Rubin, and Judith Butler, while Black feminist and womanist thinkers include Audre Lorde and bell hooks.

In 1980, Adrienne Rich examined heterosexuality through a critical lens. She wrote 'Compulsory Heterosexuality and Lesbian

Existence', arguing how heterosexuality functions as a social power and that people are pressured into seeing heterosexuality as the norm. Rich notes how 'the ideology of heterosexual romance, beamed at her from childhood out of fairy tales, television, films, advertising, popular songs, wedding pageantry' (Rich, 1980: 645), is part of social conditioning. People conform to heterosexuality, according to Rich, because they gain benefits from doing so, and there are losses to those who deviate from it. Rich coined the term 'compulsory heterosexuality' to describe how people conform, a term popularised throughout further queer texts. In her essay, Rich was highly critical of patriarchal gender relations, where men dominate. Her work introduced the idea of a 'lesbian continuum' as a way to see the bonds and relationships between women, not only as same-sex attraction. Despite its significant critical reading of heterosexuality, Rich's work was criticised for focusing solely on lesbian experience rather than wider marginalised sexualities.

As Rich focused on matters of sexuality, Gayle Rubin's influential paper 'Thinking Sex' (Rubin, 1984) explored the multidimensional nature of human sexuality in the form of a sex hierarchy. This hierarchy is regulated by different aspects of society: religion, law, the media, and mainstream culture, among others. In thinking about sex, Rubin establishes a 'charmed circle' of sex which is validated by words such as 'normal', 'natural', and 'healthy'. This charmed circle of sexuality includes sex that is heterosexual, marital, monogamous, and reproductive. In contrast, Rubin describes the negativity associated with certain types of sexual behaviours, distinguishing how stable, long-term lesbian and gay couples are nearly respectable, while 'promiscuous gay men' and 'bar dykes' are positioned much lower, near sex workers, and pornography. These 'outer limits' work in opposition to the charmed circle, and sex in these categories is deemed 'abnormal', 'unnatural', and 'unhealthy'. Rubin defines the sex hierarchy as an erotic pyramid:

> Marital, reproductive heterosexuals are alone at the top of the erotic pyramid. Clamoring below are unmarried monogamous heterosexuals in couples, followed by most other heterosexuals. Solitary sex floats ambiguously [...] Stable, long-term lesbian and gay male couples are verging on respectability, but bar dykes and promiscuous gay men are

> hovering just above the groups at the very bottom of the pyramid. The most despised sexual castes currently include transsexuals, transvestites, fetishists, sadomasochists, sex workers such as prostitutes and porn models, and the lowliest of all, those whose eroticism transgresses generational boundaries.
>
> (Rubin, 1984: 279)

The language here reflects the historical context in which Rubin was writing. The work of gay and lesbian movements was invested in assimilationist politics, as they worked for social integration. That means that such groups wanted to be similar to and have the same rights as heterosexuals. Rubin sees such assimilation as problematic, as the scramble to enter the 'charmed circle' still means that other groups are marginalised and remain at the outer limits. Such groups are then further oppressed because of this 'abnormal' status. Rubin cites organised religion, naming Christianity, as contributing to the teaching that sex is sinful.

Monique Wittig's paper on 'The Straight Mind' dates to 1978, and the English collection *The Straight Mind and Other Essays* was published in 1992. She exposes how heterosexuality forms part of the everyday practices of life: thinking, speaking, feeling. Because assumed heterosexuality is widespread, it is pervasive. This points to why non-heterosexuality has been deemed so deviant and alien. Indeed, Wittig argues that because heterosexuality is so dominant in culture, its power is invisible. Non-heterosexuals therefore examine themselves in relation to this. Wittig's work was popularised by her controversial statement that 'lesbians are not women' (Wittig, 1992: 32). She highlights that the idea of 'woman' refers to the sexual, procreative function of women. In using this idea of reproduction, Wittig states how matriarchy is just as heterosexual as patriarchy. For Wittig, being a 'woman' only makes sense in a straight world, when people think of heterosexual women, 'as "woman" has meaning only in heterosexual systems of thought' (1992: 32).

Complementing these positions were the voices of Black feminist thinkers, who raised awareness that the civil rights movement, which campaigned to end discrimination and segregation on the basis of race, had overlooked the question of gender. Comparatively, the feminist movement had also neglected issues of race. In this way, their work questioned the idea of 'identity' as a universal term, as there were wide-ranging experiences between 'women' based on class and race.

Audre Lorde was a Black lesbian feminist socialist who examines the notion of privilege between women based on class, race, and age in her essay 'Age, Race, Class and Sex: Women Redefining Difference' (Lorde, 1984). Lorde points to the actions of oppression, noting how 'it is the responsibility of the oppressed to teach the oppressors their mistakes' (1984: 114). In highlighting privilege, Lorde exposes the irony of the marginalised teaching the dominant: how Black people are expected to educate white people about race; how women educate men about gender; how gay and lesbian people educate straight people about sexuality. For Lorde, the category of 'women' had been based on the experiences of white women, to which Black women are 'other'. Lorde states:

> As a Black lesbian feminist comfortable with the many different ingredients of my identity, and a woman committed to racial and sexual freedom from oppression, I find I am constantly being encouraged to pluck out some one aspect of myself and present this as the meaningful whole, eclipsing or denying the other parts of self. But this is a destructive and fragmenting way to live.
>
> (Lorde, 1984: 120)

The term 'womanist' was coined by Alice Walker (1983) to describe Black feminists and feminists of colour, and is grounded in the history, culture, and experiences of Black women. The term removes the white assumptions of feminism. bell hooks, the American author, feminist, and socialist, published *Ain't I a Woman? Black Women and Feminism* (hooks, 1981) and *Feminist Theory: From Margin to Center* (hooks, 1984). hooks's work on gender and feminism reveals how, in the quest for women to be assimilated to men, the task is futile, as women are not all equal to one another. hooks challenges feminism to look at how issues of gender interact with race, class, and sex. Her work also insists that men must be part of the campaign for equality. Lorde's and hooks's work therefore anticipates the idea of intersectionality – how certain forms of oppression intersect with other forms of oppression; a term now understood as intersectionality, due to the work of Kimberlé Crenshaw (1989). So, an individual may be marginalised because of one identity characteristic, but that is further compacted when others are examined. Intersectionality shows how systems of oppression and discrimination are multiple. The most marginalised people, therefore, fall under multiple minority groups. Writings from feminist and womanist thinkers were critical in the development of thinking that contests categories of identity and explores issues of marginalisation which later came to characterise queer theory.

In 1990, Judith Butler's *Gender Trouble* built on the intellectual theories of French critical thinkers, feminism, and poststructuralism, including Foucault. Butler is often credited as one of the founders of queer thought, but Butler did not see herself in this position. In writing the book, Butler says how 'I understood myself to be in an embattled and oppositional relation to certain forms of feminism' (2006 [1990]: vii). Butler's thought dismantles essentialist ideas of gender, stating that gender is not solely biologically determined. People are born into bodies, but what counts as 'male' or 'female' is shaped by social and cultural ideas. Butler states how gender is socially constructed: society and culture has built ideas of what it is to be male or female, and individuals perform these ideas. On a simple level, what is thought of as masculine or feminine is performed by individuals, especially in terms of appearance and in the clothes that people wear. But Butler argues that gender is also produced through repeated acts described as 'gender performativity'. Miriam Meyerhoff offers a helpful definition of how performativity is different from performance:

> The performative quality of gender and sexuality is distinct from gendered and sexualized performance. If a performance is something controlled and possibly characterized by a degree of artifice, performativity is talking about something completely different. To say that gender is performative is simply to say that how we understand gender, and how we position ourselves as gendered or sexual beings in relation to others is achieved through the repetition and enactment of these activities.
>
> (Meyerhoff, 2014: 2)

This is not to suggest that gender can be put on and taken off at will. Gendered enactment is better understood as a *compulsive performativity*: compulsive because failure to adapt to the script carries real social risk, and because it often feels practically impossible to break free from it entirely. Perceptions of gender are therefore individual and collective repetitions. For Butler, gender is what you do (although not necessarily on our own terms), rather than who you are.

The coining of the term 'queer theory' is often attributed to Teresa de Lauretis, who used the words 'queer theory' in a special edition of the feminist cultural journal *Differences* (de Lauretis, 1991). Her title, 'Queer Theory: Lesbian and Gay Sexualities', shows how de Lauretis's focus at the time was on issues of sexuality, whereas queer theory today critiques and destabilises fixed and essentialised ideas of identity more broadly. Nonetheless, the word 'queer' quickly became applied to critical thought around issues of gender and sexuality in the 1990s. Building on the thoughts of Rich's 'compulsory heterosexuality' and Rubin's work on gender and sex, Michael Warner edited *Fear of a Queer Planet* (Warner, 1993) and popularised the word 'heteronormativity' to refer to the idea that heterosexuality had been so normalised by society. Heteronormativity describes the assumption that people are heterosexual and how society presumes heterosexuality. This includes normalising assumptions around gender binaries, monogamy, reproduction, and family structures. One way to describe the reach of heteronormativity is how non-heterosexuals or non-cisgender people 'come out'. In terms of sexuality, the act of coming out is unique to LGBTQ+ people, even today, which renders heterosexuality the norm. It is important to note that 'compulsory heterosexuality' and 'heteronormativity' differ. Heteronormativity is the assumption that everyone is straight, whereas compulsory heterosexuality describes the process and enforcement of heteronormativity through the constant messages that promote and uphold it.

Another emerging critical thinker at this time was Eve Kosofsky Sedgwick. Her essay, 'How To Bring Your Kids Up Gay' (Sedgwick, 1991), critiques how homosexuality has been pathologised and thought of as abnormal. Sedgwick calls attention to the false assumption that binary gender equates to binary sexuality. In considering how being homosexual may be seen as acceptable among adults in society, Sedgwick notes that there is an institutional agenda among psychoanalysts that children who may grow up to be gay should still be treated and dissuaded. In *Epistemology of the Closet* (Sedgwick, 1990), she states how binary definitions of gender and sexuality are far too limiting and simplistic to be able to represent human sexuality. 'The closet' is a metaphor for hidden homosexuality, where those who experience same-sex attraction attempt to hide and conceal their sexuality. Using examples taken from literature, Sedgwick shows that while leaving the closet can be experienced as liberating for some, it is not a universal or risk-free process.

There are power relations at play in the performativity of gender and the regulation of sexuality. What come to be considered 'normal' or 'natural' only do so because they have been performed by a majority and repeated. The work of the theorists highlighted above collectively reveals how gender and sexuality are no longer seen as essential or fixed, but socially constructed and fluid. In a similar way, Christianity and Christian theology have been constructed by power relations and are seen as fixed in some way only because of dominant repetitions. Queer theologies destabilise these repetitions.

Although, in its development, queer theory first concerned itself with marginalised gender and sexualities, queer theory now moves beyond this. Queer is a much-contested term and cannot be easily defined. Where definitions exist, they fail to recognise that queer is fluid; it is unfixable. David Halperin illustrates how the term queer cannot be easily defined:

> Queer is by definition whatever is at odds with the normal, the legitimate, the dominant. There is nothing in particular to which it necessarily refers. It is an identity without an essence.
>
> (Halperin, 1995: 62)

Halperin goes on to say that queer is a positionality rather than an identity. Such a positionality means that it is not limited to LGBTQ+ people but can be taken up by anyone. Anything which challenges compulsory ideas of binary gender and heterosexuality can be queer. In his edited book, *Straight with a Twist* (Thomas, 2000), Calvin Thomas explores how queer theory interrogates heterosexuality and how it includes and speaks for straight people too. This is further developed in Chapter 5.

As queer is indefinable, instead of looking at what queer *is*, it is better to look at what queer *does*. Or, even better, what queer 'undoes'. These are the most common ways queer theory has come to be applied:

[i] queer resists ideas of categorisation;
[ii] queer challenges the idea of essentialism;
[iii] queer challenges 'normal';
[iv] queer exposes the instability and limits of binary thinking and presumptions;
[v] queer exposes and disrupts power relations or hierarchies.

[I] QUEER RESISTS IDEAS OF CATEGORISATION

Queer goes beyond being a descriptor for non-heterosexual identities. Queer resists all definitions and categories. Annamarie Jagose states how 'queer itself can have neither a fundamental logic, nor a consistent set of characteristics' (Jagose, 1996: 96), so queer itself cannot be defined. To be defined is to be normalised! Queer resists definitions because any attempt to define it only limits it. Therefore, queer resists categorisation.

[II] QUEER CHALLENGES THE IDEA OF ESSENTIALISM

Essentialism refers to the idea that there is a set of fixed, uniform characteristics to identity. Identity therefore becomes universal. In her work on feminist identity, Elizabeth Spelman states how 'one's gender identity is not related to one's racial and class identity as the parts of pop-bead necklaces are related, separable and insertable in other "strands" with different racial and class parts' (Spelman, 1988: 15). Queer challenges the ideas of essentialism, therefore, as each aspect of an individual's identity cannot be 'popped off' and examined, without seeing how one part relates to another. The idea of an identity having a fixed essence is therefore false.

[III] QUEER CHALLENGES 'NORMAL'

The work of Foucault and Butler shows how identities are enmeshed within systems of social power and control, which regulate what is understood as 'normal'. Heteronormativity is socially powerful. It reveals how heterosexuality is presumed within society as the dominant expression of sexuality and this is tied up in institutional life: law, business, education, and health, among others. The same is true for gender, as cisgender has been considered the norm. Queer reveals how biological sex is not a direct correlation to gender. What is accepted as a norm has been socially constructed. What are often understood as fixed categories are, in fact, not fixed. They are largely fixed by imagination and social conditioning. Queer challenges any assumption of normal by enlarging the picture and looking at the experiences of those on the margins to see how the idea of 'normal' is ruptured.

[IV] QUEER EXPOSES THE INSTABILITY AND LIMITS OF BINARY THINKING AND PRESUMPTIONS

Identity categories such as man/woman and heterosexual/homosexual actually serve to reinforce cisnormativity and heteronormativity, as they only allow for thinking in opposites. Such categories operate around a norm; so, homosexuality, for example, operates around the norm of heterosexuality. Queer removes binary thinking and assumptions. Binaries are limiting. Queer pushes beyond binaries by showing that gender, for example, is more than just male/female. There are people who identify as trans, non-binary, agender, gender-fluid, for example.

[V] QUEER EXPOSES AND DISRUPTS POWER RELATIONS OR HIERARCHIES

Queer exposes the power relations that are often invisible in society and religion. It examines how power has been used in regulating what is considered 'normal'. Queer works against patriarchy and heteronormativity by exposing how these systems privilege certain individuals over others. Traditionally, privilege has served white, heterosexual, cisgender men. Queer exposes such privilege, and this disruption can serve as a catalyst and agent of change.

THE APPLICATION OF QUEER THEORY

Queer has come to mean different things: queer as a catch-all term for LGBTQ+ identities and queer as a theory. There has been concern about queer theory being a highly philosophical task, rather than working at a grassroots level to serve individuals who experience marginalisation. The language used in queer theory is often dense, complex, and unfamiliar to anyone starting out in the area. Biblical scholar Deryn Guest expresses concern in relation to the language used 'that this can render queer biblical and theological scholarship a heavily theorized, jargon-ridden, highfalutin language game that loses the wider audience' (Guest, 2018: 440).

Not only does this create a divide between those who have been afforded the opportunity of education to be able to tackle such challenging work, it begs the question as to whom this intellectualism is for? If it is not accessible to non-academic people, does it not lose its political power and agency? Elsewhere, Guest notes how complex language can create divisions:

> Queer will prove to be an elitist discourse, hardly accessible to the lay person or in touch with the lived realities of grassroots communities [...] Despite the argument that complex ideas require complex terminology, some feminists have long upheld a commitment to the communities they seek to represent and to present their ideas in ways that are accessible to such communities.
>
> (Guest, 2005: 51)

Guest suggests that the language of queer should be accessible. Queer theologian Marcella Althaus-Reid shares the same concerns, questioning 'queer theologies as a luxury which only privileged women in academia can afford to pursue' (Althaus-Reid, 2008: 106). Questions of education, class, and intellectualism can, therefore, create power structures of their own, as well as systems of exclusion and marginalisation.

CONCLUSION

This chapter has navigated key concepts in the development of queer studies in the 20th century. The activism, resistance, and protest from feminist, civil rights, and lesbian and gay groups called for social justice for marginalised communities. Against this backdrop, feminist theory, womanist theory, feminist theology, and gay and lesbian theologies interrogated traditional Christian understandings of gender and sexuality, exposing its patriarchal and heteronormative power structures. Queer theory exposes heteronormative assumptions within society and culture. Queer theologies undo traditional theology by deconstructing it and by critiquing the patriarchy and heteronormative assumptions at play in its production. Queer theologies seek to liberate Christianity from patriarchal, cisnormative, and heteronormative constraints. Having undertaken a brief history of the development of queer theologies, Chapter 2 explores the queering of 'traditional' theology.

FURTHER READING AND RESOURCES

Barker, M. J. and Scheele, J. (2016) *Queer: A Graphic History*. London: Icon Books.

A very accessible introduction to the development of queer theory. The text is written without complex language, and the discussion is illuminated by cartoon drawings illustrating key ideas.

Cornwall, S. (2011) *Controversies in Queer Theology*. London: SCM Press.

Cornwall examines key issues in queer theology in this detailed volume. This is a text highly recommended as the next step for those wishing to go beyond 'the basics'.

Goss, R. E. (1993) *Jesus Acted Up: A Gay and Lesbian Manifesto*. San Francisco: Harper.

Goss's manifesto calls for justice for, rather than acceptance of, lesbian and gay people by the churches. His book examines the importance for lesbian and gay Christians to reject institutional religion and embrace the Jesus found in the gospels. An iconic text in the history of Christian and sexual identities.

Shaw, S. M. and Kim, G. J. S (2026) *Feminist Theologies: The Basics*. Abingdon: Routledge.

A concise introductory text for anyone wanting to learn about feminist theologies, through exploring its histories and methods. The book also explores feminist theologies from intersectional perspectives. A useful starting point for those interested in gender studies and feminism and Christian theology.

Stuart, E. (Ed.) (2003) *Gay and Lesbian Theologies: Repetitions and Critical Difference*. Farnham: Ashgate.

This significant text offers a detailed and comprehensive overview of the histories of gay and lesbian theologies to queer theologies.

https://www.queertheology.com/

This website is aimed at Christians who are looking to reconcile their faith with their LGBTQ+ identities. It is aimed at supporting church groups in welcoming LGBTQ+ members. It does not engage with queer theology from a theoretical perspective.

REFERENCES

Althaus-Reid, M. (2008) 'The Bi/girl Writings: From Feminist Theology to Queer Theologies'. In Isherwood, L. and McPhillips, K. (Eds.) *Post-Christian Feminisms: A Critical Approach*, pp. 105–116. Farnham: Ashgate.

Butler, J. (2006 [1994]) *Gender Trouble*. Abingdon: Routledge Classics.

Carter, D. A. (2004) *Stonewall: The Riots That Sparked The Gay Revolution*. New York: St Martin's Griffin.

Comstock, G. D. (1993) *Gay Theology Without Apology*. Cleveland: Pilgrim Press.

Cornwall, S. (2011) *Controversies in Queer Theology*. London: SCM Press.

Crenshaw, K. (1989) 'Demarginalizing the Intersection of Race and Sex: A Black Feminist Critique of Antidiscrimination Doctrine, Feminist Theory and Antiracist Politics'. *University of Chicago Legal Forum*, *1*(8), pp. 139–167.

Daly, M. (1968) *The Church and the Second Sex*. Boston: Beacon Press.

Daly, M. (1973) *Beyond God the Father: Towards a Philosophy of Women's Liberation*. London: The Women's Press.

de Lauretis, T. (1991) 'Queer Theory: Lesbian and Gay Sexualities'. *Differences: Journal of Feminist Cultural Studies*, *3*(2), pp. iii–xviii.

de Saussure, F. (1966) *Course in General Linguistics*. In Bally, C. & Sechehaye, A. (Eds.), translated by W. Baskin. New York: McGraw-Hill.

Foucault, M. (1977) *Discipline and Punish: The Birth of the Prison*. Translated by A. Sheridan. Harmondsworth: Penguin (Originally published in French in 1975).

Foucault, M. (1978) *The History of Sexuality. Volume 1: The Will to Knowledge*. Translated by R. Hurley. London: Penguin (Originally published in French in 1976).

Gill, S. (1998) *The Lesbian and Gay Christian Movement: Campaigning for Justice, Truth and Love*. London: Continuum.

Goss, R. E. (1993) *Jesus Acted Up: A Gay and Lesbian Manifesto*. San Francisco: Harper.

Goss, R. E. (1998) 'Sexual Visionaries and Freedom Fighters'. In Gill, S. (Ed.) *The Lesbian and Gay Christian Movement: Campaigning for Justice, Truth and Love*, pp. 187–202. London: Continuum.

Guest, D. (2005) *When Deborah Met Jael: Lesbian Biblical Hermeneutics*. London: SCM Press.

Guest, D. (2018) 'Review of Sexual Disorientations: Queer Temporalities, Affects, Theologies, by Brintnall, K., Marchal, J. and Moore, S. (Eds.)'. *Reviews in Religion and Theology, 25*(3), pp. 439–442.

Gutiérrez, G. (1971) *A Theology of Liberation.* Maryknoll: Orbis (Originally published in Spanish in 1971).

Halperin, D. (1995) *Saint Foucault: Towards A Gay Hagiography.* Oxford: Oxford University Press.

Hampson, D. (1990) *Theology and Feminism.* London: Blackwell.

hooks, b. (1981) *Ain't I a Woman? Black Women and Feminism.* Boston: South End Press.

hooks, b. (1984) *Feminist Theory: From Margin to Center.* London: Pluto Press.

Jagose, A. (1996) *Queer Theory.* Melbourne: Melbourne University Press.

Kinsey, A., Pomeroy, W. and Martin, C. (1948) *Sexual Behavior in the Human Male.* Philadelphia: W. B. Saunders.

Kinsey, A., Pomeroy, W., Martin, C. and Gebhard, P. (1953) *Sexual Behavior in the Human Female.* Philadelphia: W. B. Saunders.

Lorde, A. (1984) 'Age, Race, Class, and Sex: Women Redefining Difference'. In Lorde, A. (Ed.) *Sister Outsider: Essays and Speeches*, pp. 114–123. California: Crossing Press.

Martin, D. and Lyon, P. (1971) 'A Lesbian Approach to Theology'. In Oberholtzer, W. D. (Ed.) *Is Gay Good? Ethics, Theology and Homosexuality*, pp. 213–220. Philadelphia: Westminster Press.

McFague, S. (1987) *Models of God: Theology for An Ecological, Nuclear Age.* Philadelphia: Fortress Press.

Meyerhoff, M. (2014) 'Gender Performativity'. In Whelehan, P. and Bolin, A. (Eds.) *The International Encyclopedia of Human Sexuality*, pp. 1–4. New Jersey: Wiley.

Oberholtzer, W. D. (Ed.) (1971) *Is Gay Good? Ethics, Theology and Homosexuality.* Philadelphia: Westminster Press.

Petrella, I. (2007) 'Theology and Liberation: Juan Luis Segundo and Three Takes on Secular Inventiveness'. In Althaus-Reid, M., Petrella, I. and Susin, L. C. (Eds.) *Another Possible World*, pp. 162–177. London: SCM Press.

Rich, A. (1980) 'Compulsory Heterosexuality and Lesbian Existence'. *Signs, 5*(4), pp. 631–660.

Rubin, G. (1984) 'Thinking Sex: Notes for a Radical Theory of the Politics of Sexuality'. In Vance, C. S. (Ed.) *Pleasure and Danger: Exploring Female Sexuality*, pp. 267–319. London: Routledge and Kegan Paul.

Ruether, R. R. (1983) *Sexism and God-talk: Toward a Feminist Theology.* Boston: Beacon Press.

Sedgwick, E. K. (1990) *Epistemology of the Closet.* Berkeley: University of California Press.

Sedgwick, E. K. (1991) 'How to Bring Your Kids Up Gay'. *Social Text, 29*, pp. 18–27.

Spelman, E. (1988) *Inessential Woman*. Boston: Beacon Press.

Stuart, E. (Ed.) (1997) *Religion Is a Queer Thing*. London: Cassell.

Stuart, E. (2003) *Gay and Lesbian Theologies: Repetitions and Critical Difference*. Farnham: Ashgate.

Thomas, C. (Ed.) (2000) *Straight with a Twist*. Urbana and Chicago: University of Illinois Press.

Walker, A. (1983) *In Search of Our Mothers' Gardens: Womanist Prose*. San Diego: Harcourt Brace Jovanovich.

Warner, M. (1993) *Fear of a Queer Planet*. Minneapolis: University of Minnesota Press.

Wittig, M. (1992) *The Straight Mind and Other Essays*. Boston: Beacon Press.

QUEERING 'TRADITIONAL' THEOLOGY

INTRODUCTION

Feminist and gay and lesbian theologies were concerned with identity-based issues. This chapter begins by examining how queer theologies move beyond identity-based theologies. Then, considering the 'indecent theology' of Marcella Althaus-Reid, the chapter looks at queer theologies that destabilise God and Christ. Indecent theologies disrupt traditional interpretations in Christianity, including doctrine, rites, and rituals. At times, queer theologies have used philosophical reason to provide arguments as to why Christianity should make space for the inclusion of LGBTQ+ people. In theology, these are called apologetic strategies, and queer theologies to date have focused on such themes. This chapter briefly considers calls in queer theologies that suggest a move away from such apologetics (Tonstad, 2018). The chapter concludes with a consideration of Christian traditions through a queer lens, discussing queer worship and queer sacraments.

Queer theologies are not a synonym for lesbian and gay theologies. Queer theologies go beyond looking at sexuality. Elizabeth Stuart states:

> Queer theology, though it usually begins with issues of sexuality, is not really 'about' sexuality in the way that gay and lesbian theology is about

DOI: 10.4324/9781003434993-3

> sexuality. Queer theology is actually about theology. In gay and lesbian theology, sexuality interrogated theology; in queer theology, theology interrogates sexuality but from a different place than modern theology has traditionally done, the place of tradition.
>
> (Stuart, 2003: 102–103)

Queer theologies, just like queer theory, move beyond queer identities. Instead of being identity-based and concerned with LGBTQ+ people, one of the insights from queer theologies is that they are anti-identity. Queer disrupts and destabilises identity categories, so there is no such thing as a queer identity in any true sense. Of course, issues of sexuality can be examined through a queer lens, but the lens is open to anyone who wishes to use the critical insights of queer theory. That said, the experiences of gay and lesbian people, alongside other marginalised individuals, are very effective in showing the powerful, hegemonic structures in Christianity which require disruption.

Gerard Loughlin's essay, 'What is Queer? Theology after Identity' (2008), offers helpful inroads to understanding what queer theologies do (or undo!). In his opening comments, he states, 'Theology is a queer thing. It has always been a queer thing' (Loughlin, 2008: 143). His argument unfolds in two directions. First, he points to the queerness of theology, using the definition of 'queer' to mean strange or odd. Loughlin comments how theology is 'strange' as it 'does not fit into the modern world' (2008: 144). Second, he points to the task of *queering*, where Christian traditions and theologies are read through a queer filter. Queering is to use a queer lens to reinterpret texts and contexts. This enterprise uses imaginative and creative tools to ask, 'what if …?' A queer lens therefore makes traditional readings unstable. Queer theologies deconstruct the building blocks of Christianity but may reshape the pieces in new, constructive ways.

As it is undefinable, like queer theory, it is more helpful to consider what queer theologies do, rather than are. Queer theologies disrupt any 'normal' or 'natural' readings of Christianity in its theological forms, including tradition, scripture, worship, fellowship, dogmas, and beliefs. Queer also removes binary thinking and presumptions, as will be observed in the idea of Althaus-Reid's 'Queer God' below. Importantly, as Christianity operates through hierarchal church structures, queer theologies expose the power relations at play within the production of theology in the institutions of the Christian churches. Queer theologies interrogate institutional hierarchies and what have been considered sources of authority in theology, such as scripture and doctrines. The Christian tradition is undoubtedly patriarchal and heteronormative. Queer theologies therefore *re-write* and *right* Christianity to some extent. As expected, the production of queer theologies has sometimes been met with disinterest or dismissal from authoritative structures within church organisations and conservative Christians. There is a real tension between queer studies and Christianity, with suspicion on both sides. Althaus-Reid states how 'on the one side there are Christians who think that queer studies offend Christianity, while on the other there is a suspicion that a too close association with Christianity will contaminate queer studies' (Althaus-Reid, 2008: 107).

Susannah Cornwall observes 'a case of queer theory and Christianity speaking in different languages, where the language-game of Christianity [...] simply does not make sense to theorists who are not themselves grounded in it' (Cornwall, 2011: 236). The different languages represent the different positions of those whose work falls under the umbrella of queer theologies. There are Christian theologians who use a queer lens while remaining faithful to the building blocks and master narratives of the tradition. In theology, systematic theology formulates ordered and reasoned accounts of Christian doctrines, looking at what the Bible teaches or what is known and true about God. Queer theologians who work systematically have their starting points and positions in the tools and languages of Christian theology, and they reveal a queer interpretation or lens within it. Using the same idea of theologies as languages, Stuart says how this option is preferable, as focusing solely on contemporary, rational, critical thought was the downfall of gay and lesbian theology:

> Gay and lesbian theology made the mistake of putting its ultimate trust in the traditions of modernity rather than the traditions of Christianity with the result that it has sometimes ceased to be recognisable as theology at all, and forfeited its place in contemporary Christian dialogue

> because it no longer speaks the same language nor does it follow the same 'grammatical' rules as its opponents.
>
> (Stuart, 2003: 105)

Another approach to queer theologies comes from the perspective that breaks free from the rules of Christianity, as queer ruptures regulation. Queer theologies can also be said to be produced in specific contexts or positions, often referred to as contextual theology. Isherwood and Althaus-Reid state that 'theology has always been contextual, and it has always depended on a theoretical framework of interpretation of the world' (Isherwood & Althaus-Reid, 2004: 4). Queer theologies in global contexts are further detailed in Chapter 3.

Queer theologies work in two ways, therefore. They show a continuation of systematic theology and a disruption of it. Althaus-Reid observes how queer theologies are an exercise of 'serious doubting' (Althaus-Reid, 2000: 5). In this, she suggests that theologians should look at the theological methods that make traditional theologies indifferent to the reality of people's contexts. The power of traditional theology is exposed in such methods. It is the traditional methods of doing theology which are exclusive and exclusionary, so queer theologies re-examine and disrupt these methods.

There has also been concern around the engagement of queer theologies with queer theory. While their entrance on the academic stage was in sync with the popularity of queer theory, it has been noted that queer theologies do not always engage with the texts and critical analyses of queer theory. Cornwall draws attention to this distinction and is concerned that 'if queer theologians do not use the term in the same way that queer critical theorists do, this may make queer theology less credible as an intellectual discourse' (Cornwall, 2011: 24).

INDECENT THEOLOGY

Marcella Althaus-Reid (1952–2009) was a Latin American liberation theologian and an eminent scholar in the field of queer theologies. She wore many hats as a theologian: feminist, liberationist, queer. Her prolific contributions to queer theologies are unparalleled and her death left a huge gap and questions for the future of queer theologies. Althaus-Reid's thought produced theologies that were completely disruptive and daring. Instead of relying on systematic order, Althaus-Reid relied on the senses and on action. Her queer theologies were passionate theologies of feeling and doing. She states that 'a Queer popular theology is an unruly one. It may bring some chaos and disorder to the effective ideology of Christian theology, but its contribution is immense' (Althaus-Reid, 2004b: 9). Her theology broke away from traditional, feminist, and liberation moulds.

A little detail about her own background provides the context for her theological projects. Althaus-Reid had left Argentina, completed her doctoral studies, and embarked on her research career in Scotland. Although some would say Althaus-Reid's theology is a cocktail of Western and Latin American ingredients, her use of Latin American contexts ensures her theologies are grounded in the living experiences of Latin American people, as she tackles issues which are relevant and important to these contexts. Leopoldo Cervantes Ortiz states:

> Though she walked the path traveled many times by other Latin American theologians who studied in Europe, her theology was not merely an academic exercise, cold, calculated, and remote-controlled to a particular audience. To understand this, we must remember her work in Argentina and Scotland among underserved communities.
>
> (Cervantes Ortiz, 2016: 29)

In 2000, Althaus-Reid released a text which would shake the foundations of theology. Her book *Indecent Theology* (2000) uncovers how 'based on sexual categories and heterosexual binary systems, obsessed with sexual behaviours and orders, every theological discourse is implicitly a sexual discourse, a decent one, an accepted one' (Althaus-Reid, 2000: 22). Her *Indecent Theology* is provocative, revolutionary, and sexually explicit. To glimpse at the radical nature of her theology, the book opens with a question about the poor women who sell lemons on the streets of her hometown in Argentina. Althaus-Reid suggests that the women do not wear underwear while they work and claims that theologians who do not wear underwear are able to challenge the 'decent' theology which has been dominant. Althaus-Reid vividly describes their poverty, their business, their interactions, and their sex. She says, 'that is the point for a theology without underwear, made by people whose sexual misfortunes, personal or political, needed to be reflected upon as part of our theological praxis' (2000: 28).

Indecent Theology also raises problems around the image of Mary within Latin American religious culture, stating that Mary's status as a virgin means that the poor women of her area are unable to identify with her. Althaus-Reid describes poor women as rarely being virgins. She notes how it is not Mary the mother of Jesus who has become significant for theology, but the construct of Mary in the Christian tradition, who has become 'the religious alien Virgin' (Althaus-Reid, 2000: 72). Mary the mother of Jesus has been sanitised by the Christian tradition, and Althaus-Reid describes her as 'the rich white woman who does not walk' (Althaus-Reid, 2004b: 30).

Fully aware of her task of 'talking obscenities to theology' (Althaus-Reid, 2000: 87), she moves from a critique of the theological ideal of Mary to how Jesus has been constructed in theology. She states how Jesus 'has been dressed theologically as a heterosexually orientated (celibate) man. Jesus with erased genitalia; Jesus minus erotic body' (2000: 114). Heterosexual masculinity is presumed and attributed to Jesus. The fact that theology has rarely considered Jesus as a sexual being 'does not allow us to see his relationship with his community or with us as instances of the way that human beings relate to each other' (2000: 114). Because of this erasure of Jesus's sexuality within Christian theology, Althaus-Reid spots a gap and uses her imagination to plug it. She says it is possible that 'Jesus may have been a transvestite, a butch lesbian, a gay or a heterosexual person' (2000: 114). Althaus-Reid imagines a Bisexual Christ, a 'Bi/Christ', which allows Jesus to be cast outside of a heterosexual identity. In 2003, she released a further text, *The Queer God*, which built on these ideas.

The work of Althaus-Reid blazed a trail in queer theologies. She states how 'in theology it is not stability but a sense of discontinuity which is most valuable' (Althaus-Reid, 2000: 4). Demonstrating how the Christian tradition is unstable is a queer strategy. Christianity only appears stable because people repeat it, thereby continuing and solidifying the idea of a tradition. Althaus-Reid was concerned with theologies from the margins that used the language of the centre. In order for theology to be truly radical it had to interrogate the centre from the margins. In *The Sexual Theologian* (2004), Isherwood and Althaus-Reid note how the position of queer theologies is at the margins:

> It is a theology from the margins which wants to remain at the margins [...] Terrible is the fate of theologies from the margin when they want to be accepted by the centre! Queer theology strives instead for differentiation and plurality [...] queer theology is a political and sexual queering of theology which goes beyond the gender paradigm of thinking of the early years of feminist theology but also transcends the fixed assumptions of gay and lesbian theology.
>
> (Isherwood & Althaus-Reid, 2004: 3)

In seeking to theologise from the margins, Althaus-Reid places value on the importance of life narratives as a source for theology. An entire chapter in *Indecent Theology* is concerned with the 'theology of sexual stories'. She states, 'the everyday lives of people always provide us with a starting point for a process of doing contextual theology without exclusion' (Althaus-Reid, 2000: 4). Chapter 5 of this book explores the queer theologies which emerge from engaging with queer lives.

QUEERING GOD/CHRIST

> Then indecent theologians may say: 'God, the Faggot; God, the Drag Queen; God, the Lesbian. God, the heterosexual woman who does not accept the constructions of ideal heterosexuality; God, the ambivalent, not easily classified sexually'.
>
> (Althaus-Reid, 2000: 95)

Althaus-Reid dared to imagine what God's and Mary's sexuality would be. Theology had largely located sexuality at the human level in relation to sexual ethics, behaviour, identity; yet, Althaus-Reid repositioned sexuality at the level of God and this shift is both theologically radical and provocative. Human understanding of sexuality often means it is a taboo subject, left out of polite conversation and better not discussed. Although sexualised images are abundant in contemporary society, including in advertising and media, talking about sex is often seen as vulgar, dirty, or indecent. Sex itself is messy. Therefore, imagining God as sexual moves away from the idea of God as sanitised. More importantly, this creates a close intimacy or relationship with God, to whom humans can relate because of their own experiences of being sexual. Imagining God as sexual is therefore an indecent task. In this spirit, Althaus-Reid asks, 'is theology the art of putting your hands under the skirts of God?' (Althaus-Reid, 2004a: 99). She states, 'God is also queer: perhaps the first queer of all' (2004a: 103).

It becomes part of Althaus-Reid's theological tactic to use shock and indecency to queer traditional ideas of God. Queer theologies are boundaryless, indecent, sexual, and do not shy away from intimacy; after all, such intimacy is part of human life. Mainstream theology has previously excluded the poor and the marginalised, who have received little space and attention in dominant theologies. Althaus-Reid's conceptions of God and Mary provide images which are far removed from traditional imaginings. Indecent theology provides dialogue between sexual, embodied contexts and the Christian tradition.

In her 2003 publication, *The Queer God*, Althaus-Reid aims to envision God outside of heterosexuality and the traditional ideas of Christianity. The book engages in a theological queering, noting how heterosexuality has shaped understanding in theology. God and Christian theology must be liberated from heterosexuality, which has become a *straight*-jacket for Christianity. Taking God out of the closet liberates God, as Althaus-Reid states: 'Queering theology, the theological task and God is all part of a coming out of the closet for Christianity which is no longer simply the high-road of classical theology' (Althaus-Reid, 2003: 4).

To engage in queer theologies, Althaus-Reid states that the task requires an honesty from theologians themselves. She explains that 'God cannot be Queered unless theologians have the courage to come out from their homosexual, lesbian, bisexual, transgendered, transvestite or (ideal) heterosexual closets. Out-of-the-closet theologians do not leave the personal aside' (Althaus-Reid, 2000: 88). Queer theologians, therefore, offer information about themselves and their background. This allows for their position and agenda to be explicit. Honesty in the production of theology means that queer theologies do not pretend to be neutral or universal.

For Althaus-Reid, queer theologies wrestle with the idea of the God of the centre. Her conception of the Queer God reflects her allegiance to liberation theologies. The Queer God is 'the stranger at the gate of churches and theology [...] God is a truly marginal God [...] the Queer God is the God who went into exile with God's people and remained there in exile with them' (Althaus-Reid, 2004b: 146). Of course, conceptualising God is a human activity, and this is one area which raises questions around the limitations of human capacity to think about God. Both Elizabeth Stuart and Althaus-Reid state how contextual theologies may fall into a tendency to create a mirror-God (Stuart, 2003: 29; Althaus-Reid, 2003: 52). Yet, imagining God in these ways is a corruption of the methods of theology, and, according to Althaus-Reid, queer theologies must 'move objects and subjects of theology around, turning points of reference and re-positioning bodies of knowledge and revelation in sometimes unsuitable ways' (Althaus-Reid, 2003: 52).

Returning to queer ideas of God, Gerard Loughlin works within the tradition and points to Thomas Aquinas's idea of negative theology. Negative theology explores the nature of what God is not, as humans are unable to state exactly what God is. Loughlin therefore works from inside the writings of traditional theology to discuss the nature of God as queer. Following Aquinas, Loughlin states:

> the most that we can say about God is that God *is* [...] In an analogous way we can say that queer *is*, even if we cannot say in what queer consists other than by pointing to the effects of its deployment.
>
> (Loughlin, 2007: 10)

He claims that the idea of queer is similar to the idea of God – that it defies definition: 'queer might be offered as a name for God' (2007: 10).

Elsewhere, Patrick Cheng's *An Introduction to Queer Theology: Radical Love* focuses on the concept of God as 'radical love' (Cheng, 2011: 50). This radical love 'breaks down fixed categories and boundaries' (2011: 51). For Cheng, the Trinity is imagined as an 'internal community of radical love' (2011: 56); Jesus 'the embodiment of radical love' (2011: 78); and Mary the 'bearer of radical love' (2011: 87). Cheng works within the Christian tradition with a confessional yet queer lens by upholding the themes of Christian theology to shape his queer reading. Via this approach, the creeds and Christian theological concepts such as sin, grace, atonement, and the sacraments provide a framework for Cheng's discussion of radical love.

QUEER TRADITION

There are a number of queer theologies that state how Christianity has always been queer, and the range of discussions is impossible to cover in this short space. I suggest that readers interested in this specific area should engage with suggested texts described in the further reading section, particularly Loughlin (2007). Among these thinkers is Stuart, who asserts that 'Christian theology was queer two thousand years before queer theory was invented' (Stuart, 2003: 102). Stuart is referring to the fact that Christianity is a religion which focuses on and displaces bodies. There are numerous examples of how theologians are able to reflect on the main beliefs of the Christian tradition and examine how they are already queer or subversive: the virgin birth, the Body of Christ as a metaphor for the church, the death of Christ through crucifixion, and the act of remembering Christ's body through the Eucharist.

By adopting this strategy some theologians use what I call a 'queer-view mirror'. Like a rear-view mirror, they reflect back on the tradition and re-examine it from the lens of the present. It is a task which looks retrospectively on the tradition with the theories and knowledge of today. Obviously 'queer' did not exist throughout the 2,000+ years of Christianity, as it is a contemporary concept. Using a queer-view mirror approach reveals multiple examples of queer readings of non-normative gender and sexuality located within the tradition, even without the current terminology and language that exist today to label them as such. The queer-view mirror provides a creative, critical, and analytical lens to offer queer readings of the tradition. Yet, queering elements of the tradition is not enough for Jeremy Carrette. He argues that, for Christianity to become truly queer, it has to queer its foundations, including its belief in one God and its exclusive possession of truth. Carrette radically proposes, 'we now need to rewrite the history of Christian theology' (Carrette, 2001: 297).

Queering the tradition has often involved queer readings of the lives and work of the early church fathers or saints. Latin American theologian Martín Hugo Córdova Quero states, 'to queer the past implies to ask different questions of it [...] attempting to find answers that go beyond what has traditionally been accepted' (Córdova Quero, 2004: 26). In an example of using a queer-view mirror, Córdova Quero re-examines the life of Aelred of Rievaulx, the English medieval monk. First, he re-examines the relationship of Aelred with a fellow monk, Simon. Following Simon's death, Aelred writes a lament of grief for his beloved friend. This lament is interpreted as an expression of both brotherly and erotic love between Aelred and Simon. Aelred develops a theology of friendship, and he allows the monks in his monastery to express their feelings physically, thereby removing feelings of guilt, sin, and shame associated with the body and same-sex physical contact with others. Córdova Quero's analysis of social orders during the period in which Aelred lived reveals how monasteries functioned as spaces 'where males engaged in homoerotic practices gathered, [monasteries] were places in which alternatives could be explored' (2004: 42).

It is not just the church fathers who are examined through this queer-view mirror. Elsewhere, Córdova Quero offers a queer reading of Mary of Magdala (Córdova Quero, 2006), exposing how Christians had trapped her in binary thinking, as a sinner or a saint. Mary represents a break in the decent story of Christianity, and Córdova Quero's examination demonstrates how Mary of Magdala went from being depicted as a sinful woman to a virtuous leader of the early church. In tracing the queerness of the treatment of Mary Magdalene and using a metaphor of 'indecent theology' borrowed from Althaus-Reid, Córdova Quero concludes that 'every *theology* is, in fact, *ideology*; ultimately there is no such thing as *innocent theology*' (2006: 82).

Within the edited volume *Queer Theology: Rethinking the Western Body* (Loughlin, 2007), there is a whole section of rich examples of queer/ing tradition. Again, the method of using a queer-view mirror helps to re-examine traditional concepts. For example, the early church father Gregory of Nyssa has been reinterpreted by Virginia Burrus (2007). She examines the notion of desire in the theology of Gregory, analysing concepts of virginity, marriage, and fatherhood. Similarly, Amy Hollywood (2007) provides a critical reading of medieval women, offering a queer reading of three mystic women – Mechthild of Magdeburg, Hadewijch of Anvers, and Marguerite Porete. Their devotion in worship is revealed as sacred eroticism, and the language of their mystical writings challenges assumptions of gender. Furthermore, Christopher Hinkle (2007) offers a queer reading of Saint John of the Cross. In resisting the temptation to read John as a gay saint, as other theologians have tended to do, Hinkle examines John's submission to the dominant God as an act of burning desire and love.

Queer theologies are not always written or text based. Other examples of queering the tradition are found in forms of queer art. Kittredge Cherry's *Art That Dares* (2007) offers dramatic new visions of a woman Christ, a gay Jesus, and saints in love. In Cherry's rich anthology, various artists are incorporated into a collection of paintings, photographs, and sculptures which offer new visual forms for spiritual and personal contemplation. The paintings include Alex Donis's images of Jesus and Lord Rama from Hindu mythology kissing passionately (Cherry, 2007: 36). The theme of kissing continues with a gay embrace depicted in the Judas Kiss by Becki Jayne Harrelson (Cherry, 2007: 42) and a passionate kiss between Mary Magdalene and the Virgen de Guadalupe (Cherry, 2007: 39, private artist). In photographic form, the work of Elisabeth Ohlson Wallin depicts an image of Jesus entitled 'Sermon on the Mount', where he is surrounded by half-naked leather-clad men wearing chains and restraints (Cherry, 2007: 74). Ohlson Wallin's work continues in her reimaging the iconic 'Pietà', where Mary is cradling the dead body of Jesus. In Ohlson Wallin's queer reconceptualisation of the piece she uses a gay man dying of AIDS in a hospital ward being cradled by a woman in blue.

Queer images are used to engage with and reflect upon queer lives. Cherry states how 'the images are arising now because the conventional Jesus is no longer adequate' (Cherry, 2007: 8). Throughout the history of Judaism and Christianity, there has always been a charge of blasphemy against those who make images of idols and icons. Within the Hebrew Bible/Old Testament, one of God's commandments to Moses was against creating images of God: 'You shall not make for yourself an image in the form of anything in heaven above or on the earth beneath or in the waters below' (Exodus, 20:4). Some Christian denominations do use images as a focus for worship, yet Cherry is keen to point out that there are power structures at play with religious images. She states, 'by controlling religious images, they control people [...] unauthorized images can be made by unauthorized people' (Cherry, 2007: 9).

BEYOND APOLOGETIC STRATEGIES

In the study of theology, apologetics does not mean apologising for one's faith. The term comes from the Greek: 'apologia' meaning a 'reasoned defence'. Therefore, traditional apologetics is the defence of Christian religious doctrines through reasoned arguments. In terms of gender and sexuality, apologetic strategies may examine theological questions relating to gender transitioning or same-sex marriage. Queer theologians who engage in apologetics look for ways to counter claims that Christianity is incompatible with LGBTQ+ identities. They may look to doctrines and to the Bible to find examples within the Christian message that appeal to queer imaginations. Gay and lesbian and queer theologies have largely been done using apologetic strategies.

In *Queer Theology: Beyond Apologetics,* Linn Tonstad is of the opinion that 'queer theology is not about apologetics, or at least that it *should* not be about apologetics' (Tonstad, 2018: 16). She states that 'Christians should stop arguing over issues of sexual morality altogether, and instead should allow the discernment of the individual conscience before God to rule' (2018: 38). Tonstad suggests how the focus of the queer project in theology is capitalism – the relationship between the economy and sex. She describes how heterosexual marriage, monogamy, and reproduction are the cogs of capitalism: 'Children are needed for the continuance and growth of capitalism: they must be born, clothed, fed, and educated, so that they, in turn, become productive workers and consumers' (2018: 81). Religion has sanctified this process, giving it 'an aura of holiness, divine will and ethical responsibility' (2018: 82).

In stating her own position, she says:

> I am a Christian theologian who works in queer theory as well. Many Christian theologians and many queer theorists believe that combination is possible. Those who think such a combination is possible often disagree about how such a task should be undertaken.
>
> (2018: 50)

She reiterates her claim that queer apologetics offers little theological value and acknowledges that her own work could be assessed as being too 'doctrine-heavy than most queer theologians would prefer' (2018: 50).

Queer cannot be pinned down. The plural term, queer theologies, is therefore much more appropriate in highlighting the different languages spoken by queer theologians, who all hold their own preferences for methods and allegiances. Queer is indefinable and unfixable. Therefore, queer theologians should exercise caution when stating what queer theologies should or should not be about, as this can be seen as an attempt to carve out a normativity. Whether apologetic strategies are used or not, queer theologies are committed to the task of disruption, removing power structures and hierarchies, and demonstrating the instability of firmly fixed objects and positions. Queer theologies are diverse and plural. Queer theologies are multiple and varied, their richness allows them to speak differently.

One of the major themes that characterises the work of queer theologies is the interplay between continuity and disruption in relation to traditional theology. Queer theologies refuse to allow a patriarchal and heteronormative tradition to continue without being examined, critiqued, subverted, and disrupted. The Christian tradition, therefore, only seems stable because it has been repeated throughout the centuries, and that repetition has firmed up its hold on power structures which regulate theologies, bodies, and beliefs. Elsewhere I call this 'Christian-normativity' (Greenough, 2018: 172). A resistance to repeating traditional Christianity is the task of queer theologies, as Althaus-Reid states: 'queer traditions are made of strange alliances of memories of discontinuity and disorder, shared by communities of people with pride and resistance' (Althaus-Reid, 2003: 10). Attention now turns to the communities of Christians as a body, where Christian worship is queer and queered.

QUEER WORSHIP

> Queer people are not outsiders to the church. Christianity has not only always had queer members, has not only always had the potential to be queered, but has from the start been a site of radical queerness.
>
> (Larrimore, 2015: 2)

In noting that queer members of the church have always existed, Mark Larrimore is in agreement with theologians like Stuart who claim that Christianity has always been queer. There are a number of questions that have become popular which relate to the inclusion of LGBTQ+ people within the churches. Why do people who are LGBTQ+ remain within the churches, whose positional statements are often biphobic, homophobic, and transphobic? How does someone reconcile being Christian with other non-normative aspects of their identity? In Chapter 5, I address some of these questions when looking at queer theologies that emerge from queer Christian lives. In this section on queer worship, I consider the important developments within Christian denominations to include marginalised people. Then, I consider how Christian worship can be seen to reflect the lives of queer people. In examining queer worship, there are two perspectives: the first reflects on the elements and relevance of worship for 'queer' people; the second reveals elements of Christian worship which are unusual, or queer.

Across a wide range of Christian traditions, denomination-specific gay and lesbian or LGBTQ+ organisations have emerged. Examples include but are not limited to Roman Catholics (Quest), the Episcopalians (Integrity), Methodists (Affirmation), the Association of Welcoming and Affirming Baptists, and Evangelicals Concerned. An increasing number of churches are making it known publicly that they are welcoming, open, and affirming, despite the positions of their institutional hierarchies. There are a number of LGBTQ+ friendly worship organisations and churches across the world whose services are designed to affirm the beliefs and identities of LGBTQ+ Christians. The Metropolitan Community Church (MCC) is an example of a church community that ministers specifically to LGBTQ+ people. The church was founded in California a year before the Stonewall riots by the Rev. Troy Perry. In addition to a presence of MCC churches in Australasia, Europe, and North America, there are also ministries within Africa (including Kenya and Nigeria) and Latin America. There has been an identified presence in Russia, where 'anti-gay' propaganda is criminalised. In Asia, important efforts in relation to LGBTQ+ inclusion and queer theologies in Christian religious communities are noted in, for example, the Jakarta Theological Seminary in Indonesia, the National Council of Churches and the United Theological College in India, MCC churches in the Philippines, Tong Kwang church in Taiwan, and Blessed Ministry Community Church and the Queer Theology Academy in Hong Kong.

In his discussion on 'queer-church', Andy Braunston details his own experiences as a founding senior pastor of an MCC congregation in the UK. Braunston notes how queer worship is able to self-fashion and re-create what church is by refusing to play by the rules of mainstream churches. This has been empowering and attractive to those who have left traditional congregations. Braunston details what queer-church and queer worship looks like:

> The thing that unites us is the feeling that we are making the rules for ourselves. We can make our own liturgies and ceremonies which mark our lives and loves [...] Our poets and musicians are now writing hymns for us [...] We are re-creating the church in a way which is powerful and meaningful to our loves and lives.
>
> (Braunston, 1997: 102)

In Christian theology, liturgy is a form of public worship which can include rites, rituals, ceremonies, and sacraments. Specific suggestions for queer liturgy come from the authors of *Religion is a Queer Thing* (Stuart, 1997). There are practical suggestions throughout the text, including exercises and reflections for use as part of worship services. The span of themes is wide, with due care and attention to make the language accessible in discussions of the Bible, God, the queer Christ, salvation, liturgy, and queer ethics. The editor, Elizabeth Stuart, is keen to include lesbian, gay, bisexual, and transgender voices in the design of queer worship. She says:

> only if queer theology reflects the reality and spirituality of those who live the reality of queer lives in the mess and muddle of the world will queer theology [... have] the potential to transform not just queer people but all men and women.
>
> (1997: 4)

In a similar vein to Stuart, Martin Stringer advocates that messy bodies and lives should be embraced as a part of worship. He is among scholars who note how Christianity has been queer, revealed in his reading of mainstream Anglo-Catholic worship as camp and drag (Stringer, 2000). Stringer observes that worship is a physical and sensory experience, and by re-centring the body, he challenges accounts that treat worship as primarily intellectual or spiritual. Indeed, Stringer points out how bodies are integral to worship: the body of Christ and the liturgical body are both widely discussed in theology, but these discussions are distanced from 'any real bodies, and particularly from any kind of "bodily functions"' (2000: 38). The body is therefore idealised, and the realities of human bodies are avoided. According to Stringer, any part of the human body that is functional, unclean, sinful, or sexual is completely ignored in discussions of the body in worship. In highlighting the camp aspects of worship, Stringer draws on parallels with drag, noting how the church sacristy is an all-male environment in which men who are about to perform adorn themselves in lace and jewels. Yet, this playful reading is serious; as Stringer concludes:

> if we are able, however, to move beyond the camp and to find alternative ways of expressing much more openly and directly our sexual selves in worship, then there may be much more hope and much more cause for rejoicing.
>
> (2000: 54)

Queer people are part of churches and worshipping communities. Siobhán Garrigan questions how significant life events in the lives of LGBTQ+ people are marked and celebrated within churches. She imagines coming-out services, re-naming ceremonies, house blessings, and blessings of same-sex unions (Garrigan, 2009: 213). Likewise, she asks 'how many times have you heard sermons in which the stories told are about LGBT people's lives?' (2009: 214). Garrigan calls for such rites to be part of whole services, rather than private and supplementary to public liturgical worship. By making something a private event, it hides its status from the community. In making this observation, Garrigan points to the fact that queer theologies have to be practical, rather than theoretical or ideological when it comes to worship. In highlighting how worship, like theology, is gendered and heteronormative, Garrigan states how worship is truly queer when masculine references to God are removed. She states, 'queer worship is at its most controversial not when it proposes the acceptability of people coming to worship dressed in leather but when it suggests calling God something other than Father' (2009: 219). Just as feminist theology held concerns about the masculine language for

God, within queer theologies descriptions of God can reflect the preferred terminology from the worshipper.

In this sense one of the most contested issues within the field is revealed: the relationship between queer-identities (LGBTQ+) and queer which serves to destabilise identities. If queer disrupts identity, how can it be supposed to represent or support queer identities? There is often a blur between identity-informed queer theologies and queer theologies beyond identity.

To respond to this difficult question, it is helpful to recall how queer theologies are not universal and not all theologians speak the same language. For some, queer theologies are intellectual and theoretical (queerly rupturing identities), while for others, they are practical (serving queer identities). Queer theologies seem to be doing two different things. In one sense, they seem to be working from a top-down approach grounded in theory, tradition, and reason, while, on the other hand, they work from a bottom-up approach grounded in the lives of queer people. Within each approach, there are complex and challenging questions, and these can lead to vagueness or to disagreements between both approaches. Yet, queer resists such binary framing; queer theologies can be both/and, rather than either/or: both theoretical and practical, both academic and lived, both apologetic and indecent, both systematic and constructive. The whole point of queer is to destabilise, so, as an academic area and approach, the possibilities beyond normativity are abundant. Queer allows for disciplinary promiscuity in a variety of ways.

Inclusion in queer worshipping communities remains a significant issue on a practical level where LGBTQ+ people have to make important choices around their access and inclusion to be able to participate in worship, including with friends and family, and in their local communities. The question of inclusion remains an important challenge to Christianity, despite theoretical or reasoned positions, precisely because of the emotional wrestling in the daily lives of people who are LGBTQ+ and Christian. Negotiating what can be seen as conflicting identities is a long, difficult, and emotional process: individuals may choose to reject the centre of mainstream Christianity on a personal level, while some wish to remain. In blending queer and practical theologies, these discussions are important to LGBTQ+ Christians.

Abandonment, rejection, or isolation from religious communities features in the lives of queer Christians. The loss of the worship community can be significant. Deryn Guest notes that there is a real loss when the religious community one has grown up in becomes a thing of the past. On leaving the Salvation Army, Guest recalls experiences of loss and grief:

> what I had not anticipated was the sheer enormity of loss that this action entailed: loss of a religious home akin to a much loved family of would-be aunts, uncles, nieces, nephews, cousins, grandparents; loss of its liturgical environments – particularly in musical and lyrical heritage, which for all its gendered stereotypes and heteronormativity, had always held profound significance for me; and the loss of relationship with God.
>
> (Guest, 2008: 202)

Religious identities are often constructed from birth, through relationships with individuals in local worship communities and surroundings. For LGBTQ+ Christians, the loss and grief can be profound, and, therefore, questions of exclusion and inclusion remain significant.

QUEER SACRAMENTS

> Queer theologies do not disregard church traditions. However, the process of queering may turn them upside down.
>
> (Althaus-Reid, 2003: 8)

Althaus-Reid reveals how the active agenda of queering Christian traditions is disruptive. In this way, Stuart has offered comprehensive queer readings of the sacraments (Stuart, 1997, 2007, 2010). The underlying principle of her scholarship is that 'the body of Christ is queer. That body is made available to Christians through the sacraments' (Stuart, 2007: 66). For Christians, sacraments are significant rites of passage, with the objective of bringing Christians closer to God. Within the Catholic and Orthodox traditions, there are seven major sacraments: baptism, Eucharist, confirmation, reconciliation, marriage, anointing of the sick, and holy orders. The Protestant view rejects five of the sacraments above, citing baptism and Eucharist as the only two important ones. In this overview of queer sacraments, I examine baptism and Eucharist as queer sacraments. I also draw attention to the controversies surrounding the marriage debate within Christian churches. Moreover, I consider how there is a non-sacramental rite of passage which can be considered queer: the concept of 'coming out' (see also Chapter 6 for rites of passage for trans people).

BAPTISM

A queer reading of baptism reveals it as a sacrament which moves Christians beyond identity. Baptism is a sacrament of initiation: it is a rite of naming an individual and their belonging to church. In some denominations, baptism is done to babies a few weeks after their birth. In others, baptism is a choice a Christian makes as an adult to become a full church member through their own free will. At their baptism, Christians believe that their sins are washed away. This is why water is an important sign of baptism. Christians therefore die to sin. In a queer reading of the sacrament of baptism, Stuart views baptism as the acquisition of a new identity, one that surpasses human markers of identity. Stuart reveals how baptism involves two simultaneous deaths: one to sin and the other to identity. She states how baptism 'reveals the inadequacy of all other forms of identity and the desire caught up in them' (Stuart, 2007: 67). Stuart's understanding of baptism is grounded in Paul's letter to the Galatians in the New Testament, where he declares: 'There is neither Jew nor Gentile, neither slave nor free, nor is there male and female, for you are all one in Christ Jesus' (3:28). For Stuart, baptism signifies taking on a new identity as Christian, one which erases categories of identity that can separate people on earth. This belief is truly realised in the afterlife. In Christian theology, eschatology is the examination of death, judgement, and afterlife. Stuart's belief is that baptism is wholly connected to the eschatological promises stated by Paul in his letter to the Galatians. She notes that the promise of eternal afterlife renders those who are baptised 'people who in their own beings carry around with them the death that society fears' (Stuart, 2007: 73). Stuart claims that queer flesh is sacramental flesh. Through baptism, she states, 'in Christ maleness and femaleness and gay and straight are categories that dissolve before the throne of grace where only the garment of baptism remains' (2007: 75).

This idea of identity erasure is considered idealistic by some. Andy Buechel finds Stuart's reading of the sacrament 'rich and compelling, but also troubling in its idealism' (Buechel, 2015: 58). He states how Stuart's notion of baptism is grounded in what happens in the afterlife, rather than what happens currently on earth. According to Buechel, Stuart's reading means that 'no longer do we relate to one another as men and women, gay and straight, or via any other human identity' (2015: 63). He responds by stating that 'it is quite obvious that Christians are still bound up in the same cultural identities as anyone who is non-baptised. In fact, it is often the non-baptised who are more successful at exposing the non-ultimacy of these identities' (2015: 63). He notes how baptism is problematic for queer Christians, especially as the promises of being included into a Christian family often prove to be false. Buechel expresses this as follows:

> the baptized are not granted some special privilege that allows them to avoid the same cultural constructions, negotiations, and maneuvers as anyone else. In fact, if we look at the controversies over sex and gender in the churches, we would be led to believe the exact opposite.
>
> (Buechel, 2015: 65)

For Buechel, the need for Christians to wait for the afterlife for issues of identity to be fixed, as Stuart suggests, is a step too far. He states that 'appeals to eschatology […] may not attend enough to questions that need to be addressed in the here and now' (Buechel, 2015: 73).

Beyond issues of identity, the links between birth and baptism are problematic too. Althaus-Reid is concerned with baptism as a rite which does not recognise, appreciate, or celebrate the human nature of an individual. In fact, she states that it does the opposite, as it is:

> a liturgical act based on a theology which devalues the human, in the sense that it assumes the incompleteness of the new-born human. However, it is also a devaluation of women, as if women are incapable of giving birth to children accepted by society as fully human.
>
> (Althaus-Reid, 2003: 136)

Simply put, the explicit need for baptism undermines the human experience of birth. The performance of baptism in Christianity is seen as superior to birth, as baptism implies that humans are not part of the Christian family until they experience this rite. She concludes that 'baptism appears here as a sacramental supplement to birth' (2003: 136).

EUCHARIST

In Christian theology, the Eucharist is a sacrament which recalls Jesus's actions at the Last Supper. For Catholics, it is called the Blessed Sacrament, as Catholics believe in transubstantiation. Transubstantiation is the belief that communion bread and wine are transformed into the actual body and blood of Jesus through the blessing of a priest. Because of this idea, a queer reading of the Eucharist brings into play ideas about bodies and blood. Such ideas relate to human embodiments and human experiences. The union of Christ and Christian in the Eucharist can be seen as a fusion of bodies, using images which are shaped by sexual ideas. The sexual imagery of intimate experiences through the Eucharist is developed by Robert Goss in his essay 'Passionate Love for Christ: Out of the Closet, Into the Streets' (Goss, 2000). Goss writes that, in celebrating the sacrament of the Eucharist, 'I envisioned making love to Jesus, felt myself become sexually aroused, and climaxed in an orgasmic union with Jesus the Christ [...] Jesus was my gay lover' (2000: 300–301). Goss continues to describe the presence of Christ in his lovemaking with his partner, Frank:

> our sex was Eucharistic, intensely passionate, and intensely spiritual. During passionate lovemaking, I felt Christ in a way that I only experienced in my solitary erotic prayer. I felt Christ in our lovemaking and did not want to give it up.
>
> (2000: 301)

Stuart too agrees that 'God is in there, rustling between the sheets, disrupting and dislocating' (Stuart, 2010: 114), but for Stuart, the satisfaction of experiencing God's presence during a sexual encounter is only temporary. Stuart warns that 'condensing God to human relating, whether in bed or not, is dangerous because human relationships simply cannot bear the weight of the divine' (2010: 114). Her queer Eucharist shows how the diversity of human characteristics and identities is part of the body of Christ:

> The chief characteristic of this body is its extraordinary diversity – all sexes, sexualities, races, classes are part of it, the decent and the indecent. The body of Christ in which our individual bodies find their meaning is the perfect queer community.
>
> (Stuart, 2010: 122)

In another queer reading, Althaus-Reid stresses the physical aspect of consuming divine flesh in the Eucharist. She labels the Eucharist as a cannibalistic event, noting how the human consumption of Christ's body and blood is both silent yet integral to Catholics. She describes this as the 'cannibalistic elements of eucharists, elegantly suppressed and represented in theology' (Althaus-Reid, 2000: 57).

MARRIAGE

There is some unease in the discussion of the sacrament of marriage as it draws attention to the complex and antagonistic positions of the churches in recognising the loving relationships and unions between same-sex couples. This discussion is expanded in Chapter 5. Stuart sees the position of the churches as an almost failing of LGBTQ+ people in allowing full membership to the sacraments; as she states, 'the church's refusal to incorporate lesbian and gay and transsexual people into marriage demonstrates a lack of engagement with the eschatological and Christological dimension of the sacrament' (Stuart, 2007: 73). Stuart was writing at a time in which terms to describe transgender people as 'transexual' or 'transvestite' were still popular. These terms have since largely fallen out of use and are now widely regarded as outdated or inappropriate.

The majority of Christian denominations still conceptualise marriage as the union between one man and one woman, with an understanding that the marriage will be sexually consummated and result in procreation. As a sacrament, it is not difficult to see why a queer reading of marriage has been important to recognise relationships between non-heterosexual identifying individuals. Moreover, it raises questions beyond same-sex discussions. What about relationships that extend beyond two people, where the relationship may include other partners? The principle of procreation is also inherently troubling for individuals who may choose not to have children or are unable to have children. How does adoption fit into the sense of marriage procreation? Susannah Cornwall offers an extensive discussion of these issues in *Un/Familiar Theology* (2017). Her un/familiar theology takes root in assessing the familiar concepts of the theological tradition, marriage, and reproduction, before highlighting the complexity of social lived experiences which may be termed as 'unfamiliar' to the Christian tradition. Yet, these experiences are 'precisely part of what the tradition may be yet to embrace. The unfamiliar is therefore both already a part of the tradition, and part of what the tradition may become' (Cornwall, 2017: 15). She rebalances the positions of those wishing to preserve the tradition by focusing on the reality of the lives of many in it. To some extent, the tradition is not stable and unchanging in any case, and on these issues, it must engage and evolve. She states:

> if same-sex marriage, for example, somewhat changes marriage, and adoptive parenting by same-sex couples or single people, for example, somewhat alters what we understand family and parenthood to be, this is not a departure to be mourned but a shift to be critically engaged.
> (Cornwall, 2017: 2)

Cornwall is bold in her examination of marriage, reminding us that 'Christians do not own marriage' (Cornwall, 2017: 45) and that 'God did not invent marriage. Humans invented marriage, and humans can and do reinvent it too' (2017: 46).

Just as the Eucharist depicts a physical relationship with the body of Christ and Christians, there has been a marriage metaphor which emerges from a study of the relationship between God and Israel within the Hebrew Bible/Old Testament. This idea of God in a relationship with his people is reinterpreted by Christians in the concept of Jesus and the church. Loughlin recalls the story in John's gospel of the wedding at Cana, highlighting how readers do not know who got married. The story is popular for recalling the miracle of Jesus turning water into wine, but Loughlin reconsiders the story, suggesting how Christ was marrying his disciple, John. He notes how this is a 'queer kind of marriage: the bonding of men in matrimony' (Loughlin, 2007: 2).

Sexual expression cannot solely be about reproduction, as traditional theologies hold. Goss notes how equating marriage with procreative sexuality denies it the pleasures of intimacy. Goss uncovers how the churches' attempts to regulate sexuality are expressions of institutional power, such that any attempt to subvert traditional marriage or to promote sex for pleasure is treated as a threat. Goss claims how these threats to marriage and family structures 'open the social construction of sexuality to innovative meanings and values' (Goss, 1993: 136). Moreover, by uncovering the social structures of sexuality and gender, Goss sees same-sex unions as free from patriarchy and heteronormative assumptions. He states, 'same sex unions are frequently without heterosexist power relations or conjugal stereotypes that are socially incorporated into the institute of marriage' (1993: 137). According to Goss, rather than recognising the union of same-sex partners, theology can learn from their relationships.

As marriage is a public event, with banns being read and celebrations with close friends and families, Cheng points to how this is an affirmation which has similarities to the experience of 'coming out'. He says, 'the sacrament of matrimony is also closely connected with coming out because coming out is precisely what makes same-sex marriages possible in the first place' (Cheng, 2011: 124). As a pivotal event unique to the lives of LGBTQ+ people, coming out has its own ritual and transformation. Coming out is a queer sacrament.

COMING OUT AS SACRAMENT

The precarious positions of LGBTQ+ people in some churches mean that some individuals have been excluded from the sacraments. Chris Glaser discusses the effects of this on the lives of LGBTQ+ people:

> We have experienced word and sacrament not as open hands reaching to welcome us but as spiritually abusive fists ready to pummel us, not as open arms ready to embrace us but as intimidating arms pushing us away, protectively shielding rather than openly sharing the Body of Christ, the church.
>
> (Glaser, 1998: 5)

Glaser argues that 'coming out' is the most important sacrament for LGBTQ+ people. It is important to note how the process of coming out as an act of self-affirmation is the total opposite of being 'outed', where an individual has no control or say in the disclosure. Glaser sees the act of coming out as spiritual; as he states, '*coming out* is our unique sacrament, a rite of vulnerability that reveals the sacred in our lives – our worth, our love, our love-making, our beloved, our communities, our context of meaning, and our God' (Glaser, 1998: 9). He highlights the role that communities play in the rituals of the sacraments, because any enactment of the sacraments involves more than an individual but their relations and support networks. Glaser states, 'just as the sacred nature of a sacrament cannot be forced on anyone who does not believe in its efficacy, coming out requires the cooperation and belief of those affected' (1998: 9–10). He sees how the act of coming out echoes each of the traditional sacraments. For example, Glaser notes how in baptism Christians die to their old lives, and how the act of coming out can mirror this death, as LGBTQ+ people are able to live more openly and become part of a new community. Glaser also describes how coming out reflects the nature of the Eucharist, insofar as the celebration of the sacrament recalls the vulnerability and sacrifice of Jesus and leads to union with God.

CONCLUSION

This chapter has provided a basic overview of scholarship on how traditional theological thought is both queer and queered. Alternative ideas of God, Christ, and Christian traditions are revealed using a queer-view mirror to re-examine traditional theology. These alternatives disrupt traditional theologies. Queer theologies are also able to serve the marginalised, who can locate their own identifications and experiences within the Christian story. Moreover, queer theologies release ideas of God and Christ from heteronormative and patriarchal assumptions. On a practical level, this chapter has engaged with the concept of queer worship and queer Christian life through the sacraments. What emerges within the production of queer theologies is the problem with the word 'queer'. Queer theologies can be seen to contradict themselves as they function in two ways: they aim to disrupt categories of identity, yet queer theologies are simultaneously concerned with LGBTQ+ identities. In many respects, queer theologies *queer* themselves because of this tension between both approaches. They undo one another. The next chapter offers further insights into the plurality and diversity of queer theologies in global contexts.

FURTHER READING AND RESOURCES

Althaus-Reid, M. (2000) *Indecent Theology.* London: Routledge.

Althaus-Reid reveals how theology is a sexual act. She calls for a theology that is committed to social justice and transformation of powerful structures in theology and in society.

Cheng, P. S. (2011) *Radical Love: An Introduction to Queer Theology.* New York: Seabury Books.

Cheng offers an overview of queer theology, examining the role of God, Jesus, and the Holy Spirit. He provides discussion of the sacraments through a queer lens, as well as a comprehensive reference list for those looking for further reading on the subject of same-sex marriage (p.125, footnote 68).

Cooper, T. (2021) *Queer and Indecent: An Introduction to the Theology of Marcella Althaus Reid.* London: SCM Press.

Thia Cooper offers an accessible and comprehensive introduction to the major themes in Althaus-Reid's work.

Loughlin, G. (Ed.) (2007) *Queer Theology: Rethinking the Western Body.* London: Blackwell.

A collection of academic essays exploring queer theologies in the West. The essays particularly offer theological reflections on Christian churches, history, and tradition.

Stuart, E. (Ed.) (1997) *Religion is a Queer Thing.* London: Cassell.

An overview of Christian faith for LGBTQ+ people. The book offers accessible insights, particularly to those working within ministry or church communities, as well as offering practical ideas for worship.

Tonstad, L. (2018) *Queer Theology. Beyond Apologetics.* Eugene: Wipf and Stock.

Tonstad details how queer theologies should no longer be about apologetic strategies. She considers what apologetic strategies look like and why they do not satisfy, before considering how queer theology is connected more widely to capitalism.

Q Spirit: http://qspirit.net/blog/

This website looks at queer readings of Christianity, transforming biblical stories and saints into queer works of art. The blog also has an up-to-date list of books and key concepts in queer theology.

REFERENCES

Althaus-Reid, M. (2000) *Indecent Theology*. London: Routledge.

Althaus-Reid, M. (2003) *The Queer God*. London: Routledge.

Althaus-Reid, M. (2004a) 'Queer I Stand: Lifting the Skirts of God'. In Althaus-Reid, M. and Isherwood, L. (Eds.) *The Sexual Theologian*, pp. 99–109. London: Continuum.

Althaus-Reid, M. (2004b) *From Feminist to Indecent Theology*. London: SCM Press.

Althaus-Reid, M. (2008) 'The Bi/girl Writings: From Feminist Theology to Queer Theologies'. In Isherwood, L. and McPhillips, K. (Eds.) *Post-Christian Feminisms: A Critical Approach*, pp. 105–116. Farnham: Ashgate.

Braunston, A. (1997) 'The Church'. In Stuart, E. (Ed.) *Religion Is a Queer Thing*, pp. 96–104. London: Cassell.

Buechel, A. (2015) *That We Might Become God*. Eugene: Cascade Books.

Burrus, V. (2007) 'Queer Father: Gregory of Nyssa and the Subversion of Identity'. In Loughlin, G. (Ed.) *Queer Theology: Rethinking the Western Body*, pp. 147–162. London: Blackwell.

Carrette, J. (2001) 'Radical Heterodoxy and the Indecent Proposal of Erotic Theology: Critical Groundwork for Sexual Theologies'. *Literature and Theology*, *15*(3), pp. 286–298.

Cervantes Ortiz, L. (2016) '"Lifting Up God's Skirt": The Postmodern, Post-liberationist and Postcolonial Theology of Marcella Althaus-Reid: A Latin American Approach'. In Panotto, N. (Ed.) *Indecent Theologies: Marcella Althaus-Reid and the Next Generation of Postcolonial Activists*, pp. 25–40. California: Borderless Press.

Cheng, P. S. (2011) *Radical Love: An Introduction to Queer Theology*. New York: Seabury Books.

Cherry, K. (2007) *Art That Dares. Gay Jesus, Woman Christ and More*. California: AndroGyne Press.

Córdova Quero, M. H. (2004) 'Friendship with Benefits: A Queer Reading of Aelred of Rievaulx and His Theology of Friendship'. In Althaus-Reid, M. and Isherwood, L. (Eds.) *The Sexual Theologian*, pp. 26–46. London: Continuum.

Córdova Quero, M. H. (2006) 'The Prostitutes Also Go into the Kingdom of God: A Queer Reading of Mary of Magdala'. In Althaus-Reid, M. (Ed.) *Liberation Theology and Sexuality* (Second Edition), pp. 81–110. London: SCM Press.

Cornwall, S. (2011) *Controversies in Queer Theology*. London: SCM Press.

Cornwall, S. (2017) *Un/familiar Theology. Reconceiving Sex, Reproduction and Generativity*. London: Bloomsbury.

Garrigan, S. (2009) 'Queer Worship'. *Theology & Sexuality*, *15*(2), pp. 211–230.

Glaser, C. (1998) *Coming Out As Sacrament*. Louisville: Westminster John Knox Press.

Goss, R. E. (1993) *Jesus Acted Up. A Gay and Lesbian Manifesto*. San Francisco: Harper.

Goss, R. E. (2000) 'Passionate Love for Christ: Out of the Closet, Into the Streets'. In Kay, K., Nagle, J. and Gould, B. (Eds.) *Male Lust: Pleasure, Power and Transformation*, pp. 297–304. New York: Harrington Park Press.

Greenough, C. (2018) *Undoing Theology: Life Stories from Non-normative Christians*. London: SCM Press.

Guest, D. (2008) 'Liturgy and Loss: A Lesbian Perspective on Using Psalms of Lament in Liturgy'. In Burns, S., Jagessar, M. N. and Slee, N. (Eds.) *The Edge of God: New Liturgical Texts and Contexts in Conversation*, pp. 202–216. London: Epworth Press.

Hinkle, C. (2007) 'Love's Urgent Longings: St John of the Cross'. In Loughlin, G. (Ed.) *Queer Theology: Rethinking the Western Body*, pp. 188–199. London: Blackwell.

Hollywood, A. (2007) 'Queering the Beguines: Mechthild of Magdeburg, Hadewijch of Anvers, Marguerite Porete'. In Loughlin, G. (Ed.) *Queer Theology: Rethinking the Western Body*, pp. 163–175. London: Blackwell.

Isherwood, L. and Althaus-Reid, M. (2004) 'Queering Theology'. In Althaus-Reid, M. and Isherwood, L. (Eds.) *The Sexual Theologian*, pp. 1–15. London: Continuum.

Larrimore, M. (2015) 'Introduction'. In Talvacchia, K. T., Pettinger, M. F. and Larrimore, M. (Eds.) *Queer Christianities. Lived Religion in Transgressive Forms*, pp. 1–10. New York: New York University Press.

Loughlin, G. (2007) 'Introduction: The End of Sex'. In Loughlin, G. (Ed.) *Queer Theology: Rethinking the Western Body*, pp. 1–34. London: Blackwell.

Loughlin, G. (2008) 'What Is Queer? Theology after Identity'. *Theology & Sexuality, 14*(2), pp. 143–152.

Stringer, M. (2000) 'Of Gin and Lace: Sexuality, Liturgy and Identity among Anglo-Catholics in the Mid-Twentieth Century'. *Theology & Sexuality, 13*, pp. 35–54.

Stuart, E. (Ed.) (1997) *Religion Is a Queer Thing*. London: Cassell.

Stuart, E. (2003) *Gay and Lesbian Theologies: Repetitions and Critical Difference*. Farnham: Ashgate.

Stuart, E. (2007) 'Sacramental Flesh'. In Loughlin, G. (Ed.) *Queer Theology: Rethinking the Western Body*, pp. 65–75. London: Blackwell.

Stuart, E. (2010) 'Making No Sense: Liturgy as Queer Space'. In Isherwood, L. and Petrella, I. (Eds.) *Dancing Theology in Fetish Boots: Essays in Honour of Marcella Althaus-Reid*, pp. 113–123. London: SCM Press.

Tonstad, L. (2018) *Queer Theology. Beyond Apologetics*. Eugene: Wipf and Stock.

3

QUEER THEOLOGIES IN GLOBAL CONTEXTS

INTRODUCTION

This chapter draws attention to the social backdrops and global contexts in which queer theologies are produced. First, attention turns to the relationship between queer theory and postcolonial criticism. Throughout the discussion, the ideas of fusion and encounters between cultures are prominent. The chapter then provides brief overviews of queer theologies developing in a range of global contexts, spanning Asian American, Asian, African, Latin American, Black and womanist traditions, as well as scholarship from the North Atlantic, Australia, and Aotearoa (New Zealand). While the overviews in each section provide examples of queer theologies in situated contexts, they are by no means comprehensive.

POSTCOLONIAL AND QUEER CRITICISMS

Throughout history, different countries have exercised their control over others. Colonialism refers to the political control of one country by another, through populating it with migrants, taking resources, and exploiting inhabitants in terms of labour. It also involves the imposition of the coloniser's culture, beliefs, norms,

DOI: 10.4324/9781003434993-4

language, and values on the colonised, often erasing or marginalising Indigenous traditions. Postcolonialism examines the impact this has had. It uncovers the lasting effects of colonialism in former colonies. Within this framework, postcolonial theology examines the impact of colonialism in relation to Christianity, particularly as aspects of the tradition have also engaged in colonisation through missionaries who promoted Christianity in foreign lands. The version of Christianity they brought was based on Western contexts and values, rather than local contexts, values, and practices.

Hong Kong-born feminist theologian Kwok Pui-lan offers a reading of postcolonial theologies from a feminist perspective in her book *Postcolonial Imagination and Feminist Theology* (Kwok, 2005), where she examines the relationship between postcolonialism and issues of sexuality and gender. She states how theology is 'almost a generation behind postcolonial studies in other fields' (2005: 149). One of her aims in this project is to 'write back to a masculinist theological tradition defined by white, middle-class, Eurocentric norms' (2005: 144). She sees this as a task which welcomes wider participation from those who are feminist or pro-feminist and are committed to working with a postcolonial lens. Kwok states how reading theology with a postcolonial lens requires theologians to think in new ways. The task is one of 'redoing theology' (2005: 144). In a reading of queer theologies, Kwok is saddened that the existing scholarship 'gives the erroneous impression that the struggles of gay, lesbian, bisexual and transgendered people are transhistorical and everywhere the same' (2005: 142). The point of contextual theology is to show how beliefs about God and the practices of those beliefs are not the same everywhere, nor have they always been the same throughout history.

Kwok sees the work of writers such as Robert Goss's *Jesus Acted Up* (1993) and Elizabeth Stuart's *Religion is a Queer Thing* (1997) as 'white queer theology' (Kwok, 2005: 141). She goes further back in the lineage of queer theory, noting how both Michel Foucault and Judith Butler did not take race or colonialism into account in their work. From its inception, queer theory has been considered to be white and Western. In fact, the idea that queer theologies have been a largely Western practice is highlighted in the subtitle of Loughlin's volume, *Queer Theology: Rethinking the Western Body* (Loughlin, 2007). Cornwall notes how there are differences and tensions between queer and postcolonial theologies. She cautions wisely that queer may 'be responsible for reinscribing a normativity of its own' (Cornwall, 2016: 15), where that normativity is thought of as white and Western.

Can queer and postcolonial critiques come together? Intercontinental philosophy, post-structuralist thought, and contextualisation have provided platforms for both approaches. Jeremy Punt (2008) explores these intersections, while cautioning against overlooking the tensions between them and emphasising the need to recognise the complexity and diversity of each approach. Punt identifies several points of connection. First, both queer and postcolonial thought operate from the margins of society, challenging what is considered conventional, normal, traditional, or fixed. Second, both queer and postcolonial thought give weight to questions of identity and social location, thereby acknowledging the possibility of hybrid or multiple identities. Punt also observes that each critique holds what he calls a 'prophetic vision for the world' (2008: 24.7). Finally, both frameworks share a commitment to questioning universal claims and dominant norms. While there are shared struggles between queer and postcolonial approaches, attention must be paid to the distinct histories and realities that shape them. Punt cautions that 'the theoretical and other conflicts between them should not be diminished, or the complex and conflicted, the diverse and hybrid natures of Postcolonial and Queer theories denied' (2008: 24.2).

In her work on postcolonial criticism, Sharon Bong describes Christianity in Asia as part of 'its colonial heritage and its burden', and that the Bible is 'the colonial text' (Bong, 2006: 497). Bong discusses how the word 'post-colonial' is problematic, as it derives from 'colonialism', so the word 'post-colonial' is subordinate to the category 'colonialism'. According to Bong, postcolonialism 'ironically reinstates the structures of domination that it purports to avoid' (2006: 511). Following Sara Ahmed, Bong highlights a further problem with the term 'post-colonialism' as it implies that 'colonialism has been overcome in the present' (Bong, 2006: 498; Ahmed, 2000: 10). Bong emphasises the importance of exploring the needs of particularised contexts, as this 'serves as a touchstone in authenticating theologizing by, of and for Asians' (Bong, 2006: 511). She states that 'theologizing in a "post-colonial" context … involves strange encounters' (2006: 498).

In Indian contexts, Rasiah Sugirtharajah (2004) draws on the idea of a blending of cultures in his work on postcolonial theology. He notices the reluctance of systematic theology to address the relationship between colonialism and the field of study. Sugirtharajah exposes how there was a reluctance in parts of India to criticise colonialism, as the Christian missionaries offered welfare to many people disadvantaged due to the caste system. He notes how many early converts sought to present themselves as patriotic Indians, claiming how Christianity was not a strange religion but a part of the Vedic tradition. In doing this, Sugirtharajah states how 'they raided their own textual archives to demonstrate that these Vedic texts were already Christian or modernist, so that conversion to Christianity was not in any way an act of disloyalty to India' (Sugirtharajah, 2004: 31). He suggests that Christian theologies in India were formed in response to colonialism, but also as an act of nation building. Sugirtharajah discusses how theologies in India 'are mainly about belonging and identity and how Indian Christians have negotiated and continue to negotiate an Indian-Christian identity' (2004: 35). He writes how 'it appears that a theological imagination need not be in harmony with a specific geographic terrain' (2004: 36). One option is 'to blend creatively cosmopolitan and vernacular cultures' (2004: 37). He advocates that this does not involve blending into someone else's culture, which leads to a loss of identity and history, but 'the blending into one's own culture some of the liberative elements of someone else's' (2004: 37–38).

Bong and Sugirtharajah are not alone in drawing on the idea of encounters, fusion, and interaction. Gloria Anzaldúa pays attention to this in her work *Borderlands/La Frontera: The New Mestiza* (Anzaldúa, 1987). In drawing on her identities as lesbian and chicana (a woman of Mexican origin), Anzaldúa exposes the idea of invisible 'borders' that exist between various groups of people: Latinas/os–non-Latinas/os, men–women, heterosexuals–homosexuals, and other groups. Anzaldúa uses the term 'mestiza', which usually describes a woman of Indigenous and Spanish ancestry. But here, she uses it to represent a new way of thinking that embraces complexity and mixed identities. She writes about a *mestiza* consciousness that challenges binary thinking by placing value on coexistence rather than choosing between cultures.

Marcella Althaus-Reid observes how postcolonial theologies and liberation theologies risk becoming a 'theme park' of theology (Althaus-Reid, 2000). She reveals how postcolonial theologies can be seen by some in the West as novelties or area categories. She says, 'people in the West are encouraged to visit them as if going to a botanical garden' (2000: 42), warning that they may be regarded as an excursion. According to Althaus-Reid, 'the fact of being presented as a theme park accentuates the imaginary aspect of the construction of regional theologies. They highlight by their mere native presence the fact that real theologies are elsewhere' (2000: 42). This is one area in which queer and postcolonial theologies are a catalyst for disruption to the systematic theology of the West. Althaus-Reid continues, 'the point is precisely one of opening borders and tunnels under the theoretical construction of the West' (2000: 45). In turn, queer and postcolonial theologies are able to challenge the dominant and hegemonic nature of systematic theology within the discipline.

One common approach that queer and postcolonial theologies share is that they are a form of practical theology, engaging with individuals and communities. What follows are brief overviews of key themes and concerns in queer theologies as they emerge across different cultural, racial, and geographic contexts, including Asian American, Asian, African, Latin American, Black and womanist queer theologies, as well as queer theologies from Canada, the UK, the USA, Australia, and Aotearoa (New Zealand). In these overviews, rather than presenting a 'theme park' description, I focus on how these theologies work to disrupt traditional theology and work on a practical level in their various contexts. One of the limitations in this discussion is that the texts referenced are written in English. I am aware of the limitations of my scope in being unable to access texts which may be written in the native languages of these locations. I am also conscious that my aim is not to offer a ventriloquist voice when discussing queer theologies in global contexts. To avoid this pitfall, I have drawn heavily on global scholarship in queer theologies, and I encourage readers to explore these texts for themselves. Moreover, there is a risk that the global locations described below are interpreted as monolithic. I agree with Mary Ann Tolbert who states that there is 'no one feminist perspective or feminist reading of a text … no one womanist perspective, no one Hispanic perspective, no one Asian perspective, no one lesbian perspective, and so on' (Tolbert, 1995: 273). Tolbert is not attempting to deny the importance of social location and identity, rather she cautions how these experiences should not be thought of as entirely representative of each particular context. The reading of the different queer theologies in global contexts in this chapter follows this principle: that social locations, identities, and contexts allow for a range of plural experiences, identities, and voices. Moreover, queer ruptures categories of essentialism, so queer readings should not be thought of as universal or homogenised in any way.

ASIAN AMERICAN QUEER THEOLOGIES

Patrick Cheng is a leading researcher of Asian American queer theologies. His work 'marks and celebrates an emerging theological and religious scholarship among people of Asian descent who self-identify as "queer" – that is, lesbian, gay, bisexual, transgender, intersex, queer, questioning, and two-spirited folk, as well as our allies' (Cheng, 2011: 236). Using the metaphor of the rainbow, he explores the themes of multiplicity, diaspora, and hybridity in examining the experiences of queer Asian North American people of faith and suggests what queer Asian theologies may look like. In his examination of multiplicity, Cheng explores the coexistence of multiple identities – Asian, queer, spiritual, religious. He notes how even within each of these markers of identity there are further multiple identities. The idea of diaspora features prominently in his work, as it describes the reality of the experiences of many Asian North Americans who never feel quite at home. Cheng says, 'we constantly experience the annoying questions of "where are you *really* from?" or "where are you *originally* from?"' (2011: 244). The idea of diaspora also extends to the fact that within the corpus of LGBTQ+ literature on religion and spirituality 'there has been virtually no reflection on the experiences of queer Asian people in those works' and that they 'are almost uniformly silent on the queer Asian experience' (2011: 245). The sense of hybridity in queer Asian North American identities relates to similar ideas noted above from Bong, Sugirtharajah, and Anzaldúa from their different geographical locations. Cheng states how 'queer Asians of faith live and exist in a "third space" that is created by the intersections of our sexualities on the one hand, and our racial identities on the other' (2011: 246).

For Cheng, marginalisation and oppression are intersectional, and he refers to the experiences of discrimination through belonging to multiple minority groups. His reading of queer is in relation to sexual identities, rather than engaging with the theory of queer being anti-identity. In describing his own self-identification, Cheng is a 'rainbow theologian. Not a liberation theologian, not a post-colonial theologian, and not a queer theologian, although I do draw upon – and am indebted to elements of – each of those traditions' (Cheng, 2011: 248). For Cheng to self-identify as a rainbow theologian is to reflect the complexities of his position: multiple markers of identification, a sense of being displaced, and the occupation of a liminal, third space, where the complexities of competing or potentially incompatible identities are played out.

In outlining Asian American queer theologies, Cheng uses a method of reflecting on how the Christian tradition is already multiple. He offers numerical examples by referring to four gospel writers and the Trinitarian idea of God as three in one. The experience of diaspora is described as the feeling of not being at home due to one's race and sexuality, but also due to the focus on family values in Asian communities. This exclusion becomes a double exclusion in the church and Christian theology – 'a world that often refuses to understand how the Gospel is inextricably tied to both our sexual and racial identities' (Cheng, 2011: 251).

How the concept of hybridity informs queer Asian practices, according to Cheng, is seen in his description of how he brings Asian meditation practices into Christian worship. Cheng envisages an Asian Christology in the form of Christ as a '"third thing", between the divine and the human' (2011: 253). The idea of 'rainbow theology' is not unique to Asian people, and it requires deeper engagement with queer Black, Latin American, and African American communities and contexts. This theology 'must continue to be rooted in praxis and social activism'

(2011: 258). For Cheng, rainbow theology must also engage with questions of class and economic justice.

ASIAN QUEER THEOLOGIES

Joseph N. Goh is committed to exploring queer theologies in Asia. In his research, Goh describes the Malaysian *mak nyahs*, who are male-to-female trans people, some of whom are also sex workers. The *mak nyahs* experience discrimination and persecution because they challenge the cisnormative and heteronormative values of both Islamic and Christian traditions in Malaysia. Goh's work draws parallels between how Malaysian society often attempts to regulate the bodies of the *mak nyahs* in a similar way to how Christian theology has regulated the body of Mary, making her virginity sacred. With enforced regulation on their bodies, the *mak nyahs* reveal how their gender becomes a vehicle that allows them to express their spirituality. Goh sees this as connected to Mary's story, as for both Mary and the *mak nyahs* 'bodily and godly experiences are inexorably intertwined, even if these experiences are sometimes fraught with ambivalent views and feelings' (Goh, 2012: 229). Goh argues that their bodies are treated as sites of sacred meaning and regulation. Elsewhere, Goh also works on exploring the intersections of sexuality and faith in Malaysian gay and bisexual men (Goh, 2018).

In Hong Kong, Yip Lai-shan (2012) conducts research through interviews with non-heterosexual individuals exploring sexuality and faith, examining the experience of queer Catholics. Also, a study by Chan Pui-man (2018) examines three pro-LGBT religious groups in Hong Kong, exploring how some organisations are working towards inclusive membership that welcomes diverse social minorities. Chan's research details the fellowship and activities within the alliance of 'The Rainbow Covenant'. In one example from an inclusive church, pastor Susan comments:

> Happy enough, today's bread has been added with dried grapes and berries, various kinds of ingredients. It is exactly like how our God wants us to be, that is, having and embracing differences. Regardless of your sexuality, gender, race, occupation, and identity, we welcome you to our Holy Holy Communion [*sic*].
>
> (Chan, 2018: 1461)

Kwok notes how 'sexual theology has a relatively short history in Asia, and many Asian churches still find it embarrassing to discuss sexual issues in public' (Kwok, 2010: 40). She states that the task for queer Asian theologies is not only to examine the body and sexuality from the Christian tradition, but also from the cultural heritage of Asia. She cites the work of Bong (2007) as an example of a queer revisionist from Asian heritage. Bong uses the images of the lesbian mother and lesbian nun to contest the idea of womanhood, motherhood, and heterosexuality in Christianity. The queer theologies that emerge in Asia are primarily concerned with exploring sexuality and gender through lived experiences. In many ways, queer Asian theologies engage in a project that reads religion and its impact on the lives of Christians through the lenses of their gender and sexuality.

Queering Migrations: Towards, From, Beyond Asia (Córdova Quero, Goh & Sepidoza Campo, 2014) examines the intersections of ethnicity, migration, sexuality, and religion. Looking towards, from, and beyond Asia, the authors engage with the living experiences of LGBTQ+ people. In one example, Kunisuke Hirano (2014) tells the stories of those he calls 'sexiles', who are people who leave their country because of their sexual identifications. For the 'sexiles', migration offers promises of a better life, as the expectation that people are heterosexual still holds strong in Japanese culture and society. Although the authors are less concerned with queer theologies or queer religion, the text illuminates the lives of individuals through the intersection of queerness with race and ethnicity. What holds strong in this discussion is how the social and cultural assumptions of heterosexuality are inextricably linked to religion, as if heterosexuality is divinely sanctioned desire and any deviation from this is a crime against God. Also in Japan, Yuri Horie (2007) explores the relatively invisible existence of lesbian people in public discussions of homosexuality. She describes the mobilisation of women's activism in response to homophobic discrimination experienced by a gay man in the United Church of Christ in Japan, a Protestant church. Forms of resistance activism were mobilised by women, including lesbians, bisexuals, and heterosexuals, as Horie notes that the women saw parallels between the sexism they experienced and this case of homophobia. She situates women's activism in this context within the thought of

Adrienne Rich's 'lesbian continuum' (see Chapter 1 for more on Rich).

In India, George Zachariah and Vincent Rajkumar work to bring LGBTQ+ voices into dialogue with Christian communities. Their edited book, *Disruptive Faith, Inclusive Communities: Church and Homophobia* (Zachariah & Rajkumar, 2015), presents a collection of chapters seeking to transform Christian faith communities and to promote inclusion and justice for LGBTQ+ people. In a similar vein to working with church communities in India, Philip Kuruvilla is editor of a volume entitled *Christian Responses to Issues of Human Sexuality and Gender Diversity: A Guide to the Churches in India* (Kuruvilla, 2017). His volume is aimed primarily at church leaders and church communities, but is also for parents, families, teachers, and allies who wish to understand more about LGBTQ+ issues and lives.

AFRICAN QUEER THEOLOGIES

Adriaan van Klinken and Lilly Phiri observe that 'Africa is now widely associated with homophobia and is even considered to be the worst continent to be gay' (van Klinken & Phiri, 2015: 36). The idea that queer theologies could emerge from such a setting seems to be at odds with the legal situations in a large number of African countries, as well as the 'traditional' views on Christianity held across the continent.

During the 19th century, Christianity was introduced to many parts of Africa through missionary activity. Missionaries sought to spread Christianity and encourage Indigenous peoples to convert, bringing with them strict views on sex and sexuality shaped by moral frameworks from 19th-century Europe. These views influenced Christian teachings and attitudes towards sexuality in many African contexts. It is therefore important to remember that discussions of sexual relationships and Christianity in Africa are often shaped by these missionary and colonial legacies, rather than originating solely from African cultures themselves. These attitudes have taken hold and have been repeated socially and culturally in many contexts. To a large extent, these conservative values have been adopted and are now entwined with some contemporary African Christian moral frameworks. These values create ideas of 'decency' which are firmly held and which often exclude non-heterosexual activities as not Christian and, therefore, not African. This seems somewhat ironic, as it appears that in many precolonial contexts, attitudes to same-sex relationships were less hostile than they are today. Van Klinken and Chitando observe the following:

> Indigenous African societies and cultures were characterised by a relative culture of discretion, allowing a certain space for ambiguous gender identities and non-heterosexual practices, which was then restricted by the imposition of strict gender and sexual norms by missionaries and colonial administrators.
>
> (van Klinken & Chitando, 2016: 4)

Where Christian values have become intertwined with cultural and social attitudes towards same-sex relationships, it seems that there is a common perception that homosexuality is an import from Western society and is therefore un-African. Moreover, these traditional values are often debated and contested on the world stage, as African Christianity plays a major role in the global Anglican Communion. In this context, religious leaders from African countries have often publicly opposed progressive stances regarding LGBTQ+ acceptance within church communities.

One of the first texts tackling the subject of same-sex desire, relationships, and Christianity in South Africa was *Aliens in the Household of God: Homosexuality and Christian Faith in South Africa* (Germond & De Gruchy, 1997). The book explores the challenges, prejudices, and discrimination experienced by gay people in South Africa, noting that the problem is not homosexuality but heterosexism. The book contains various accounts and testimonies from people's lives and their relationships with the church and community in South Africa.

In working with African church leaders and theological educators, Gerald West, Charlene van der Walt, and Kapya John Kaoma note that the new site of struggle for Christianity in Africa is the presence of LGBTQ+ people and homophobia (West, van der Walt & Kaoma, 2016). They state how the lived realities of LGBTQ+ experiences are important for theologies on sexualities. They call for a process of 'people's theology' that 'seeks to acknowledge the sacredness of all human beings, even those who are rendered invisible, as the image of the Creator' (West, van der Walt & Kaoma, 2016: 2). Traditional theology and the Bible 'have usually been whips to chastise' LGBTQ+ people (West, van der Walt & Kaoma, 2016: 2), and focusing on the centre 'is to participate in the violence perpetrated by the centre' (2016: 3). The authors call for queer Christians to reclaim their presence in theology: 'queer Christians must be thoroughly theologically equipped to re-encounter the very tradition that has tormented and traumatised them' (2016: 3).

Van Klinken has become a prominent scholar on the issue of non-normative sexuality and emerging queer theologies in Africa. His 2013 book, *Transforming Masculinities in African Christianity: Gender Controversies in Times of AIDS,* explores African Christian theological discussions around the ideas of gender, specifically masculinity in light of the HIV/AIDS epidemic. Van Klinken's work forms part of 'the emerging (but contested) body of queer studies in Africa' (van Klinken 2015: 948). Queer studies have been contested as a possible site of inquiry within Africa due to their history and their perception as white, Western thought. Van Klinken discusses the '(im)possibility of African queer studies' (van Klinken, 2017: np), referring to scholars who consider queer studies a Western project and who question whether such approaches could work in African contexts at all. He states, 'queer studies, if it really takes seriously African queer subjectivity, must contend with the fact that many LGBT people in Africa identify with the same religious traditions that are so vocal against them' (2017: np).

Van Klinken and Phiri's work explores the development of queer theologies in African contexts. Like many queer theologies emerging in global contexts, for van Klinken and Phiri, the queer project must begin with real lives of marginalised sexualities, so they focus on gay men in Zambia for their study. They point to the importance of grounding theology about non-normative sexualities in marginalised, contested settings:

> queer theology puts sexuality in all its varieties central in the understanding of the image of God. This is certainly relevant in African contexts where certain forms of sexuality have recently become heavily policed and politicized, and where same-sex loving people have been excluded and marginalized.
>
> (van Klinken & Phiri, 2015: 44)

Within the Zambian context of the study, participants believe that discrimination against homosexuality is a result of dominant Pentecostal Christian beliefs and that gay people are viewed as 'the

Devil or the Antichrist' (van Klinken & Phiri, 2015: 45). Gay participants in the study believe God created them as children of God and that 'God is indifferent to sexuality' (2015: 47). Van Klinken and Phiri acknowledge that a grassroots study of gay Christian men does not set the standard for African queer theologies, and they state how other people from the LGBTQ+ community need to have their voices heard. An African grassroots theology allows people to think about being made in the image of God in contextual queer ways. Readers are warned to pay particular attention to context in formulating queer theologies, as 'queer theology in Africa is possible and timely – but only if it takes cognizance of the social, cultural and political specificities and sensitivities in African contexts' (2015: 45). This question of specificities and sensitivities must extend to the labelling of Africa as a homophobic continent. Ryan Thoreson (2014) is keen to point out that local understandings of same-sex attitudes can differ and that homophobia is difficult to define, making it hard to assess whether it is increasing or decreasing across African contexts. Thoreson states that to describe Africa as a homophobic continent would be racist as it would 'leave little room for the nuance and specificity of sexual politics' (Thoreson, 2014: 24).

Despite the fact that religion is often cited as being a source for homophobia in African contexts, van Klinken notes how religion is also a source for self-affirmation: 'while religion is generally considered a key factor contributing to homophobia in contemporary Africa, it also appears to be a resource for queer subjectivity and empowerment' (van Klinken, 2015: 960). Further examples of empowerment from grassroots contexts are found in the daily lives and experiences of queer Africans. Stories of African queer lives are also found in narratives, such as *Stories of Our Lives* (The Nest Collective, 2015), where several of the narratives engage with the topic of Christianity. Additionally, *Sacred Queer Stories: Ugandan LGBTQ+ Refugee Lives and the Bible* (van Klinken, Stiebert with Brian & Hudson, 2021) draws on the lived experiences of Ugandan LGBTQ+ refugees to show how biblical texts are re-read as sources of survival and sacred meaning in contexts of displacement and violence.

In a commitment to mobilising living experience as a source for theology, van Klinken uses autobiography as a source for African queer theologies (van Klinken, 2018). In adhering to prioritising context, he develops grassroots queer theologies in which individuals recall their own queer experiences and identities, countering claims that queer is 'un-African' and 'un-Christian'. He states how 'Queer stories remain generally untold and queer voices remain largely muted in African theology' (2018: 128). The turn to life story research demonstrates how African queer theologies are not a theoretical task: 'African queer theology is not to be developed "out of the blue" but is already present in the stories of African LGBTI people of faith' (2018: 213). Van Klinken states how 'African theology should be written in such a way that African queer people can locate themselves within it, and that queer life stories are the starting point for this' (2018: 217). The task to locate and tell these stories is one which is beginning to take shape. As van Klinken states, 'queer storytelling is key to the development of grassroots African queer theologies and to disrupting the silence and taboo surrounding sexual diversity in hegemonic African Christianities and theologies' (2018: 229). The importance of sharing stories as a wider strategy for queer theologies is discussed further in Chapter 5.

LATIN AMERICAN QUEER THEOLOGIES

Born in Rosario, Argentina, Marcella Althaus-Reid was a Latin American theologian whose work had a profound effect on the areas of liberation, feminist, and queer theologies. The influence of her living experiences in Latin American contexts runs throughout her scholarship (see Chapter 2). In grounding her theologies in real lives, she describes her style of theology as a *caminata* – a walk with others. She states how 'this theological journey involves taking risks' (Althaus-Reid, 2004: 2), as queer theologians embark on 'a path from the margins of sexual and economic exclusion' (2004: 4). The path signposts two issues which have been taboo in Christian theology: sexuality and poverty. This is one of the main reasons why liberation theology and, subsequently, queer theologies have engaged with issues of the economy and capitalism.

Gabriela González Ortuño describes Althaus-Reid's theology as shockingly refreshing, 'a bucket of cold water' (González Ortuño, 2016: 94). By basing her theology in the lives of everyday marginalised people in Latin America – such as the poor lemon vendors, the frequenters of gay bars who carry rosaries, or the fetishists – Althaus-Reid searches for theological explanations that 'bring us closer to the idea of a queer God; that is, a God which does not reflect the dominant male in the work of most theologians' (2016: 90). For Althaus-Reid then, there is a need for sexual honesty in theology:

> Queer theology is a process of Outing Theology as a method for action and reflection, in the sense that, first of all, Classical theology needs to come clean with its real sexual identity, from where goals and objectives can be worked out. I have said elsewhere, that all theology is sexual theology, it is just that traditionally theology doesn't admit it. It is still in the closet about its true sexual nature.
>
> (Althaus-Reid, 2001: 60)

Althaus-Reid's innovations, insights, and passions are further revealed by the authors of the essays edited by Nicolas Panotto, *Indecent Theologians: Marcella Althaus-Reid and the Next Generation of Postcolonial Activism* (Panotto, 2016). Some of the essays and contributions are grounded in Latin American contexts, and many essays were translated from the original languages in which they were written. These essays demonstrate that there is much more indecent theologising to do. In one example, reflecting on the real lives of the poorest people in Brazil, Claudio Carvalhaes echoes Althaus-Reid's previous claims that liberation theology has shied away from talking about 'the body and the sexual themes in the life of the poor: desire, sexual drives, unfitted sexual behaviors, sexualized notions of the subject, sexual (dis)orientations, transgressions' (Carvalhaes, 2016: 157). Carvalhaes cites the problems of patriarchy, racism, and homophobia as reasons why such themes have been ignored. Significantly, he reveals how the history of postcolonialism has had a major impact on the self-understanding of Latin American people: 'the represented *self*, constructed and imposed by the *conquistador* over the colonized bodies and minds of Latin American people, has still affected the ways in which we see ourselves' (2016: 206).

The idea of listening to life stories and experiences of queer people is a feature of the work by James B. Nickoloff. He cites relationality, homosexuality, community, and family as important features in US Latino/a theology. Nickoloff states that the effect of listening to the voices of the sexually marginalised does more for the wider community than it does for the individuals telling their story. He states, 'it would make the community more genuinely "Hispanic" – that is, more truly mestiza, more deeply interconnected, and more authentically loving' (Nickoloff, 2003: 32).

In working with families and communities, Miguel De La Torre authored a bilingual book entitled *A La Familia: A Conversation about Our Families, the Bible, Sexual Orientation and Gender* (De La Torre, 2011). The book seeks to promote the inclusion of LGBTQ+ people in Latin American communities. The text was created by Latin American communities for their communities. It has three main aims: to offer advice on approaching healthy conversations among Latin American families with regards to sexual orientation, gender identity, and religion; to build Latin American communities; and to encourage Latin American leaders of faith to strive for full inclusion.

In *The Wiley Blackwell Companion to Latino/a Theology* (2015), Robyn Henderson-Espinoza's essay tackles Latin American theology from a queer perspective. In the essay, 'Queer Theory and Latina/o Theologizing' (Henderson-Espinoza, 2015), characteristics of Latin American theology are highlighted. *Cotidiano* relates to a theology of everyday life, while *conjunto* is theology done together, in community. Henderson-Espinoza discusses how narrative has been used as an organising feature in Latin American theology in order to tell a story. Using the gender-neutral adjective Latin@, Henderson-Espinoza explains how Latin@ queer theologies use storytelling to draw attention to the role of sexuality, desire, and identity. Building on the idea of a Anzaldúa's *mestiza*, Henderson-Espinoza uses the term to describe how mixing and in-betweenness are characteristic of queerness. Henderson-Espinoza notes how the idea of being mixed or in-between becomes a useful methodology as it allows for intersections of theory, race, ethnicity, and theology. In one example, the idea of the family is developed as a *mestiza*, as queer people may need to choose between biological family or the family developed through friendships, and this in itself queers the idea of the traditional family.

BLACK AND WOMANIST QUEER THEOLOGIES

Black is often written with a capital B to refer to people from African heritage, black with a small b is simply a colour: this is a custom I adopt here as the majority of authors I engage with follow this practice. Moreover, a similar practice does not exist with 'white', so there is no reason to capitalise. Black and womanist theologies emerged in the USA, confronting questions of race and ethnicity. Black theology emerged as a liberation theology. In brief, Black theology is concerned with the experience of being Black in the world as well as economic deprivation, given that Black history is so heavily punctuated with the history of enslavement. In 1969, James Cone authored *Black Theology and Black Power.* For Cone, Black theology begins with the experience of African Americans in their churches. Against a backdrop of the civil rights and Black Power movements in the USA, Cone describes 'being Black in America has little to do with skin color. Being Black means that your heart, your soul, your mind, and your body are where the dispossessed are' (Cone, 1969: 151). Later, however, Cone examines the theme of race a little more closely. He authors an essay entitled 'White Theology Revisited' in his book *Risks of Faith* (Cone, 2000), in which he criticises the white church for failing to adequately address issues of race. Black theology is rooted in Black culture, so sources from African American culture form part of the theology, including writings, music, and spirituals. A spiritual is a Christian song which describes the hard and difficult oppressions experienced under enslavement. The spirituals encompass aspects of identity, faith, and the tribulations of Black people, describing the emotion and physical burden of enslavement. Some spirituals, known as jubilees, look hopefully to a future of freedom.

Delores Williams described the earlier work of Cone as sexist, stating how he failed to account for the experiences of Black women. In 1993, she re-envisioned Black theology from a feminist perspective. As feminist theology related to the experience of white women, and Black theology was concerned with the experience of Black men, Williams became a significant figure in the development of womanist theology. The term *womanist* is used to describe feminist writings developed by Black women that centre their lived experiences. Delores S. Williams, in her text *Sisters in the Wilderness: The Challenge of Womanist God Talk* (1993), argues that womanist theology takes:

> Black women's experience to provide the lens through which we view sources, to provide the issues that form the content of our theology,

> and to help formulate the questions we ask about God's relation to Black American life and the world in general.
>
> (Williams, 1993: 12)

Williams' text demonstrates the intersectionality of being marginalised as a woman, and then again as a Black woman. In terms of discussing sexuality, Kelly Brown Douglas's pivotal text *Sexuality and the Black Church* (Douglas, 1999) explores why the themes of sexuality are considered so taboo in Black culture. Pamela Lightsey humorously describes her delightful response on picking up Douglas's book for the first time, noting how 'we couldn't wait to get the book home, set aside our dull readings written by dead white men, and read about Black preachers having sex' (Lightsey, 2015: 4). Douglas's intention was to break the silence on Black sexuality, and she writes about the impact of HIV/AIDS on the Black community. Exposing the topic of HIV/AIDS and sex means that the issues can no longer be silenced. Douglas examines how the church has regulated sex, thereby devaluing and demonising human sexuality. She says how, through the eyes of the church, sexual activity is viewed as 'passionate, irrational and even satanic behaviour' (Douglas, 1999: 29). This has enabled the church to have incredible power and control in the regulation of sexuality. In further examining the links between sexuality and power, Douglas reveals how white culture has exercised control over Black sexuality by viewing Black bodies as sensual and exotic, and for women, this has resulted in vulnerability and attacks on their bodies. The colonisation of white culture on Black sexuality positions Black women as seducers and Black men as sexual predators. Douglas stands with lesbian, gay, and bisexual people by calling out homophobia as an area which also regulates sexuality within the Black community and church.

There has been a tendency within some Black communities and churches to frame homosexuality as a social or moral threat. Being gay, therefore, is associated with sin. Roger Sneed's *Representations of Homosexuality* (Sneed, 2010) draws attention to the religious experiences of Black gay men. Sneed unveils how religion and theology have seen homosexuality in Black churches as a problem to be solved; therefore, gay people are demonised in some way. Sneed sees the Black church as heteronormative, and, even in spaces where the congregations claim to be accepting, 'Black liberation theology had not progressed much beyond simplistic statements such as "God loves you"' (2010: 6). His work highlights how gay theologians have not examined Black gay experiences, and how liberation and womanist theology have not adequately engaged with the question of sexuality. Sneed states that 'Black liberation and womanist theologies have substantively little to offer Black queers other than a rhetoric of mere tolerance' (2010: 177). According to Sneed, Black theologies have failed to recognise that queer Black experiences exist. Sneed argues that exclusion and homophobia produce harm, marginalisation, and spiritual alienation. He discusses 'different conceptions of God and spirituality that are open rather than closed' and how Black queer theologies dare 'to call into question the presumptive goodness of God and the efficacy of the Black church in ameliorating crises in Black sexual identity' (2010: 190). In outlining the exclusion of non-heterosexual people in liberation, Black, and womanist theologies, Sneed points to the fact that all theologies move on: 'there is no theology or ethics that remains static, unchanging and unalterable' (2010: 176).

Black women tend to make up the majority of the congregants in Black churches, although leadership is still dominated by men. In one queer interpretation of Black theology, Stephen Finley accounts for the absence of Black men from churches, suggesting how they may struggle to enter into a bodily relationship with Jesus. Finley sees 'a conflict between a masculine Black-body construct and a same-sex symbolic relationship with an all-powerful male Divinity' (Finley, 2007: 305). In his queer reading of heterosexuality, Finley engages in fieldwork research with men in a Baptist church in the USA. Using sexual metaphors, he states how some religious heterosexual Black men were unable to submit to a male God through worship, as this 'places the male in the "feminine" or passive recipient position of the relationship' (2007: 317).

What do Black queer theologies look like? EL Kornegay argues that 'we must accept that Black (race) is already queer. Blackness and Black theological discourse has yet to accept its own queerness' (Kornegay, 2012: 331). Race, according to Kornegay, 'rests uncomfortably in our souls' (2012: 333), and he demonstrates how queer theory exposes 'mismatches' in our identifications: gender, sex, race, religion. Such mismatches have been examined by liberational theology using a tool which stretches the imagination, and an example of this is the image of the Black Christ. Kornegay describes this elasticity with method as what makes 'Black theology queer by definition' (2012: 334). In 2013, Kornegay wrote *A Queering of Black Theology: James Baldwin's Blues Project and Gospel Prose*, which examines writings from Baldwin, the Black novelist and social critic. Kornegay states how the book's aim is to engage in Black theology in ways that are post-civil rights, post-liberation, and postmodern. This, in turn, will enable 'faith and flourishing for the multiple representations of gendered and sexualized bodies within the black church and community' [*sic*] (2013: 1).

In offering an example of Black queer theologies which are grounded in sexual themes, Brittney Cooper sets out a Black feminist theology of pleasure. She describes how her previous writings on such matters had alienated her from her church communities, as she received hateful responses because of her work on desire and Christianity. Cooper notes how 'many other Black women who read the piece called me everything but a child of God, hurled scripture like knives, and basically condemned me to hell for leading other women astray' (Cooper, 2018: 193). In highlighting how sex is somehow sinful, and connected to issues of guilt and shame for Black women, Cooper says how 'they would have sex on Saturdays and put those same "sins" on the altar on Sundays' (2018: 198). Rather than see sex as something of a demon, Cooper's aim is to show it as divine. Her Black theology of pleasure releases women from experiences of any guilt connected to sexual pleasure. Notably, its reach goes beyond the pleasure of Black women to encompass queer lives. Black queer theologies, therefore, demand 'a forthright engagement with the politics of the Black female, queer, trans, and/or gender non-conforming body' (2018: 199).

Pamela Lightsey is a prominent figure in the writing of queer womanist theology and puts forward 'a queer womanist departure from Anglo-American queer studies' (Lightsey, 2012: 340). Rather than building her queer womanist theologies on white queer thinkers, her project is grounded in the lives and experiences of the African American community. She sees the word 'queer' as a problem, especially when used to refer to identity rather than theory. She uses humour to describe how people in the Black community respond to her when she says she is queer: '"Wha' da hell you mean 'queer'? Shiiit dat muthafucka jus' funny!"' (2012: 341). Lightsey finds use of the term 'queer' as a marker of self-identification too ambiguous and too weak. She states that, for the Black queer community, the church must come out: 'until the Black church "comes out" and really loves its Blackness [...] it cannot love God, itself, nor its many diverse members as it ought' (2012: 347).

Lightsey also authored a text contextualising womanist queer theology, *Our Lives Matter* (2015), adopting the slogan from the 'Black Lives Matter' campaign and national protests in the USA against police mistreatment of Black people. Womanist queer theologies are not only concerned with Black women, Black culture, and Black churches, as Lightsey notes:

> It would, nevertheless, be incorrect to suggest the only concern of womanist theology is Black women and Black culture. We are interested in exposing discrimination of Black women in particular and women in general. We are concerned about Black communities in particular but Creation in general. Nowadays our work is expansive addressing ecological needs, the struggle for quality education, self-care, quality of care for the poor and oppressed and so forth.
>
> (Lightsey, 2015: 13)

Intersectional concerns become part of the project of queer theologies. Together, queer and intersectional approaches reach beyond identity-based issues by examining social concerns such as poverty, education, and the environment.

NORTH ATLANTIC QUEER THEOLOGIES (CANADA, UK, AND USA)

Within the North Atlantic context – the UK, the USA, and Canada – queer theologies trace their lineage back to early lesbian and gay theologies (see Chapter 1). In highlighting the roots of this development, US theologian Robert Goss says 'the explosion of activism in the late 1980s and 1990s transformed gay theology into queer theologies and widened their dialogue partners' (Goss, 1998: 189). He draws attention to the inclusive potential of queer theologies that was lacking in gay and lesbian theologies. Goss offers one of the earliest definitions of queer relating to theology. He states:

> Queer as a verb means 'to spoil the effect of, to interfere with, to disrupt, harm, or put in a bad light'. Queering is a deconstructive critique of the homophobic and heterosexist political theology that already excludes us. It inverts cultural symbols, perverts and disrupts valued theologies and church practices that are already spoiled for us. Queering imaginatively reconstructs theology, spirituality and church practices in new, inclusive configurations.
>
> (Goss, 1998: 194)

Sexuality underpins lesbian and gay theologies, and also queer theologies. Yet, the focus is often different: lesbian and gay theologies address sexuality through identity and inclusion, whereas queer theologies interrogate sexuality itself as a system of power, normativity, and regulation. In 1979, US theologian James Nelson published *Embodiment*, and the phrase 'sexual theology' began to emerge. Nelson states how 'sexual questions are also religious questions' (Nelson, 1979: 15) and advocates a move beyond looking at questions of sexual ethics within theology, to examining how human sexual experience can be a grounding for theology. Nelson's thinking was courageous and groundbreaking in positioning theology from a non-traditional space that many would consider taboo. His theology looks specifically at a range of sexual practices: fantasy, masturbation, intercourse, and sado-masochism. In 1988, a further text authored by Nelson was published which examines male sexuality, *The Intimate Collection* (Nelson, 1988). Nelson's books are considered to be classic texts on sexual theology.

In the UK, Adrian Thatcher presents a Christian sexual theology in his book *Liberating Sex* (1993). Thatcher states that the book is about 'a *remaking*, an *unmaking* and a *merrymaking*' (Thatcher, 1993: 1). He notes how humans, as sexual beings, are made in the image of God, and 'in *remaking* us as sexual beings, God, through the Holy Spirit, gives us the power and the vision to make relationships which resemble those relationships existing eternally with God' (1993: 2). The process of *unmaking* exposes the legacy of patriarchy on the Christian tradition, while *merrymaking* 'is an antidote to the deadening seriousness that has attached itself to sexual activity in much of Christian history' (1993: 3). Thatcher engages in comprehensive discussions of human sexuality and sexual ethics based on traditional Christian theology, critical theory, and contemporary lives. The work, as a forerunner in Christian sexual theology, discusses sexuality, marriage, same-sex relationships, celibacy, masturbation, and safe sex. Elsewhere, in his edited volume *From Queer to Eternity* (Sweasey, 1997), Peter Sweasey takes up the relationship between spirituality and sexuality, the fluidity of sexuality and gender, how the church relates to queer people, and how focusing on the erotic and embodied self can inform theology. Sweasey's collection of essays spans different religions, beliefs, and spiritualities, yet he refuses to make arguments in defence of homosexuality, precisely because it needs none, as it is as valid as heterosexuality.

In North Atlantic contexts, lesbian and gay theologies have emerged alongside the development of queer theologies that are grounded in sexual ethics, political activism, and challenges to heteronormativity. A group of scholars turn their attention to reading how traditional theology is already queer in *Queer Theology: Rethinking the Western Body* (Loughlin, 2007). Gerard Loughlin sees theology as queer, as it is already strange and does not fit in the modern world. He observes how the call for reflection on embodiment and sexuality is one that comes from within the Christian tradition (see Chapter 2). Loughlin asserts that 'queer theology is also queer because it finds – like queer theory – that gay sexuality is not marginal to Christian thought and culture, but oddly central […] The most orthodox turns out to be the queerest of all' (2007: 9). Loughlin observes how Christianity has always been queer: 'the queer interests that were always at play in the Spirit's movement, in the lives and devotions of saints and sinners, theologians and ecclesiastics' (2007: 9). Mark Jordan shares the same opinion as Loughlin, stating 'queer theology does not come after queer theory […] it was there all along inside queer theory – and, indeed, before queer theory, as its competing parent, its disciplinary root and rival' (Jordan, 2007: 573).

UK-based scholar Susannah Cornwall has made significant contributions to the field of queer theologies, most notably in her book *Controversies in Queer Theology* (Cornwall, 2011). In a commitment to extending queer theologies beyond academic settings, Cornwall has authored church-based resources, including *Sexuality: the Inclusive Church Resource* (Cornwall, 2014). The resource is aimed at clergy and church organisations, drawing on references from the Church of England's debates on sexuality. Cornwall notes the need for church teachings and theologies to change. She states the following:

> Each time and culture throw up new possibilities and new challenges – a set of new contexts in which the Christian path must be outworked. The Bible does not pronounce on the use of hook-up apps such as Tinder and Grindr, or the ethics of internet dating. It does not explicitly condemn paedophilia – indeed, we might be surprised if it did, given the prevalence of sexual relationships between men and boys in the Greco-Roman world. It is also silent on sex toys and BDSM play, and muted on masturbation, oral and anal sex.
>
> (Cornwall, 2014: 59–60)

Cornwall observes how debates on sexuality raise questions beyond same-sex relationships. Her extensive scholarship in the field includes pioneering contributions relating specifically to intersex and transgender theologies.

Canadian scholar Margaret Robinson focuses on bisexuality and theology. She notes how 'traditionally, Christian theology has ignored bisexuality, instead defining homosexuality as encompassing all same-sex attraction and expression' (Robinson, 2015: 644). According to Robinson, however, gay, lesbian, and queer theology has also not given adequate space to the inclusion of bisexuality and has actually produced scholarship which can be interpreted as 'biphobic' (2015: 646). She observes three key issues in bisexual theology:

> (1) a holistic view of human sexuality [...]; (2) a tendency towards synthesis, unifying what are often seen as opposite categories; and (3) using an intersectional lens to examine how sexuality is shaped and constructed by categories such as class, race, or gender.
>
> (Robinson, 2015: 649)

Interestingly, Robinson sees that one of the strengths of bisexual theology is that it tends not to take up a category of its own. She states: 'bisexual theology's greatest contribution may be manifested not in developing our own theological discourse – another box labelled "bisexual theology" – but in having our theological insights taken up by all theologians' (Robinson, 2015: 653).

QUEER THEOLOGIES IN AUSTRALIA AND AOTEAROA (NEW ZEALAND)

In Australian contexts, examples of queer theologies are found in the works of Michael Bernard Kelly and Jillian Cox. Kelly's work explores the contemporary spirituality of gay men in two of his books, *Seduced by Grace: Contemporary Spirituality, Gay Experience and Christian Faith* (Kelly, 2007) and *Christian Mysticism's Queer Flame: Spirituality in the Lives of Contemporary Gay Men* (Kelly, 2018). Kelly's earlier work (2007) begins from his own autobiographical perspective, detailing the forced end of his career in the Catholic education service in Australia because he is gay. *Seduced by Grace* is a collection of different forms of writing – letters, articles, and essays – exploring the individual and personal experiences of reconciling faith and sexuality. His later work (2018) details the spiritual and life journeys of eight gay men, although the participants come from the USA.

Cox's commitment to queer theologies is demonstrated in her scholarship relating to queering traditional theology, specifically focusing on the letters of Martin Luther and Paul. Although it does not focus on Australian contexts, her work is an example of scholarship that re-examines traditional theology using the lens I call a queer-view mirror (see Chapter 2). In subverting what has been considered traditional or normative theology, Cox demonstrates how this can benefit queer theologies. In her reading of Luther, Cox maintains a commitment to his theology yet argues that his ethical approach is one which 'should be extended to theological response to lesbians and gays, and queer people broadly, and that the tools are present in the Lutheran tradition to achieve this' (Cox, 2013: 366). Moreover, she notes how, at the time, Luther challenged biblical and traditional theologies, and examined theologies grounded in new contexts similar to the approach of queer theologies. In her reading of Paul's letters to the Romans and Corinthians, Cox reveals how love should surpass human preoccupation with knowledge. The title of her article, 'Love is Better than Knowledge' (Cox, 2015), makes this clear. Underpinning her scholarship, Cox states:

> My argument is that a theology needs to engage scripture and tradition with secular thought to be relevant and transforming for people of faith and their communities, and that doing so will proffer better visions of what it means to be human.
>
> (2015: 54)

In Aotearoa New Zealand, queer theologies engage with queer lives, as lived experience of faith. Sander and Wilson's work explores the spiritual lives of gay men in Aotearoa New Zealand (Sander & Wilson, 2020). Using qualitative interviews, they examine how participants construct and negotiate the themes of belonging and exclusion in their religious communities. Many of the participants had left institutional churches, often after explicit rejection, while others sought to maintain spiritual practices or more flexible church connections. The themes of rejection or negotiation are described for two participants as follows, 'For James, coming out as gay led to his suspension from his religious community at the time, while John recalls going back in the closet because he wanted to stay involved with his church' (Sander & Wilson, 2020: 49). The research highlights how belonging is therefore partial and conditional. It involves negotiation and conditions, resulting in gay men occupying an in-between space of neither total inclusion nor total exit.

Michael Jonathan Toy's doctoral research explores the everyday theologies of queer Christians, Indigenous Māori, and migrant Samoan communities, with the aim of surveying how minority theologies are formed in response to dominant religious and social structures (Toy, 2025). Toy's work notes how the power structures of the physical world also exist in digital spaces. He writes 'heteronormativity embedded throughout New Zealand society is not the only major structure against which queer Christians push back – these major structures are extended online, rippling back into the offline world with material consequences' (2025: 28). Toy equally describes the refusal of a priest to bless the partnership of two participants in the study, Steve and Andrew. The priest simply told them, 'Sorry, but you can't have your blessing here because of your sexuality' (2025: 68). The stories of queer lives show how churches are often symbolically 'inclusive' but remain structurally conservative. The 'welcome' afforded to queer people is conditional, as long as institutional rhythms are not disrupted.

Instead, Toy frames queer theology as an act of ongoing dissent and a refusal to stabilise. This often requires queer people to engage in ongoing internal negotiation and to navigate complex relationships with religious institutions.

Byron Rangiwai offers a further example of contextual theological reflection in response to public debates on sexuality. Writing from a Māori perspective, Rangiwai notes how colonial Christianity brought strict regulation on sexuality to the Māori world. He raids Christian texts and teachings to attempt to negotiate sexual and religious identities. He writes, 'as a Christian – I have experimented with several denominations, I have experienced the torment of coming to terms with my sexuality in light of some common (mis)understandings of Christian theology' (2020: 5). His work demonstrates how theology in Aotearoa New Zealand is shaped by local histories, identities, and encounters between Christianity and Indigenous worldviews. Rangiwai is not doing theology as apologetics only in response to public debates, but his queer theological work is also deeply autobiographical and pastoral, and here, he foregrounds embodied experience as a theological source. Further exploration of lived theologies can be found in Chapter 5.

CONCLUSION

One emerging theme in postcolonial theologies is the notion of hybridity in relation to identity. This idea surfaces in different contexts in the following examples: Cheng's idea of 'third space' (2011), Bong's 'strange encounters' (2006), Anzaldúa's *mestiza* (1987), and Sugirtharajah's notion of 'blending' (2004). What queer and postcolonial theologies have in common is their relationship to what has been thought of as 'mainstream' or 'traditional' Christianity. Queer and postcolonial theologies expose that what is thought of as mainstream or traditional theology is only considered as such because it is being performed and repeated by dominant global powers. Queer and postcolonial theologies question and critically examine traditional Christian theology. Yet, Cornwall notes how the genealogy of queer theologies may continue to be problematic for some. She states:

> Queer theology is not inherently white and Western – that is, it is not condemned to be white and Western, nor to exclude non-white

> cultures – but it must recognize that its genealogy in Western lesbian, gay and feminist theologies (and, most significantly, in Western Christianity) may prejudice it in this direction. It is therefore possible that there will always be people who do not feel able to place themselves under this umbrella because of uncomfortable associations with elements of its history.
>
> (Cornwall, 2011: 105)

Cornwall goes on to say that postcolonial and queer theologies use a similar language in focussing on experience and resistance.

This chapter has considered the conflicts and shared agendas of queer and postcolonial criticism, as both interrogate the theological mainstream using the tools of post-structuralist thought and through prioritising practical theologies grounded in living experiences in different contexts. This takes us beyond what has been established and controlled in traditional theology, as Dickinson and Toomey note:

> To queer theology, then, is to take up a posture of resistance, an attitude of questioning, and an intellect informed by deconstruction [...] A theology that is queer calls us to go beyond what is known, to move past what is established, and to relinquish control over such structures totally.
>
> (Dickinson & Toomey, 2017: 13)

Given the sustained emphasis on intersectionality within feminist and queer theory, the absence of such engagement in contemporary queer theologies is difficult to justify. Through a commitment to intersectionality and to practical theology in global contexts, queer theologies are 'grassroots theology' suggested by van Klinken and Phiri (2015), prioritising the voices and experiences of individuals and communities. Theologising from experience requires the type of walk, *caminata*, advocated by Althaus-Reid (2004). The attention which must be given to Christian lives in the production of queer theologies is further explored in Chapter 5. In the following chapter, attention turns to queer biblical criticism.

FURTHER READING AND RESOURCES

Isherwood, L. and Córdovo Quero, H. (2025) *DARE Primer on Global Queer Theologies*. London: SCM Press.

This text covers case studies in queer Christian theologies from Malaysia, Rwanda, India, the USA, the UK, Colombia, Nigeria, Mexico, and El Salvador.

Campos, M. S., Cornelio, J., Von Marthin Elraphoma, E., Goh, J. N., 'Jerlo' Jaropillo, A. C., Marasigan, J., ... & Wei-Hsien, W. (2024). Symposium: From coming out to coming in: Roundtable conversation among Southeast Asian queer theologians. *Critical Research on Religion, 12*(3), 350–364. https://journals.sagepub.com/doi/10.1177/20503032241277508

A roundtable conversation via Zoom, bringing together teachers, pastors, and academics that focuses on Southeast Asian contexts that shape and critique queer identities.

ASIAN AMERICAN QUEER THEOLOGIES

Cheng, P. S. (2013) *Rainbow Theology: Bridging Race, Sexuality, and Spirit.* New York: Seabury Books.

Cheng provides illuminating discussion on queer and people of colour theologies, including queer Black theologies, queer Asian American theologies, and queer Latina/o theologies, as well as two-spirit indigenous scholarship.

ASIAN QUEER THEOLOGIES

Queer Theology Academy (Hong Kong): www.queertheo.com

An Asia-specific queer theology online resource. It was founded in 2009 by Hong Kong theologians and ministers to develop and practise queer theology in the Asian Christian context.

Goh, J. N. (2021). *Doing Church at the Amplify Open and Affirming Conferences: Queer Eccleseologies in Asia.* Cham: Springer Nature.

This book takes a deep dive into a series of open and affirming Christian conferences in Asia. These conferences offer worship, support, fellowship, collaboration, and networking for LGBTIQ-affirming churches.

AFRICAN QUEER THEOLOGIES

Van Klinken, A. and Obadare, E. (Eds.) (2019) *Christianity, Sexuality and Citizenship in Africa.* Abingdon: Routledge.

This book looks at the relationship between Christianity, sexuality, and citizenship in sub-Saharan Africa, paying attention to the crisis of HIV and AIDS and the growing visibility of LGBT communities.

LATIN AMERICAN QUEER THEOLOGIES

Panotto, N. (Ed.) (2016) *Indecent Theologies: Marcella Althaus-Reid and the Next Generation of Postcolonial Activists*. California: Borderless Press.

An edited collection of essays, which focuses mainly on queer theologies in Latin America.

BLACK AND WOMANIST QUEER THEOLOGIES

Douglas, K. B. (1999) *Sexuality and the Black Church*. New York: Orbis Books.

One of the first texts exploring the importance of sexuality in the Black church. Douglas exposes how and why sexuality has been seen as taboo in Black culture, and what the churches should do to engage with issues of sexuality.

Lightsey, P. R. (2015) *Our Lives Matter: A Womanist Queer Theology*. Eugene: Pickwick Publications.

Lightsey offers an overview of the issues of sexuality and race in Black churches, as well as an introduction to queer theology from a womanist perspective. This text is accessible and clearly written.

REFERENCES

Ahmed, S. (2000) *Strange Encounters: Embodied Others in Post-Coloniality*. London: Routledge.

Althaus-Reid, M. (2000) 'Gustavo Gutiérrez Goes to Disneyland: Theme Park Theologies and the Diaspora of the Discourse of the Popular Theologian in Liberation Theology'. In Segovia, F. F. (Ed.) *Interpreting Beyond Borders*, pp. 36–58. Sheffield: Sheffield Academic Press.

Althaus-Reid, M. (2001) 'Outing Theology: Thinking Christianity Out of the Church Closet'. *Feminist Theology*, *9*(27), pp. 57–67.

Althaus-Reid, M. (2004) *From Feminist to Indecent Theology*. London: SCM Press.

Anzaldúa, G. E. (1987) *Borderlands/La Frontera: The New Mestiza*. San Francisco: Aunt Lute.

Bong, S. A. (2006) 'Post-colonialism'. In Sawyer, J. F. A. (Ed.) *The Blackwell Companion to the Bible and Culture*, pp. 497–514. Oxford: Blackwell.

Bong, S. A. (2007) 'Queer Revisions of Christianity'. In Brazal, A. M. and Si, A. L. (Eds.) *Body and Sexuality: Theological-Pastoral Perspectives of Women in Asia*, pp. 234–249. Quezon City: Ateneo de Manila University Press.

Carvalhaes, C. (2016) 'Oppressed Bodies Don't Have Sex: The Blind Spots of Bodily and Sexual Discourses in the Construction of Subjectivity in Latin American Liberation Theology'. In Panotto, N. (Ed.) *Indecent Theologies: Marcella Althaus-Reid and the Next Generation of Postcolonial Activists*, pp. 155–212. California: Borderless Press.

Chan, P-M. (2018) 'Desexualizing Sexual Identity Politics: The Framing of Pro-LGBT Christian Organizations in Hong Kong'. *Sexuality & Culture, 22*(4), pp. 1452–1465.

Cheng, P. S. (2011) 'The Rainbow Connection'. *Theology & Sexuality, 17*(3), pp. 235–264.

Cone, J. (1969) *Black Theology and Black Power.* New York: The Seabury Press.

Cone, J. (2000) *Risks of Faith: The Emergence of a Black Theology of Liberation, 1968–1998.* Boston: Beacon Press.

Cooper, B. (2018) 'How Sarah Got Her Groove Back, or Notes Toward a Black Feminist Theology of Pleasure'. *Black Theology, 16*(3), pp. 195–206.

Córdova Quero, H., Goh, J. N. and Sepidoza Campo, M. (Eds.) (2014) *Queering Migrations: Towards, From, Beyond Asia.* New York: Palgrave Macmillan.

Cornwall, S. (2011) *Controversies in Queer Theology.* London: SCM Press.

Cornwall, S. (2014) 'A Theology of Sexuality'. In Cornwall, S. (Ed.) *Sexuality: The Inclusive Church Resource*, pp. 53–112. London: Darton, Longman and Todd.

Cornwall, S. (2016) 'Strange Encounters: Postcolonial and Queer Intersections'. In Panotto, N. (Ed.) *Indecent Theologies: Marcella Althaus-Reid and the Next Generation of Postcolonial Activists*, pp. 3–24. California: Borderless Press.

Cox, J. E. (2013) '"The Only Safe Guide Is Love": Models of Engaging Luther's Ethical Hermeneutic for Theological Responses to the Affirmation of Same-Sex Sexuality'. *Dialog: A Journal of Theology, 52*(4), pp. 365–372.

Cox, J. E. (2015) 'Love is Better than Knowledge: Paul, Luther and a Theology of Being Human'. *Theology & Sexuality, 21*(1), pp. 53–69.

De La Torre, M. (2011) *A La Familia: A Conversation about Our Families, the Bible, Sexual Orientation and Gender.* Available at: https://assets2.hrc.org/files/assets/resources/A_La_Familia_Final_Curriculum_Nov_2011.pdf_ga=2.233047390.1165034153.1558376633-1850997694.1558376633 (Accessed: January 2026).

Dickinson, C. and Toomey, M. (2017) 'The Continuing Relevance of "Queer" Theology for the Rest of the Field'. *Theology & Sexuality, 23*(1–2), pp. 1–16.

Douglas, K. B. (1999) *Sexuality and the Black Church.* New York: Orbis Books.

Finley, S. (2007) 'Homoeroticism and the African-American Heterosexual Male: Quest for Meaning in the Black Church'. *Black Theology, 5*(3), pp. 305–326.

Germond, P. and De Gruchy, S. (Eds.) (1997) *Aliens in the Household of God: Homosexuality and Christian Faith in South Africa*. Claremont: David Philip Publishers.

Goh, J. N. (2012) 'Mary and the Mak Nyahs'. *Theology & Sexuality, 18*(3), pp. 215–233.

Goh, J. N. (2018) *Living Out Sexuality and Faith: Body Admissions of Malaysian Gay and Bisexual Men*. Abingdon: Routledge.

González Ortuño, G. (2016) 'Sexual Dissidence, Faith and Release in Marcella Althaus-Reid'. In Panotto, N. (Ed.) *Indecent Theologies: Marcella Althaus-Reid and the Next Generation of Postcolonial Activists*, pp. 87–104. California: Borderless Press.

Goss, R. E. (1993) *Jesus Acted Up. A Gay and Lesbian Manifesto*. San Francisco: Harper.

Goss, R. E. (1998) 'Sexual Visionaries and Freedom Fighters'. In Gill, S. (Ed.) *The Lesbian and Gay Christian Movement: Campaigning for Justice, Truth and Love*, pp. 187–202. London: Continuum.

Henderson-Espinoza, R. (2015) 'Queer Theory and Latina/o Theologizing'. In Espín, O. O. (Ed.) *The Wiley Blackwell Companion to Latino/a Theology*, pp. 329–346. Chichester: Wiley.

Hirano, K. (2014) 'In Search of Dreams: Narratives of Japanese Gay Men on Migration to the United States'. In Córdova Quero, H., Goh, J. N. and Sepidoza Campo, M. (Eds.) *Queering Migrations: Towards, From, Beyond Asia*, pp. 77–97. New York: Palgrave Macmillan.

Horie, Y. (2007) 'Possibilities and Limitations of "Lesbian Continuum"'. *Journal of Lesbian Studies, 10*(3–4), pp. 145–159.

Jordan, M. (2007) 'Religion Trouble'. *GLQ, 13*(4), pp. 563–575.

Kelly, M. B. (2007) *Seduced by Grace: Contemporary Spirituality, Gay Experience and Christian Faith*. Melbourne: Clouds of Magellan.

Kelly, M. B. (2018) *Christian Mysticism's Queer Flame: Spirituality in the Lives of Contemporary Gay Men*. New York: Routledge.

Kornegay, E. (2012) 'Baldwin on Top'. *Black Theology, 10*(3), pp. 328–338.

Kornegay, E. (2013) *A Queering of Black Theology: James Baldwin's Blues Project and Gospel Prose*. New York: Palgrave Macmillan.

Kuruvilla, P. (Ed.) (2017) *Christian Responses to Issues of Human Sexuality and Gender Diversity; A Guide to the Churches in India*. Bangalore/Delhi: CISRS/ISPCK.

Kwok, P-L. (2005) *Postcolonial Imagination and Feminist Theology*. London: SCM Press.

Kwok, P-L. (2010) 'Body and Pleasure in Postcoloniality'. In Isherwood, L. and Petrella, I. (Eds.) *Dancing Theology in Fetish Boots: Essays in Honour of Marcella Althaus-Reid*, pp. 31–43. London: SCM Press.

Lightsey, P. R. (2012) 'Inner Dictum'. *Black Theology, 10*(3), pp. 339–349.

Lightsey, P. R. (2015) *Our Lives Matter: A Womanist Queer Theology*. Eugene: Pickwick Publications.

Loughlin, G. (Ed.) (2007) *Queer Theology: Rethinking the Western Body*. London: Blackwell.

Nelson, J. B. (1979) *Embodiment*. Minneapolis: Augsburg Publishing House.

Nelson, J. B. (1988) *The Intimate Collection*. Philadelphia: The Westminster Press.

Nickoloff, J. B. (2003) 'Sexuality: A Queer Omission in U.S. Latino/a Theology'. *Journal of Hispanic/Latino Theology, 10*(3), pp. 31–51.

Panotto, N. (Ed.) (2016) *Indecent Theologians Marcella Althaus-Reid and the Next Generation of Postcolonial Activists*. California: Borderless Press.

Punt, J. (2008) 'Intersections in Queer Theory and Postcolonial Theory, and Hermeneutical Spin-Offs'. *The Bible and Critical Theory, 4*(2), pp. 24.1–16.

Rangiwai, B. (2020) '"My Heart Goes Shut Up, Shut Up!": Gay Marriage to an Indian Man – One Year On'. *Te Kaharoa, 15*(1), pp. 1–16.

Robinson, M. (2015) 'Bisexual People'. In Thatcher, A. (Ed.) *The Oxford Handbook of Theology, Sexuality and Gender*, pp. 640–656. Oxford: Oxford University Press.

Sander, D. and Wilson, J. (2020) 'The Weaving of the Garment that I'm Wearing: The Spiritual Lives of Gay Men in Aotearoa New Zealand'. *New Zealand Journal of Counselling, 40*(1), pp. 45–61.

Sneed, R. (2010) *Representations of Homosexuality: Black Liberation Theology and Cultural Criticism*. New York: Palgrave Macmillan.

Stuart, E. (Ed.) (1997) *Religion Is a Queer Thing*. London: Cassell.

Sugirtharajah, R. S. (2004) 'Complacencies and Cul-de-sacs: Christian Theologies and Colonialism'. In Keller, C., Nausner, M. and Rivera, M. (Eds.) *Postcolonial Theologies: Divinity and Empire*, pp. 22–38. St. Louis: Chalice Press.

Sweasey, P. (Ed.) (1997) *From Queer to Eternity. Spirituality in the Lives of Lesbian, Gay and Bisexual People*. London: Cassell.

The Nest Collective (2015) *Stories of Our Lives*. Nairobi: The Nest Arts Company.

Thatcher, A. (1993) *Liberating Sex. A Christian Sexual Theology*. London: SPCK.

Thoreson, R. R. (2014) 'Troubling the Waters of "A Wave of Homophobia": Political Economies of Anti-Queer Animus in Sub-Saharan Africa'. *Sexualities, 17*(1/2), pp. 23–42.

Tolbert, M. A. (1995) 'Reading for Liberation'. In Segovia, F. F. and Tolbert, M. A. (Eds.) *Reading From This Place, Vol. I. Social Location and Biblical Interpretation in the United States*, pp. 263–276. Minneapolis: Fortress Press.

Toy, M. J. (2025) *Digital Religion in Aotearoa: Minority Theologies of Flourishing.* PhD thesis. Te Herenga Waka—Victoria University of Wellington. Available at: https://openaccess.wgtn.ac.nz/articles/thesis/Digital_Religion_in_Aotearoa_Minority_Theologies_of_Flourishing/28728629?file=53410061 (Accessed: January 2026).

van Klinken, A. (2013) *Transforming Masculinities in African Christianity: Gender Controversies in Times of AIDS*. Abingdon: Routledge.

van Klinken, A. (2015) 'Queer Love in a "Christian Nation": Zambian Gay Men Negotiating Sexual and Religious Identities'. *Journal of the American Academy of Religion, 83*(4), pp. 947–964.

van Klinken, A. (2017) 'Queer Studies and Religion in Contemporary Africa: Decolonizing, Post-secular Moves', *Scholar & Feminist Online, 14*(2).

van Klinken, A. (2018) 'Autobiographical Storytelling and African Narrative Queer Theology'. *Exchange, 47*, pp. 211–229.

van Klinken, A. and Chitando, E. (Eds.) (2016) *Public Religion and the Politics of Homosexuality in Africa*. Abingdon: Routledge.

van Klinken, A. and Phiri, L. (2015) ' "In the Image of God": Reconstructing and Developing Grassroots African Queer Theology from Urban Zambia'. *Theology & Sexuality, 21*(1), pp. 36–52.

van Klinken, A. S., Stiebert, J., Sebyala, B. and Hudson, F. (2021) *Sacred Queer Stories: Ugandan LGBTQ+ Refugee Lives and the Bible*. Rochester: Boydell & Brewer.

West, G., Van der Walt, C. and Kaoma, K. J. (2016) 'When Faith Does Violence: Reimagining Engagement Between Churches and LGBTI Groups on Homophobia in Africa'. *HTS: Theological Studies, 72*(1), 1–8.

Williams, D. (1993) *Sisters in the Wilderness: The Challenge of Womanist God Talk*. New York: Orbis.

Yip, L-S. (2012) 'Listening to the Passion of Catholic Nu-tongzhi: Developing a Catholic Lesbian Feminist Theology in Hong Kong'. In Boisvery, D. and Johnson, E. (Eds.) *Queer Religion: Homosexuality in Modern Religious History*, pp. 63–80. Santa Barbara: Praeger.

Zachariah, G. and Rajkumar, V. (Eds.) (2015) *Disruptive Faith, Inclusive Communities: Church and Homophobia*. Bangalore/Delhi: CISRS/ISPCK.

QUEER BIBLE

INTRODUCTION

This chapter focuses on the act of reading and interpreting the Bible queerly. There are many exciting explorations in the field of queer biblical studies, where lesbian, gay, bisexual, intersex, and transgender interpretations offer innovative approaches to biblical studies, as well as the methods of analysis that come from queer criticism. The chapter is ordered in three parts. The first part of the chapter interrogates the authority of the Bible, before looking at biblical interpretations relating to lesbian, gay, bisexual, and intersex lives. Trans readings are covered more fully in Chapter 6. Then, the second part of the chapter draws on extensive scholarship in this area, and three queer approaches in biblical studies are discussed: (i) biblical hermeneutics and same sex relationships; (ii) queering the Bible; and (iii) queer ways of telling. Examples of queer readings are included throughout the chapter. In the third part of the chapter, attention is given to queer readings from global contexts, focusing on reader responses from Asian American, Asian, African, and Latin American contexts, as well as Black and womanist readings.

DOI: 10.4324/9781003434993-5

PART 1: QUEERING AUTHORITY AND QUEER READINGS

Historically, the Bible has played an important role in the development of society and culture. In today's society, its influence is still prominent. Indeed, its authority is presumed in public life, as it is used to swear an oath in court in many countries. The Bible is frequently invoked in contemporary debates around gender and sexuality. Deryn Guest notes how the Bible is 'a cultural artefact of considerable significance and influence, which is regularly deployed politically to bolster statements on such matters as transsexuality, civil partnerships, anti-discrimination law, gay adoption and parenting and so on' (Guest, 2012: 29). Its significance in the public sphere cannot be overestimated. Therefore, it is of great importance that biblical studies must engage with questions of sexual diversity and gender identities.

Despite its influence on public, social, and cultural spheres, the status and authority of the Bible is often misplaced in Christianity. Adrian Thatcher points out that the Bible does not claim to be the Word of God. He says, 'once the Bible is identified with the Word of God the text of scripture rivals or even replaces the Word of God, which is Jesus Christ' (Thatcher, 2008: 4). In this way, Christians who elevate the status of the Bible to a point where it is worshipped commit bibliolatry – worship of the Bible instead of God. Thatcher warns how this, according to the Bible itself, is disastrous, as 'the letter kills, but the Spirit gives life' (2 Corinthians 3:6). Moreover, there are arguments which state that the Bible cannot have any significance or authority for LGBTQ+ identified people. For example, Elizabeth Stuart says:

> the Bible is the creation of the early church, a church whose patriarchal assumptions we no longer share. It can therefore have little authority for us, instead we need to develop a new canon of sacred writings which reflect our experience of God.
>
> (Stuart, 1997: 45)

It is clear so far that queer serves to disturb and disrupt. Queer biblical studies, therefore, places into question the status and authority of the Bible. More importantly, queer biblical studies offers transformative readings of biblical texts, and the queer

Bible 'turns the Bible from being an enemy to a friend' (Stuart, 1997: 45). Timothy Koch advocates the process of queer reading as 'highly selective work' (Koch, 2006: 373) and explicitly refuses to allow traditional hermeneutics or church authority to decide on the meanings of the texts:

> we, as LGBT persons, come with our own questions, our own need for resources, our own limited energies; when we regard biblical texts as *resources* for us [...] We can find our own concerns, emotions, goals and fears reflected throughout these pages; we can find role models, cautionary tales, ribald stories and points to ponder that can illuminate our own journeys.
>
> (Koch, 2006: 373)

LESBIAN, GAY, AND BISEXUAL THEOLOGIES AND THE BIBLE

Gay, lesbian, and bisexual readings of the Bible draw on inclusive and affirming interpretations of scripture, challenging heteronormative assumptions within biblical interpretation. They often emphasise themes of love, justice, and acceptance, while directly responding to discriminatory readings that portray LGBTQ+ identities as sinful. Derrick Sherwin Bailey was an English Christian theologian. His book, *Homosexuality and the Western Christian Tradition* (Bailey, 1955), offers one of the first explorations into how biblical texts have shaped theological thought in relation to homosexuality. Bailey argues that Christian teaching on homosexuality is based on a misreading or a selective reading of scripture. He submitted his text to the Wolfenden Committee in the UK, which, in 1957, concluded that same-sex sexual acts between men in a private capacity should no longer be criminalised.

Phyllis Trible was a pioneer in feminist biblical interpretation, exposing misogyny within scripture and also how this has resulted in misogyny by religious organisations. Trible authored a book entitled *Texts of Terror* (Trible, 1984), where she published her ideas. She focuses primarily on the interpretation of texts (rather than on institutional theology per se), but her approach has influenced broader critiques of how religious organisations interpret scripture in ways that uphold patriarchal norms. The idea that the Bible is used against people as a 'text of terror' was then applied to the biblical texts which are used to oppose same-sex relationships.

Robert Goss uses the term 'texts of terror' (1993: 90) to refer to biblical passages which are used to condemn homosexuality. The terror is connected to how the Bible can be weaponised against people, and this, in turn, causes harm. For many LGBTQ+ people who are on the receiving end of harmful interpretations of such texts, this constitutes a form of spiritual abuse. Goss states:

> The majority of Christian traditions believe that the Bible opposes homosexuality. The Bible has been used as a weapon of terror against gay men and lesbians. It has been interpreted to legitimize oppression against same-sex practices throughout Christian history. Biblical texts have been used by fundamentalist churches in their homophobic attacks upon gay men and lesbians in hate campaigns.
>
> (Goss, 1993: 90)

One of the earliest major considerations for gay and lesbian theology was how the Bible was used as a weapon to justify homophobic attitudes. The Bible is problematic, in this sense, and much work has been done to look at the original basis and contexts for the claims against same-sex relations. There are a number of biblical verses which are used by conservative Christians to condemn homosexual lifestyles and relationships. These have often been referred to as 'clobber texts', as they are commonly used to describe homosexuality as a sin. Here are some of the passages (NIV translations):

> Do not have sexual relations with a man as one does with a woman; that is detestable.
>
> (Leviticus 18:22)

> If a man has sexual relations with a man as one does with a woman, both of them have done what is detestable. They are to be put to death; their blood will be on their own heads.
>
> (Leviticus 20:13)

> Because of this, God gave them over to shameful lusts. Even their women exchanged natural sexual relations for unnatural ones. In the same way the men also abandoned natural relations with women and were inflamed with lust for one another. Men committed shameful acts

> with other men, and received in themselves the due penalty for their error.
>
> (Romans 1:26–27)

> Or do you not know that wrongdoers will not inherit the kingdom of God? Do not be deceived: Neither the sexually immoral nor idolaters nor adulterers nor men who have sex with men.
>
> (1 Corinthians 6:9)

> They called to Lot, 'Where are the men who came to you tonight? Bring them out to us so that we can have sex with them.' Lot went outside to meet them and shut the door behind him and said, 'No, my friends. Don't do this wicked thing. Look, I have two daughters who have never slept with a man. Let me bring them out to you, and you can do what you like with them. But don't do anything to these men, for they have come under the protection of my roof.'
>
> (Genesis 19:5–8 (Sodom and Gomorrah))

A further example exists in 1 Timothy 1:10.

In asking the question 'what does the Bible say about…?', there is an assumption that there is a definitive answer to be found in the Bible that will carry authority or relevance. Yet, biblical studies and biblical interpretation offer much more than being able to locate a biblical passage and claim bottom-line responses which are deemed to carry ultimate truth. Postmodern biblical studies brings into question the role, position, and power of the author, the text itself, and the reader, alongside engaging with critical theory and contemporary issues.

Daniel Helminiak, a Roman Catholic priest, published a landmark and accessible study about biblical interpretation and homosexuality. In his book, *What the Bible Really Says About Homosexuality*, (2000, first published in 1994), he draws a simple conclusion that nowhere in the Bible is there explicit condemnation against homosexuality as it is know it today. How could there be? It is important to remember that the word 'homosexuality' did not become popularly used until the late 19th century; and, since then, its cultural and contextual meanings have changed significantly. His premise is based on a distinction between 'homosexuality' (identity, orientation, how people of the same sex relate to one another romantically and lovingly), and 'homogenitality' (the engagement of same-sex acts). He focuses on a number of texts that are used against LGBTQ+ people, beginning with an overview of the story of Sodom and Gomorrah (Genesis 19), where the 'sin' is not same-sex acts, but inhospitality. The 'abomination' of Leviticus 18:22 has to do with a state of purity rituals and an uncleanliness that is forbidden, rather than actual same-sex acts. Helminiak equally addresses Paul's words that have been used to comment on same-sex relationships in Romans 1:26–27, 1 Corinthians 6:9, and 1 Timothy 1:10.

Helminiak's book is a bold defence against wielding scriptures to condemn LGBTQ+ people, and he writes how it is 'outrageous for any educated person to quote the Bible to condemn homosexuality' (2000: 13). The author is clear that there are no simple answers to be found in the Bible when it comes to contemporary issues. There is an ethical implication to this project, as Helminiak suggests that using the Bible to condemn homosexuality is an act of justifying prejudice and discrimination against LGBTQ+ people. For LGBTQ+ people, what is at stake is less about a choice between religion and sexuality, but between being themselves and their faith.

There are examples where the texts of terror are reshaped by offering reparative readings. In Nancy Wilson's publication of *Our Tribe: Queer Folks, God, Jesus and the Bible* (1995), she offers a space for biblical readings to be combined with a focus on experiences from lesbian, gay, and bisexual perspectives. Wilson encourages LGBTQ+ people of faith to take back the Bible:

> I believe that it is essential for gay men, lesbians, and bisexuals to take back the Bible. If we are not included among the stories and characters of the Bible, then it cannot be our book [...] Years from now, none of this will be shocking or unusual [...] As gay and lesbian biblical scholars come out, do the scholarship, and pay the price, the texts will be healed.
>
> (Wilson, 1995: 164)

Wilson talks about cutting out the passages in the Bible which oppress. She underlines the fact that, throughout Christian traditional biblical interpretation, troublesome parts of the Bible are often glossed over or ignored, as gay and lesbian people engage in '"picking and choosing" only the parts of the Bible that support our point of view' (Wilson, 1995: 70). Yet, those parts which are cut out, states Wilson:

> serve as very important reminders, as documentation of the history of oppression and the source of our struggles. They, too, are part of our tribal memory. For this reason – that *we may never forget* – it is still important for gay and lesbian people to understand how the Bible has been misused to oppress us.
>
> (Wilson, 1995: 70)

Wilson speculates on the idea of there being a special place in hell for those who misuse the Bible to hurt or alienate others, acknowledging the irony in her own statement because she believes that hell does not really exist. Rather than thinking of the Bible as the divine Word of God, or as an untouchable and revered sacred text, Wilson states that the Bible offers a lot to speculate on. She describes an uncomfortable experience speaking on the theme of 'Outing the Bible' at her former college. The responses from her audience members were polite, yet hostile to her thinking. Her work exposes the challenges involved in attempting to open up people's interpretive imaginations, as she writes, 'it would be so much easier for these students if we gay and lesbians would just continue to hate ourselves and the Bible' (Wilson, 1995: 75). She refuses that position, stating:

> For me, the Bible is an elastic, resilient friend who bounces back and even talks back when I question it [...] The Bible belongs to anyone who will love it, play with it, push it to its limits, touch it, and be touched by it – and the same is true for God.
>
> (1995: 75)

Wilson's call to 'take back the Word' can be related to the edited collection of essays, published in 2000, entitled *Take Back The Word: A Queer Reading of the Bible* (Goss & West, 2000). The aim of the volume is for LGBTQ+ people to be able to read the Bible as a friend, rather than an enemy, given the fear and complex relationships many queer people have towards scripture. By 'taking back the Word', its authors are able to liberate the Bible from fundamentalist, exclusionary, and violence uses that seek to harm LGBTQ+ lives and communities through weaponising the Bible. The authors remind people that Hebrew and Christian texts do not simply belong to heterosexual people, but to all people of faith.

The strategies of approaching the Bible through a queer-inclusionary lens is vital. Outside of biblical studies and theology, research into how lesbian, gay, and bisexual Christians view the scriptures details the continuing relevance of scripture for LGBTQ+ people. Sociologist Andrew Yip explored the beliefs, attitudes, and lives of lesbian, gay, and bisexual Christians (Yip, 2003). In one study, out of the 565 people questioned, 94.9% of gay men stated that the Bible cannot be taken literally, while 96.2% of lesbians said the same. Yip's study illuminates how, while 'the Bible was considered still relevant to everyday life, it is nevertheless considered an insufficient guide for Christian living' (2003: 151). The research sheds light on the question of authority of the Bible in relation to religious and sexual identities.

Similarly, Alex Toft's work on bisexual Christians (2009) revealed that 87% of respondents agreed that the Bible is often misinterpreted on the theme of sexuality. That said, only 12% of bisexual Christians in his study claimed the Bible was incompatible with modern life (Toft, 2009: 83). This points to the fact that bisexual Christians, like lesbian and gay Christians, still feel that the Bible has relevance to them but should not be taken literally. One of Toft's participants, Adam, puts it as follows: 'It makes me so bloody angry that the Church is hypocritical, and they will use this excuse of "well the Bible says", and it's cherry picking' (2009: 84).

The pick 'n' mix approach to reading biblical texts is a popular strategy among queer Christians. Melissa Wilcox calls this strategy a 'biblical buffet' (Wilcox, 2002: 501). Her research with LGBTQ+ Christians reveals how people take from the Bible what is relevant to them, what pleases them, and they disregard anything which does not appeal. One of the interviewees in her study is a bisexual man who says just that: 'I take from the Bible what I can use, and I disregard a lot of what I can't use' (2002: 501).

INTERSEX READINGS OF THE BIBLE

There are a number of biblical texts which enforce the distinction between male and female identities, as well as those which blur such distinctions. Genesis 1:27 states: 'So God created mankind in his own image, in the image of God he created them; male and female he created them'. This verse has often been used to highlight the differences and enforce the distinctions between the sexes in Christian belief. Conservative Christians may use the texts to point out that there seems to be no room for ambiguity in terms of gender. Sally Gross provides a closer reading of Genesis 1:27, and she says that the verse should be read in context (Gross, 1999). According to Gross, the fact that Abraham and Sarah were unable to have children may reveal the possibility of Sarah's intersex body. Moreover, Gross is keen to mobilise the scriptural texts themselves to advocate for contemporary intersex bodies. Currently, many babies born into intersex bodies, where genitalia are ambiguous at birth, undergo medical procedures to align their genitalia with what are perceived as traditionally male or female bodies. Intersex activists reject the idea of such surgery on young bodies on the grounds that it is medically unnecessary, as the surgery is often cosmetic. There are arguments that such surgery is, in fact, genital mutilation. Gross says how scripture can support arguments against surgical interventions:

> biblical literalists should be persuaded by the letter of Scripture to be very suspicious indeed of genital surgery imposed upon intersexed infants when no intrinsic risk to life and physical health demands it. The removal of gonads and other such surgery is explicitly forbidden by Scripture (see Deut. 23.1, for example).
>
> (1999: 74)

The presence of eunuchs in the biblical texts may demonstrate the presence of intersex bodies within the scriptures. This discussion is also one that is found in trans biblical interpretation (see Chapter 6). A eunuch was usually thought to be a castrated male or an individual with ambiguous genitalia. The verse from Deuteronomy 23:1 – 'No one who has been emasculated by crushing or cutting may enter the assembly of the Lord' – is an argument that can be raised to object to early surgery in intersex children, but the very same scripture is used by Christians who oppose sex reassignment surgery for trans people. There seems to be an obsession with emasculation and the erasure of male genitalia within such scriptures, and this is read alongside the numerous verses relating to male circumcision. There is a clear focus on the penis and its function to procreate, yet the scriptures do not give such attention to female genitalia for procreation. There are other positive references to eunuchs within the Bible (NIV):

> For this is what the Lord says: 'To the eunuchs who keep my Sabbaths, who choose what pleases me and hold fast to my covenant— to them I will give within my temple and its walls a memorial and a name better than sons and daughters; I will give them an everlasting name that will endure forever.'
>
> (Isaiah 56:4–5)

> For there are eunuchs who were born that way, and there are eunuchs who have been made eunuchs by others – and there are those who choose to live like eunuchs for the sake of the kingdom of heaven. The one who can accept this should accept it.
>
> (Matthew 19:12)

> As they traveled along the road, they came to some water and the eunuch said, 'Look, here is water. What can stand in the way of my being baptized?' And he gave orders to stop the chariot. Then both Philip and the eunuch went down into the water and Philip baptized him. When they came up out of the water, the Spirit of the Lord suddenly took Philip away, and the eunuch did not see him again, but went on his way rejoicing.
>
> (Acts 8:36–39)

The texts demonstrate a more inclusive reading for intersex individuals, and conservative Christians could focus on these texts as a model for inclusion. Yet, a word of caution is needed. The verse from Matthew 19:12 shows variation in the reasons as to why people were eunuchs. Often castration was involuntary as eunuchs were enslaved, and, although their presence was significant enough to be referenced in scriptural texts, there certainly did appear to be a lot of stigma around eunuchs in ancient times. The eunuch therefore becomes a symbol, a trans-cestor (see Chapter 6). Susannah Cornwall's work provides examples of how intersex people engage with such scriptures; as one of her participants, David, says:

> Of course I scoured the Bible to find out anything to do with intersex and I was thrilled when I discovered that Jesus spoke about it. My interpretation of what Jesus said about eunuchs ... I thought that was wonderful, yes. And that was the springboard for my faith. I thought, 'Jesus knows I exist! I'm not on my own'. Because I thought I was the only one in the world, you see.
>
> (Cornwall, 2015: 225)

PART 2: QUEER APPROACHES IN BIBLICAL STUDIES

There are three main contemporary approaches to queer biblical scholarship. The first approach examines biblical hermeneutics with regard to same-sex relationships and works sensitively within traditional methods. The second approach looks at strategies to queer the Bible, including the reception of the Bible by readers, who bring their own contexts and positions to their readings. The third approach is imaginative and creative, offering a retelling of the stories by recasting characters, events, plots, and contexts. Although they are discussed separately here for ease of explanation, these approaches are often combined and cross over.

[i] Biblical hermeneutics and same-sex relationships

One of the first lenses in which queer readings of the Bible have troubled the idea of sexuality and gender has been through an analysis of linguistic and literary structures. This approach may also treat the Bible in the same way as any other text of literature may be examined, focusing on language, style, content, and genre. Trained scholars in ancient biblical languages have re-examined texts and their translations. For example, in 1 Corinthians 6:9–10, the Greek word often translated as 'homosexuals' is *arsenokoitēs*. But this is an extremely difficult word to translate as it is composed of two parts – *arsen* (man) and *koite* (bed) – so 'manbedders' would be a rough fit. Some interpretations look at this word as referring to non-consensual sexual activity between men, such as rape, or an abuse of status and privilege from one man to another.

A second lens has been to examine the histories of the ancient contexts in which the texts were produced, demonstrating how radically different society and culture were. In biblical studies, historical-critical interpretation is a method which seeks to uncover the world behind the texts, exploring the histories and contexts of the time in which they were produced. Therefore, the method explores the themes of sexuality, gender, and examples of identity disruption in ancient contexts. The historical-critical method helps to create an understanding of what life was like for the authors and characters in the stories. The writing of ancient texts was a task carried out by those who were educated and therefore literary skilled. Authors of the biblical texts are privileged in some way, and their experiences and practices shape the texts.

Certainly, gender and sexuality as understood today are radically different from what would have been thought of at the times the texts were written. The sexual imagination in ancient times was therefore unlike today's understandings of sexuality. Nowadays, there are sexual activities and discussions of sexual topics for which no explicit biblical reference exists, including, for example, discussions of pornography. The biblical texts pertaining to sexuality reveal how, in ancient times, the dominant themes of marriage, rape, incest, and prostitution formed part of the laws on which Judaism, and later Christianity, viewed sexuality. Indeed, feminist biblical studies has examined the patriarchy and power at play in how these ancient concepts have been upheld, to the detriment of women and sexually marginalised individuals.

Other interpretations which are found in queer hermeneutics include the positive same-sex relationships described in the biblical texts. The interactions between David and Jonathan and Naomi and Ruth become examples of same-sex relationships. Therefore, exploring the narratives in this way does not necessarily expose David and Jonathan as a gay couple engaging in sexual acts, but points to the value of same-sex relationships:

> After David had finished talking with Saul, Jonathan became one in spirit with David, and he loved him as himself. From that day Saul kept David with him and did not let him return home to his family. And Jonathan made a covenant with David because he loved him as himself. Jonathan took off the robe he was wearing and gave it to David, along with his tunic, and even his sword, his bow and his belt. Whatever mission Saul sent him on, David was so successful that Saul gave him a high rank in the army. This pleased all the troops, and Saul's officers as well.
>
> (1 Samuel 18:1–5 (NIV))

In 1 Samuel 16:18, David is chosen for his good looks. Chapter 18:1 describes Jonathan's love for David as they become one in spirit. By verse 3, this love is cemented in a covenant Jonathan makes with David: a commitment to one another in the form of a union. This text does not require a reader to have finely tuned gaydar to be able to see it as an example of same-sex commitment. The emotional attachment between the two men is undeniable, and the fact that their relationship was publicly condoned by the men in the army is significant.

Further on, in 2 Samuel 1:26, David grieves for Jonathan, saying, 'Your love for me was wonderful, more wonderful than that of women'. In 2 Samuel 6:20, David dances semi-naked before the ark of the Lord. This leads to disgust on the part of Michal, David's wife. Michal's repulsion lies in the fact that she has witnessed a series of relationships between David and Saul, then Jonathan, and now the Lord:

> David said to Michal, 'It was before the Lord, who chose me rather than your father or anyone from his house when he appointed me ruler over the Lord's people Israel—I will celebrate before the Lord. I will become even more undignified than this, and I will be humiliated in my own eyes ...' And Michal daughter of Saul had no children to the day of her death.
>
> (2 Samuel 6:21–23 (NIV))

Given Michal's annoyance and David's relationships with Jonathan and then the Lord, perhaps it is not too difficult to speculate on why she remained childless!

In the book of Ruth, there is a similar intense and loving bond between Naomi and Ruth. Ruth is the daughter-in-law of Naomi. The text is pivotal in exploring the relationship and bond between the two women, which move away from the backdrop of the male-dominated society and culture of ancient contexts where women were dependent on men. Marriage often equated to economic security and protection for women, and to some extent Boaz (Ruth's husband) offers a third element which helps to triangulate this bond in an economic sense. Deborah Kahn-Harris uses the term polyamory to consider this relationship (Kahn-Harris, 2023). Yet, there are no words of love or commitment between Ruth and Boaz, only Ruth and Naomi. The relationship demonstrates a same-sex loving commitment to one another:

> But Ruth replied, 'Don't urge me to leave you or to turn back from you. Where you go I will go, and where you stay I will stay. Your people will be my people and your God my God. Where you die I will die, and there I will be buried. May the Lord deal with me, be it ever so severely, if even death separates you and me.'
>
> (Ruth, 1:16–17 (NIV))

Ironically, the statements of commitment and love between Naomi and Ruth are often used in heterosexual wedding ceremonies. Wilson notes the popularity of Ruth's declaration in opposite-sex weddings and claims that 'these stories of committed faithful love, filled with risk taking, are moving, powerful biblical stories for gay and lesbian people. We must take them back' (Wilson, 1995: 156).

Similar stories exist elsewhere in the Bible; for example, the relationships between Mary and Martha and Jesus and Peter, among others, could be read with a queer eye. Yet, sympathetic literary approaches to same-sex relationships do not focus on the physical expression of their love through any same-sex activity. Whether David/Jonathan are gay, or Naomi/Ruth lesbian, contemporary readers simply cannot not know. Wilson suggests that 'they could have had a deep platonic friendship that was also romantic in a homoerotic but not homosexual way' (Wilson, 1995: 156). In developing further the idea about sexuality and acting upon it, Guest highlights how focusing on this 'could play to the Church's game of distinguishing between a sexual orientation (which is acceptable) and acting upon it (which, in the case of homosexuality, is usually negatively evaluated)' (Guest, 2005: 185). Indeed, as Guest suggests, denying the possibility of genital acts between these characters only reinforces a negative opinion of same-sex acts.

Exploring readings of same-sex relationships provides a way in for queering biblical hermeneutics; as Teresa Hornsby states, 'queer theory often enters a party on the arm of a more traditional guest' (Hornsby, 2006: 412). The limitations of a literary approach to same-sex relationships mean that the level of acceptability is drawn as long as the same-sex couples do not engage sexually. There is, of course, the potential to go beyond literary readings, and queer the texts even further, thereby offering the potential for more sexualised or intimate readings of the relationships. There is creative abundance in queering biblical studies in this way, which is discussed in both sections below.

[ii] Queering the Bible

In biblical studies, the term *reception criticism* is used to refer to how the text is interpreted by the reader. The reader therefore engages in an act of creating their own meaning from the text that emphasises their own particular responses to it. Reception criticism can be thought of as a reader response. The Bible moves away from being considered as a timeless text, with a clear and universal meaning embedded within its pages, which is accepted and holds significance for all eternity. Instead, it becomes part of a process in which the text is picked up by the reader who locates it in their particular contexts, interests, and concerns.

Reception criticism looks at the impact the text has on an individual reader or reading community. In this method, the reception of the text may take priority over reconstructing the text's original meaning. Perhaps only some aspects of the biblical text will be selected for discussion by the reader. Timothy Koch suggests a queer reader-response approach in which biblical texts are reinterpreted by 'cruising the scriptures' (Koch, 2001). Cruising refers to an activity where a person seeks out a partner for sex, and it is a popular term in gay culture. Cruising therefore offers a measure of excitement and a degree of risk. The risk is keeping an eye open for attackers or haters, while the excitement is located in the thrilling encounter. Koch applies this as a method to approach the biblical text, describing how biblical texts can be picked up according to tastes, connections, instincts, and experience. He says 'choosing to cruise means taking our own authority and responsibility for following up on whatever comes our way, for it is this which speaks to our desires' (2001: 175).

For queer biblical studies, the way in which LGBTQ+ individuals read and devise commentaries on the biblical texts in their own contexts results in lesbian, gay, bisexual, and transgender reception criticism. The most significant example of this is *The Queer Bible Commentary* (Guest et al., 2006; revised 2022). In this volume, each biblical text is not given verse by verse analysis, as is found in more traditional Bible commentaries, but portions of the text are selected which have relevance for the lives and interests of each commentator. Therefore, a queer commentary does not seek to offer answers to questions, but it offers creative, innovative, and empathic approaches to queer interpretations of scripture.

In order to examine the importance of queer reception criticism, attention now turns to strategies offered by biblical scholars. Deryn Guest has been a pioneer in lesbian, queer, and trans biblical studies. In developing lesbian biblical hermeneutics, Guest advocates the principles of four Rs: resistance, rupture, reclamation, and re-engagement (Guest, 2005: 110), which are discussed below with reference to practical examples found in other queer readings.

Resistance

Guest's work shows how reading texts with suspicion has been used in liberation, feminist, womanist, and postcolonial critiques. Guest offers a strategy of reading the text in a way which is suspicious of the presumed heterosexuality of the biblical characters and their relationships, *hetero-suspicion* (Guest, 2005: 124), and this can be mobilised for all non-normative gender or sexual identities. Reading in this way is an act of resistance. The method of hetero-suspicion encourages the reader to be suspicious of how heteronormativity and patriarchy have introduced bias in the texts themselves, and then in how the texts have been interpreted throughout history.

Examples of queer reception criticism which show resistance and suspicion of the presumed heterosexuality of the characters include the stories of the relationships between David/Jonathan and Naomi/Ruth, as noted in the previous section. Another, more sexualised, example can be found in the reading of Moses in the book of Exodus by Rebecca Alpert (2006). She describes Moses as bisexual, in that he is married but is intimate with a male God. Alpert's reading looks specifically at the intimacy of the relationship between God and Moses. She points to the Jewish tradition where Moses was kissed by God and was called to have this special relationship with God. Alpert's commentary suggests how Moses and God's relationship becomes more sexually and erotically charged throughout the text, and therefore, her reading demonstrates a commitment to a hermeneutic of hetero-suspicion, as suggested by Guest above. Alpert sexualises this hetero-suspicion, as Moses becomes 'the feminine, submissive partner who begs for God's attention, opens his orifice, and clings to God's rod' (Alpert, 2006: 71).

Rupture

Guest's second principle, rupture, focuses on how religious institutions and traditions have drawn upon certain biblical texts to enforce a binary of heterosexuality and homosexuality. The texts have been manipulated to demonstrate how one side of the binary, heterosexuality, is God-ordained. Similar to the use of the texts of terror, the other side of the binary, homosexuality, is used to indicate disapproval from God. As noted previously, the texts of terror have been re-examined using historical contexts and linguistic analyses to demonstrate how their references to homosexuality are more complex and nuanced than previously thought.

Guest's method of rupturing sex or gender binaries can be seen in further work on the 'transgender gaze' (Guest, 2016: 47). Guest states how 'the trans gaze in biblical studies is owned by those whose in-house knowledge and experiences provide the trigger for critical observation and insights' (2016: 57). Justin Tanis, self-identifying as a trans man, offers an example of a trans reading, saying, 'it never occurred to me that God would not accept me, but I was very afraid that God's representatives within the Church might reject me' (Tanis, 2000: 44). Recalling the New Testament story of the woman at Canaan who approached Jesus to help heal her daughter, the disciples suggested Jesus should send her away. With a transgender gaze, Tanis reinterprets the story. His reception sheds light on contemporary concerns about people presenting as non-binary in public. He ruptures the text by stating that 'the woman approaching Jesus to help her daughter was like a drag queen approaching a bunch of teenagers on a street corner to call 911 after her sister has been beaten' (2000: 45). See Chapter 6 for more on trans readings.

Reclamation

The third principle, reclamation, works in conjunction with each of the other strategies, as Guest describes how a queer gaze interprets the scriptures, noting how the biblical texts often come alive for lesbian and gay readers. This allows for reclamation in the sense that the texts are then interpreted in ways which have not previously been explored, and this is a fundamental aspect of reception criticism. Exodus is one story which has been reclaimed and re-interpreted in light of LGBTQ+ contexts. The book of Exodus describes how the Israelites were freed from enslavement through the strength of God/Yahweh. Led by the prophet Moses, the Israelites were offered the promised land in return for their faithfulness. Mona West sees the process of coming out of enslavement as similar to the process of coming out in the lives of LGBTQ+ individuals. West states, 'the themes of enslavement, exodus, wilderness wanderings, promised land, and exile parallel the stories of queer Christians who risk the security of their closets to find wholeness in relation to God and the believing community' (West, 2000: 73). The closet can be a secure environment; West highlights that coming out is not safe for everyone to do. So, rather than being an event which is celebratory, for some people it is an impossible task. West states: 'Queers die [...] often at their own hands when the only way out of the closet is suicide' (2000: 74). For those who are able to come out of the closet, there is a liberation similar to the Exodus story where LGBTQ+ people are able to affirm their own sexuality/gender and begin living authentically. In West's reading of Exodus, 'coming out, crossing over the boundaries of silence and homophobia, gay and lesbian Christians come home to God' (2000: 70).

Re-engagement

Guest's fourth strategy is to call for re-engagement with biblical texts. The emphasis here is on how the task is to exonerate or pardon scripture, to wrestle with scripture, and to reject the authority of the scriptures. In this way, it has not been the scriptures themselves that have caused harm to LGBTQ+ people, but the finger of wrongdoing is pointed towards previous interpreters and their interpretations. Guest highlights the need to study the actual texts themselves and to question the existing translations. According to Guest, this task means the scriptures themselves can no longer be harmful, as it blunts 'their capacity to kill by arguing it is the interpretation of the scriptures, not the scriptures themselves that have been condemnatory' (Guest, 2005: 247). Many individuals may use their own position to wrestle with the text itself. Guest notes that this is a place 'where one's inner conviction plays a pivotal role in discerning the priorities of the scriptures' (2005: 251).

The book of Lamentations is a bleak account of undeserved suffering. Guest's own reading of Lamentations sees the text as offering a voice to those who have suffered or been oppressed by the abuse of the Bible. Lamentations is an expression of anger, and Guest notes how the text offers a voice for the hurt caused by organised religion through homophobic and transphobic statements. Guest relates this to the experience of LGBTQ+ people in affirming their own sexual and gender identities. For those in churches that are not accepting or affirming of their gender or sexuality, Guest suggests that readers follow the example of Lamentations in which they are all 'invited to share in the expression of outrage and distress' (Guest, 2006: 403). Guest sees this anger as a pathway for LGBTQ+ people to negotiate their faith and to hold God and faith communities to account in their inclusion of LGBTQ+ people. Guest raises the question of allegiance and belonging for those who wish to remain faithful to their churches, asking 'is the continued effort to engage with scripture and one's religious tradition ultimately tantamount to collusion?' (Guest, 2005: 256). Those who remain within the tradition and uphold the authority of the scriptures could be accused of 'colluding' with the oppressor. Yet, each individual has a right to make their own choices. Having considered the principles of queer reception criticism and looked at various queer commentaries, the next section offers examples in which queer texts have been overhauled and rewritten using a queer lens.

[III] QUEER WAYS OF TELLING

So far, it is clear how queer commentaries on the Bible offer both engagement with and disruption of the reading of texts. Queer readings have allowed LGBTQ+ people to resist, rupture, reclaim, and re-engage with the biblical texts, as noted in the previous section. A further approach in queer biblical studies is one in which the biblical texts are *queered*. To queer something means to disturb or to disrupt it, to turn it upside down. This approach allows for an entirely imaginative retelling of the biblical texts using creative tools of writing. It allows for a style of biblical reading which is creative, original, and unique.

Within the field of queer biblical studies, there are a number of examples to demonstrate how this queering works in practice. In one of the essays in *Queer Commentary and the Hebrew Bible* (Stone 2001), Roland Boer rewrites the entire relationship between God/Yahweh and Moses as one which is gay. In doing this, he does not write an academic essay in the conventional style of traditional biblical scholars; rather, he writes the story in narrative prose. His essay begins with a queering of the biblical genre by including everyday situations and camp humour. For example, on greeting one another, Moses says to Yahweh, 'big fucking mountain you've got here, Yahweh', to which Yahweh responds, 'Must impress the other gods, dear, can't let appearances slip' (Boer, 2001: 76), and then, Yahweh makes tea for them. There is loose engagement with some of the original biblical narrative in Exodus in terms of plot:

> 'Well', continues Yahweh, 'we need to have a chat, since I want you to make me a beautiful tent, a tabernacle where you and your Israelites can worship me.'
>
> 'Great, just what we need ...' begins Moses.
>
> (Boer, 2001: 76)

Moving beyond features of the original storyline, further queer additions are described in the form of sexual suggestiveness. Boer describes sexual tensions in their relationship, as Moses starts to find Yahweh attractive. Later in the story, Boer narrates:

> All this talk of tingling clothing, pomegranates and bells and hems, has made Moses horny; he is already at the half husky, dying for a look beneath those furs that Yahweh insists on wearing on this unbearably hot mountain. I'm sure he's got a great, pert, upright butt, he asserts.
>
> (Boer, 2001: 78)

Queer theory, with its roots in post-structuralist thought, demonstrates how texts are not stable, and this includes the Bible. Mary Ann Tolbert notes 'how creatively and even joyously queer readers of the Bible reclaim some of its texts by destabilizing them, playing with them, laughing at them, allegorising them, tricking them' (Tolbert, 2000: ix). Elizabeth Stuart does exactly that, by encouraging a strategy of laughing in the face of scriptures used to oppress, such as the texts of terror. She states, 'laughing at those texts is a strategy that subverts their efforts of destructiveness and distances us from the pain of being a target' (Stuart, 2000: 23). Retelling biblical stories in this way breaks down barriers between previous hostile and traditional interpretations, and thereby offers contemporary ways of reading and engaging with scripture for LGBTQ+ people.

James Martin uses imaginative storytelling as a queer approach, describing an encounter with Jesus. Martin loosely tells the story of Jesus's appearance following the resurrection, including a fictitious meeting between Jesus and a gay man. The encounter focuses on the love between the protagonist, Joseph, and Jesus. The story is told from the first-person perspective of Joseph. Jesus asks if he can meet Joseph's mother, and Joseph is hesitant as his mother considers him 'an abomination'. In Martin's telling of the story, Jesus is a faithful and encouraging friend who accompanies Joseph to confront this situation: 'as we walked along, and he pulled me close to him. He looked deeply into my eyes, as though he were looking into my soul, and he whispered to me again that everything would be fine' (Martin, 2000: 221). The queer retelling concludes:

> As I made my way home that evening, it all left me: all my fear, all my failings, all my self-doubt, all my embarrassment, all my pain, all the emptiness, all the loneliness, all of it was gone. His resurrection was my resurrection, you see. All because he loves me.
>
> (2000: 225)

A queer way of reading can be found using queer-coded language in the form of Polari. Polari is considered a form of gay slang once used in the UK. It is a hybrid form of words from romance languages and London slang, and was often used by people in performance, at sea, and in gay subcultures. It is believed to be connected to Punch and Judy puppet performances, as they used Polari to converse. It is therefore fitting that the Bible has been rewritten in Polari (Greening-Jackson, 2025) by a nun in the Manchester Sisters of Perpetual Indulgence (more on the Sisters of Perpetual Indulgence in Chapter 5). Here is an example reading of the opening of Genesis:

1. In the beginning *Gloria* created the heaven and the earth.
2. And the earth was *nanti* form, and void; and *munge* was upon the *eke* of the deep. And the *Fairy* of *Gloria trolled* upon the *eke* of the *aquas*.
3. And *Gloria cackled*, let there be *sparkle* and there was *sparkle*.

(Greening-Jackson, 2025)

The retelling of texts clearly does not adhere to the traditional, established methods used in biblical studies, but that is the point of the queer project. Queer retellings disrupt the assumption that all characters are heterosexual and cisgender. Alternative tellings are possible. Queer approaches in biblical studies breathe fresh air into texts saturated in patriarchy, misogyny, and negativity towards same-sex relationships and transgender lives.

PART 3: QUEER READINGS IN GLOBAL CONTEXTS

The Bible is a significant text that is read by individuals across cultures and locations. As the missionaries brought Christianity to various places across the globe, they also brought with them accepted interpretations of the Bible. Queer biblical studies must place such interpretations under a microscope and examine, expose, and disrupt them. Queer postcolonial biblical studies welcomes voices from groups which have historically been marginalised in multiple ways. The following sub-sections contain examples of queer readings of the Bible in specific global contexts. These include readings and interpretations given by LGBTQ+ individuals or a disruption of the texts based on the settings in which they are read.

ASIAN AMERICAN QUEER READINGS OF THE BIBLE

In his reading of Galatians in the *Queer Bible Commentary* (2006), Patrick Cheng describes his location as queer and Asian as 'a minority within a minority' (Cheng, 2006: 624). In this queer Asian reading, Galatians represents dominant white queer culture attempting to colonise those from minority ethnic backgrounds. In the letter to the Galatians, Paul talks about whether male followers of Jesus need to be circumcised or not, and he states that there is no need for circumcision. Cheng reframes the question, observing how compulsory circumcision is like compulsory heterosexuality and therefore not needed to be a Christian. He states how Galatians speaks powerfully to queer Asians, and he observes how the Gentiles' obsession with circumcision was similar to queer Asians who search for affirmation. He describes the alternative spiritual workshops he offers to gay men of Asian descent, where they share and connect with one another's bodies.

In a short essay which reflects on the experiences of Asian Americans and the Bible, You-Leng Leroy Lim wonders 'Why folks don't just call themselves Holy Biblians instead of Christians?' (Lim, 2002: 316). Like Thatcher, Lim refers to how people state that the Bible is the Word of God, rather than Jesus Christ being the Word of God. Lim's essay is called 'The Bible Tells Me to Hate Myself', and it recounts his experience as a university chaplain and his encounter with a young Christian man who had questions about homosexuality. The profound statement Lim uses as a title was the response a student gave to him when discussing faith. In pointing out how Asia is a vast continent – including India, Japan, and China – Lim appeals to religious leaders of Asian Christianity to blend the experience of Christianity with ancient wisdom practices of Asian traditions. Lim highlights the role of religious leaders in their use and abuse of the Bible, stating, 'the question is not about finding out which passages of scripture are relevant to Asian Americans, but what kinds of leaders and leadership qualities are needed by Asian Americans' (2002: 319), and he points out that the Bible tells the story of a good leader.

ASIAN QUEER READINGS OF THE BIBLE

Missionaries used selective passages from the Bible to demonstrate how Christianity was superior to local spiritual practices. Local expressions of religion were deemed uncivilised or inferior by the missionaries. One example of this use of the Bible is observed when the British occupied Hong Kong in 1842, and missionaries began to preach in the seaports.

Queer Asian readings of the Bible must pay due attention to LGBTQ+ lives and the Asian cultures and contexts in which the Bible is read. Joseph N. Goh explores its reception in Malaysia, where 9.2% of the population are Christian and where same-sex relations are illegal. The Christian churches there are widely disapproving of homosexuality, advising celibacy, counselling or so-called 'conversion' to heterosexuality for gay-identifying individuals. In his study of the Bible among non-heterosexual identifying men, Goh brings together biblical texts with the life-texts of sexuality (Goh, 2016). One of the participants, Artisan, sees the Bible as a message in which the idea of love surpasses any idea of disapproval or discrimination:

> Artisan: Ya ... you know that being a gay man is sinful in the mainline church context. And to me, is not, because on the bible, on John 3, 16 that for God so loved the world, and to me the world is inclusive of gay men, and not just straight men, certain sector of the society, is the world ... every human being, is loved by God and I don't think, and I strongly believe that I'm not excluded at all [*sic*].
>
> (Goh, 2016: 45)

Another of Goh's participants, Skidiver, follows the verse in Leviticus 18:22 which prohibits a man from lying with a man, as a man lies with a woman. In practice, Skidiver says this does not prohibit sexual activity between consensual men, but that penetration should be avoided, as that is what he reads in the Leviticus reference. In his conclusion, Goh recommends that 'Christian communities and churches need to realize how important it is to confront, challenge and transform traditional interpretations of the bible' [*sic*] (Goh, 2016: 49).

In Chinese, the word *tongzhi* has been used to describe LGBTQ+ people, but without referring to a particular gender identity or sexuality. It also means 'comrade'. Kwok Pui-lan (Kwok, 2010: 35) notes how the term is almost similar to 'queer' in the West, but it is preferred in Chinese because it is different from the English word. She describes how homosexuality had been criminalised in Hong Kong through laws of sodomy inherited from British colonialism. In one example of queer Asian readings of the Bible, Tat-siong Benny Liew talks about Jesus's body in the gospel of John and describes it as 'cross-dressing' (Liew, 2009: 261). This reading of John's gospel aims 'to redress the wrongs suffered by people who have not been gendered strictly as male or female' (2009: 261). The text, therefore, comes alive for the gender-fluid, trans, or intersex reader. Liew also states how John's gospel is queer as it recounts how Jesus is beaten, flogged, nailed, and pierced; he states how Jesus has 'a body that is being opened to penetration' (2009: 266). The text is queered in that Jesus's passion is positioned as a sexual encounter with a masochistic Father.

AFRICAN QUEER READINGS OF THE BIBLE

In Africa, the Bible was introduced by missionaries who also brought along theological conservativism. Sub-Saharan Africa is now the global centre for Christianity, seeing a growth in church populations which are steadily declining in other countries. In the Anglican Communion, the Bishops of Africa remain one of the strongest opponents to LGBTQ+ rights. The conservative attitudes from the Western missionaries in Africa about sex and sexuality have now become so embedded that they are considered African values. This is often highlighted by those who are advocates for LGBTQ+ rights, recognising that conservative Christian values and readings of the Bible were a Western import. In this way, the argument that homosexuality is against African values becomes flawed and unconvincing (see Chapter 3). The Bible is used as a justification to oppose LGBTQ+ rights, especially in the African countries in which homosexuality is illegal. The Bible has become a battlefield on which the question of LGBTQ+ rights is being fought against Christian conservatism.

Given such a culture of hostility, what methods do queer Africans use as they engage with the Bible? Queer African readings demonstrate a shift from institutional readings to individual interpretations. This means that queer African individuals are able to find their own meaning in the texts, rather than focusing on the authority of church bodies. The shift is indicative of general approaches to how LGBTQ+ people view tradition and scripture, as understandings of religion are personalised. This personalisation means that individual believers have direct access to texts and can construct their own interpretations and meanings.

Within Adriaan van Klinken's research on Christian Zambian gay men, all interviewees recognise God as love, and this is more important to their beliefs than scriptural readings. They worship God, rather than the text. One participant notes:

> Jesus Christ to me preached love, tolerance, hope, you know. That's what I chose to believe in, which is why I could embrace my Christianity and am not moved by what the Bible says about gay people ... You see people raising the Bible to say, 'God hates fags' – but the word 'hate' has never come out of the Lord's mouth. So they are the ones, those who are saying this, who are involved in blasphemy.
>
> (van Klinken, 2015: 958)

An extensive study on the Bible and homosexuality in Africa, and specifically in Zimbabwe, was carried out by Masiiwa Ragies Gunda in 2010. Gunda states that it is not surprising that the majority of biblical scholarship on the question of sexuality has emerged from South Africa, as an African country with legislation in place to protect against discrimination on the basis of gender, sex, and sexuality. Focusing on the Bible as used by missionaries, Gunda points out a particular irony: the Bible was used by Western missionaries to claim how many things in African culture were unbiblical, yet the Bible is used today by Africans to say how many things in Western culture are unbiblical (Gunda, 2010: 36).

From a Kenyan perspective, stories of queer readings reveal how the Bible is seen as a tool to control people. Within *Stories of Our Lives: Queer Narratives from Kenya* (The Nest Collective, 2015), the section on spirituality and religion tells one story of a Christian who is unable to read the Bible because of the damage it does. One story says, 'Maybe there is another way of reading the Bible. I think the Bible is more than just a punishment structure for sinners' (2015: 302). Another story focuses on different biblical verses which can be used to empower queer people. Using the verse from Proverbs 13:20, one story writer says, 'walk with the wise and become wise, for a companion of fools suffers harm' (2015: 306). The idea of wisdom is linked to education, as several stories in the collection talk about reading widely and wisely, including philosophical texts or texts from other religious traditions.

LATIN AMERICAN QUEER READINGS OF THE BIBLE

There has been a trend in Latin American scholarship to use the biblical text to advocate for social justice. This emerged during the time of liberation theology, where concern for the poor and marginalised was a focus. At its beginning, the marginalised of liberation theology did not consider sexually marginalised people or women. The move beyond liberation theology to feminist and queer theologies began to recognise those excluded because of their gender, sex, or sexual identities. Popular themes in Latin American biblical scholarship include liberation, postcolonialism, and the ideas of borderlands. In attending to voices from the margins, these themes also serve to work with other queer approaches.

Fernando Candido da Silva (2012) observes how queer people have been excluded from Latin American biblical interpretations, and he calls for an approach in which the queer community in São Paulo, Brazil, can re-examine the bible. Da Silva calls for a use of lowercase 'b' when writing 'Bible' as this decreases its authority, and the text serves among many other spiritual writings used by queer folk. His idea of a queer community 'is based in multiple friendship networks, such as "families we choose"' [*sic*] (da Silva, 2012: 213). This community acknowledges differences, but there is an alliance. Da Silva states how 'for the queer community the biblical text cannot represent supreme authority. This is, of course, a matter of survival' (2012: 214). Together, there is an awareness of the community, of its differences, and of the threat posed in reading 'the bible'.

The idea of a community reading of the Bible echoes the work of Latin American theologian Marcella Althaus-Reid. She thought of theology and biblical engagement as a community project and called this a *caminata* (a walk). This requires a 'different engagement with the Bible, new questions concerning the patriarchal structures of sin [that] needed to be unveiled in the Scriptures' (Althaus-Reid, 2004: 12). The structures relate to wealth, power, authority, and readings of the biblical texts. They also relate to gender, sex, and sexuality. A *caminata* allows for a different sort of engagement, and this is a task done in solidarity with the community.

Focusing on Jesus's clothes in the gospel of Mark, Althaus-Reid locates him as one of the transvestites who is persecuted by church and state. Jesus, dressed in royal purple and a crown of thorns, becomes the subject of laughter and mocking. This is similar to the transvestite in Buenos Aires or a Brazilian slum who 'attracts laughter and derision for her gender-fucking' (Althaus-Reid,

2006: 518). The story is retold within Latin American contexts of homophobia and transphobia. Althaus-Reid says:

> we need to read the life of Jesus with the same eyes that we read stories in the tabloids about homosexual people being killed. Unless we can locate Jesus' passion in the real life of people we will not be able to understand the meaning of incarnation nor the subversion of bodies that resurrection implies.
>
> (2006: 519)

Staying briefly with Mark's gospel, Oscar Cabrera uses reflections from Guatemala to re-read the story of Bartimaeus (Mark 10:46–52). Cabrera notes how Bartimaeus was excluded, yet he stands firm in his resistance. The crowd is loud and insensitive, trying to drown out Bartimaeus and other excluded voices. Cabrera states 'Jesus, who hears the voicing of the needy, restores the dignity that was snatched from Bartimaeus' (Cabrera, 2016: 251). Cabrera encourages Guatemalan theologians 'to think indecently, undisciplined, and in rebellious ways' (2016: 255).

BLACK/WOMANIST QUEER READINGS OF THE BIBLE

As the Bible has been used to support arguments against LGBTQ+ lives, conservative Christians often use the bottom-line response 'because the Bible says so'. Within the Black community, it is not uncommon for Black preachers to be theologically conservative, having based their ministries on popular evangelical movements of the 20th century, such as that of Billy Graham. Graham made popular his repeated phrase about the authority of the Bible – 'God said it, I believe it, that settles it' – and this gives absolute authority to scripture. This common phrase, in use in Black churches to this day, was consequently used to denounce LGBTQ+ identities and relationships. In her work on sexuality, Kelly Brown Douglas notes how 'scripture is often the cornerstone of homophobia in the Black community' (Douglas, 1999: 90).

The Bible played a major role in the lives of African American enslaved people, who were often illiterate. The interpretation of the Bible was often what was handed down, and it was received without question. This meant that stories from the Bible which pointed to freedom caught the imagination of African American enslaved people. The Bible, therefore, offered hope, reflecting on stories where the oppressed are set free through faithfulness to God. The stories heard were used in prayers, spirituals, and testimony as they provided words that reflected African American experiences of struggle and survival. The Exodus story, describing the struggles and experience of the Israelites as enslaved, served as a text which provided hope and comfort for African American people. It is a text which shows God's care and favour on those who are struggling or who are oppressed in some way. As many enslaved people were unable to access the Bible for themselves, they were unaware that there are biblical texts that serve to justify enslavement. In contemporary society, there is increased access to the texts as more people are literate and therefore able to read the stories for themselves.

Black and womanist queer readings of the Bible approach traditional interpretations with multiple suspicions. Given this double bind, why do Black and womanist queer people bother with the Bible at all? Pamela Lightsey notes how the Bible has been part of moral, social, and political life, especially as a large number of Black Americans belong to Christian religious traditions. She states, 'Scripture is not only a written instrument but also a way of life for many African Americans. We turn to the Bible for comfort, guidance and nurture' (Lightsey, 2015: 41).

CONCLUSION

The Bible is a significant source for Christian theology, and therefore, queer theologies must disarm it of its potential to be used to hurt and abuse others. Queer biblical studies serves to re-examine and re-tell the Bible in light of queer lives. Queer interpretations use queer identities to uncover how the texts speak to, for, and with LGBTQ+ people. Queer biblical studies works with queer identities and queer theory. The Bible is disrupted and queered by focusing on gender, sex, and sexual identities which are not explicit in literal readings of the scriptures. Against its use as a weapon to bolster arguments against LGBTQ+ lives and relationships, queer biblical readings allow the terror to be blunted. This allows LGBTQ+ Christians of faith to be able to re-engage with the texts. As Goss and West say, 'When queers "take back the Word", we see within the Scriptures visions of hope and dreams of liberation' (Goss & West, 2000: 7). The queer Bible allows for freedom and prioritises the reader. Yet, one final word of caution: queer readings of the Bible are multiple, creative, and have endless possibilities, but no queer reading of the Bible can become a stable or authoritative text. Queer means that all texts are unstable, as are all readers.

FURTHER READING AND RESOURCES

Greenough, C. and Blyth, C. (Eds.) (2026) *T&T Clark Handbook of Sexualities in the Bible and its Reception*. London: Bloomsbury.

A contemporary collection of essays examining LGBTQI+ identities, heterosexuality, marriage, sexual violence, and circumcision, but the volume also engages with issues that tend to receive less scholarly attention, including asexuality, homoeroticism, voyeurism, sex work, masturbation, menstruation, pornography, disability, mental health, and reproductive justice.

Guest, D. (2005) *When Deborah Met Jael: Lesbian Biblical Hermeneutics*. London: SCM Press.

Guest explores the instability of the label 'lesbian' and offers significant elements which constitute a lesbian reading of scripture.

Guest, D., Goss, R. E., West, M. and Bohache, T. (Eds.) (2006) *The Queer Bible Commentary*. London: SCM Press.

A comprehensive commentary to the Bible with relevance for LGBTQ+ readers. Each book of the Bible is examined with a queer lens, offering fresh ways of looking at the biblical texts. The 2022 revised Second Edition (edited by Mona West and Robert E. Shore-Goss) contains a large proportion of the original essays, with some updated chapters and bibliographies.

Helminiak, D. A. (2000 [first published 1994]). *What the Bible Really Says About Homosexuality*. New Mexico: Alamo Square Press.

A clear survey of scholarly literature and biblical passages used in relation to homosexuality. This book is written in clear ways to a wide audience. The 'sources' section at the back of the book is essential for anyone seeking a chronological overview of the studies relating to homosexuality and biblical interpretation.

Thatcher, A. (2008) *The Savage Text: The Use and Abuse of the Bible*. London: Wiley-Blackwell.

An accessible, jargon-free book which exposes how the Bible has been used to discriminate against minority groups, including women, enslaved people, children, and people of colour.

REFERENCES

Alpert, R. (2006) 'Exodus'. In Guest, D., Goss, R. E., West, M. and Bohache, T. (Eds.) *The Queer Bible Commentary*, pp. 61–76. London: SCM Press.

Althaus-Reid, M. (2004) *From Feminist to Indecent Theology*. London: SCM Press.

Althaus-Reid, M. (2006) 'Mark'. In Guest, D., Goss, R. E., West, M. and Bohache, T. (Eds.) *The Queer Bible Commentary*, pp. 517–525. London: SCM Press.

Bailey, D. S. (1955) *Homosexuality and the Western Christian Tradition*. London: Longmans.

Boer, R. (2001) 'Yahweh at Top: A Lost Targum'. In Stone, K. (Ed.) *Queer Commentary and the Hebrew Bible*, pp. 75–105. London: Sheffield Academic Press.

Cabrera, O. (2016) 'A Postcolonial Reading of the Bartimaeus Story: Contributions Towards the Construction of Another Hermeneutical Model'. In Panotto, N. (Ed.) *Indecent Theologies: Marcella Althaus-Reid and the Next Generation of Postcolonial Activists*, pp. 241–259. California: Borderless Press.

Cheng, P. S. (2006) 'Galatians'. In Guest, D., Goss, R. E., West, M. and Bohache, T. (Eds.) *The Queer Bible Commentary*, pp. 624–629. London: SCM Press.

Cornwall, S. (2015) 'Laws "Needefull in Later to Be Abrogated": Intersex and the Sources of Christian Theology'. In Cornwall, S. (Ed.) *Intersex, Theology, and the Bible. Troubling Bodies in Church, Text, and Society*, pp. 147–172. New York: Palgrave Macmillan.

da Silva, F. C. (2012) 'An Abominable and Perverted Alliance? Toward a Latin-American Queer Communitarian Reading of Deuteronomy'. In Brenner, A. and Yee, G. A. (Eds.) *Exodus and Deuteronomy*, pp. 205–236. Minneapolis: Fortress Press.

Douglas, K. B. (1999) *Sexuality and the Black Church*. New York: Orbis Books.

Goh, J. N. (2016) 'Survivalist Sexuality-faith Strategies in Biblical Meaning-Makings: Non-heteronormative Malaysian Christian Men and

Negotiations of Sexual Self-affirmation'. *QUEST: Studies on Religion & Culture in Asia, 1*, pp. 38–53.

Goss, R. E. (1993) *Jesus Acted Up. A Gay and Lesbian Manifesto.* San Francisco: Harper.

Goss, R. E. and West, M. (Eds.) (2000) *Take Back the Word: A Queer Reading of the Bible.* Cleveland: Pilgrim Press.

Greening-Jackson, T. (2025) *The Polari Bible.* Available at: www.polaribible.org/bible/index.html (Accessed: January 2026).

Gross, S. (1999) 'Intersexuality and Scripture'. *Theology & Sexuality, 11*, pp. 65–74.

Guest, D. (2005) *When Deborah Met Jael: Lesbian Biblical Hermeneutics.* London: SCM Press.

Guest, D. (2006) 'Lamentations'. In Guest, D., Goss, R. E., West, M. and Bohache, T. (Eds.) *The Queer Bible Commentary*, pp. 394–411. London: SCM Press.

Guest, D. (2012) *Beyond Feminist Biblical Studies.* Sheffield: Sheffield University Press.

Guest, D. (2016) 'Modelling the Transgender Gaze'. In Hornsby, T. J. and Guest, D. (Eds.) *Transgender, Intersex, and Biblical Interpretation*, pp. 45–80. Atlanta: SBL Press.

Guest, D., Goss, R. E., West, M. and Bohache, T. (Eds.) (2006) *The Queer Bible Commentary.* London: SCM Press.

Gunda, M. R. (2010) *The Bible and Homosexuality in Zimbabwe. A Socio-historical Analysis of the Political, Cultural and Christian Arguments in the Homosexual Public Debate with Special Reference to the Use of the Bible.* Bamberg: University of Bamberg Press. Available at: https://core.ac.uk/download/pdf/144484344.pdf (Accessed: January 2026).

Helminiak, D. A. (2000 [1994]) *What the Bible Really Says About Homosexuality.* New Mexico: Alamo Square Press.

Hornsby, T. (2006) 'Ezekiel'. In Guest, D., Goss, R. E., West, M. and Bohache, T. (Eds.) *The Queer Bible Commentary*, pp. 412–426. London: SCM Press.

Kahn-Harris, D. (2023) *Polyamory and Reading the Book of Ruth.* London: Lexington Books.

Koch, T. R. (2001) 'Cruising as Methodology: Homoeroticism and the Scriptures'. In Stone, K. (Ed.) *Queer Commentary and the Hebrew Bible*, pp. 169–181. London: Sheffield Academic Press.

Koch, T. (2006) 'Isaiah'. In Guest, D., Goss, R. E., West, M. and Bohache, T. (Eds.) *The Queer Bible Commentary*, pp. 371–385. London: SCM Press.

Kwok, P-L. (2010) 'Body and Pleasure in Postcoloniality'. In Isherwood, L. and Petrella, I. (Eds.) *Dancing Theology in Fetish Boots: Essays in Honour of Marcella Althaus-Reid*, pp. 31–43. London: SCM Press.

Liew, T-s. B. (2009) 'Queering Closets and Perverting Desires: Cross-Examining John's Engendering and Transgendering Word Across Different Worlds'. In Bailey, R. C., Liew, T-s. B. and Segovia, F. F. (Eds.) *They Were All Together in One Place? Toward Minority Biblical Criticism*, pp. 251–288. Atlanta: Society of Biblical Literature.

Lightsey, P. R. (2015) *Our Lives Matter: A Womanist Queer Theology.* Eugene: Pickwick Publications.

Lim, Y-L. L. (2002) 'The Bible Tells Me to Hate Myself': The Crisis in Asian American Spiritual Leadership. *Semeia, 90–91*, pp. 315–322.

Martin, J. (2000) '"And Then He Kissed Me": An Easter Love Story'. In Goss, R. and West, M. (Eds.) *Take Back the Word: A Queer Reading of the Bible*, pp. 219–226. Cleveland: Pilgrim Press.

Stone, K. (Ed.) (2001) *Queer Commentary and the Hebrew Bible.* London: Sheffield Academic Press.

Stuart, E. (Ed.) (1997) *Religion Is a Queer Thing.* London: Cassell.

Stuart, E. (2000) 'Camping Around the Canon: Humour as a Hermeneutical Tool in Queer Readings of Biblical Texts'. In Goss, R. and West, M. (Eds.) *Take Back the Word: A Queer Reading of the Bible*, pp. 23–34. Cleveland: Pilgrim Press.

Tanis, J. (2000) 'Eating the Crumbs that Fall from the Table: Trusting the Abundance of God'. In Goss, R. and West, M. (Eds.) *Take Back the Word: A Queer Reading of the Bible*, pp. 43–56. Cleveland: Pilgrim Press.

Thatcher, A. (2008) *The Savage Text: The Use and Abuse of the Bible.* London: Wiley-Blackwell.

The Nest Collective (2015) *Stories of Our Lives. Queer Narratives from Kenya.* Nairobi: The Nest Arts Company.

Toft, A. (2009) 'Bisexual Christians'. In Hunt, S. (Ed.) *Contemporary Christianities and LGBT Sexualities*, pp. 67–86. Farnham: Ashgate.

Tolbert, M. A. (2000) 'Foreword'. In Goss, R. E. and West, M. (Eds.) *Take Back the Word: A Queer Reading of the Bible*, pp. vii–xii. Cleveland: Pilgrim Press.

Trible, P. (1984) *Texts of Terror: Literary-Feminist Readings of Biblical Narratives.* Philadelphia: Fortress Press.

van Klinken, A. (2015) 'Queer Love in a "Christian Nation": Zambian Gay Men Negotiating Sexual and Religious Identities'. *Journal of the American Academy of Religion, 83*(4), pp. 947–964.

West, M. (2000) 'Outsiders, Aliens, and Boundary Crossers: A Queer Reading of the Hebrew Exodus'. In Goss, R. and West, M. (Eds.) *Take Back the Word: A Queer Reading of the Bible*, pp. 71–80. Cleveland: Pilgrim Press.

Wilcox, M. (2002) 'When Sheila's a Lesbian: Religious Individualism among Lesbian, Gay, Bisexual, and Transgender Christians'. *Sociology of Religion, 63*(4), pp. 497–513.

Wilson, N. (1995) *Our Tribe: Queer Folks, God, Jesus and the Bible*. San Francisco: Harper Collins.

Yip, A. K. T. (2003) 'Spirituality and Sexuality: An Exploration of the Religious Beliefs of Non-Heterosexual Christians in Great Britain'. *Theology & Sexuality*, *9*(2), pp. 137–154.

5

QUEER THEOLOGIES FROM QUEER LIVES

INTRODUCTION

There seem to be two main concerns in the production of queer theologies: the first focuses on issues of non-normative sexuality, representing LGBTQ+ people from where the term 'queer' emerged; and the second moves beyond identity or is anti-identity, as a critical approach. There is concern with the idea that queer theologies are an intellectual project, rather than an activity that looks at the negotiations and renegotiations of queer lives in Christianity. Of course, as an academic area of study, queer theologies are rich in terms of the intellectual gains which come from studying queer theory and theology. But what about LGBTQ+ Christians? The lines between LGBTQ+ theologies and queer theologies have been blurred. Within queer theologies, there still needs to be space to explore bottom-up theologies that emerge from queer people. Many people who come to study queer theologies do so precisely because of their own self-identification, personal location, or a commitment to issues of social justice relating to gender and sexuality. Indeed, attention must be paid to individual lives; as Marcella Althaus-Reid states, 'it is from human sexuality that theology starts to search and understand the sacred, not vice-versa' (Althaus-Reid, 2000: 146).

DOI: 10.4324/9781003434993-6

Before considering queer theologies that emerge from queer lives, an examination of the relationship between the churches and LGBTQ+ people helps to set queer lives in context. In addition to discussing the academic literature relating to queer theologies from life stories, this chapter briefly engages with the body of literature relating to religion and LGBTQ+ sexualities in the academic discipline of sociology of religion. Most importantly, this chapter offers insights into the genuine life experiences of LGBTQ+ Christians, including lesbian, gay, bisexual, and intersex voices (see Chapter 6 on trans theologies). Attention is also given to the following 'queer' theologies of sexuality: asexuality, celibacy, 'straight' queers, kinky Christians, and the order of queer nuns known as the Sisters of Perpetual Indulgence.

THE CHURCHES' POSITIONS

The churches' positions on non-normative gender and sexuality have caused controversial debates across the mainstream Christian denominations. Within the Anglican Communion, there are rifts between more progressive voices against conservative voices. An analysis of the pronouncements and debates relating to LGBTQ+ lives from all main denominations is beyond the scope of this chapter, but to highlight the impact of the churches' positions in relation to gender and sexuality, I consider briefly two mainstream denominations: the Roman Catholic Church and the Anglican Communion. In this discussion, 'homosexuality' is the language used by the official church documents to refer to same-sex attraction. It is widely acknowledged that this use of language is formal, with 'gay', 'lesbian', 'bisexual', and 'same-sex' being more commonly used. One of the reasons for such traditional language is that the churches have not moved from their original positions or pronouncements.

The Roman Catholic Church is based in Rome, as its name suggests. It is headed by the Pope and is the oldest of Christian institutions. In terms of same-sex attraction, the Roman Catholic position declares that to have an inclination towards homosexuality is not a sin, but 'it is a more or less strong tendency ordered toward an intrinsic moral evil and thus the inclination itself must be seen as an objective disorder' (Congregation for the Doctrine of the Faith, 1986). This idea of 'disorder' has echoes to past ideas about homosexuality being a psychological disorder. Here, the Roman Catholic position in 1986 uses similar language and has not been updated or revised since.

The Roman Catholic position, therefore, recognises that people have an inclination towards homosexuality and this is not a sin, but acting on this inclination and having same-sex relationships is sinful. Gay, lesbian, and bisexual people therefore should not engage in same-sex activities and are called to celibacy. The Roman Catholic Church calls for people not to discriminate, as the doctrine also says, 'Such persons must be accepted with respect, compassion and sensitivity. Every sign of unjust discrimination in their regard should be avoided' (Catechism of the Catholic Church, 1993).

The Roman Catholic Church does not recognise or celebrate same-sex marriage. In 2003, the publication of 'Considerations Regarding Proposals to Give Legal Recognition to Unions Between Homosexual Persons' offers further examples of the Church reiterating its position:

> There are absolutely no grounds for considering homosexual unions to be in any way similar or even remotely analogous to God's plan for marriage and family. Marriage is holy, while homosexual acts go against the natural moral law. Homosexual acts close the sexual act to the gift of life. They do not proceed from a genuine affective and sexual complementarity. Under no circumstances can they be approved.
>
> (Congregation for the Doctrine of the Faith, 2003)

The Vatican's position on ordaining even celibate gay-identifying men was clarified in 2005 with the document 'Instruction Concerning the Criteria of Vocational Discernment Regarding Persons with Homosexual Tendencies in View of Their Admission to Seminaries and Holy Orders'. The document, authorised by former Pope Benedict XVI, states how the Church:

> cannot admit to the seminary or to holy orders those who practice homosexuality, present deep-seated homosexual tendencies or support the so-called 'gay culture'. Such persons, in fact, find themselves in a situation that gravely hinders them from relating correctly to men and women.
>
> (Congregation for Catholic Education, 2005)

Pope Francis said in 2012, 'If a person is gay and seeks God and has good will, who am I to judge?' Yet, he reaffirmed the Roman Catholic Church's position that homosexual acts were sinful, but homosexual people should be treated with dignity (BBC News, 2013). The Roman Catholic Church has not updated its official doctrinal positions to date, and such doctrines are hostile to the lives of LGBTQ+ people. Moreover, these positions have psychological and emotional effects on LGBTQ+ Catholics who seek to reconcile their gender or sexual identities with their religion.

The situation in the Anglican Communion is a little more complicated and there is not sufficient space to detail the positions and practices of all provinces. The Anglican Church came into being when Henry VIII separated the Church from Rome in England. The Anglican Communion is how it has come to be known, a group of worldwide churches historically based on the Church of England. The Communion is diverse, and the large majority of its members are currently in the Global South, where it is experiencing growth – yet in the Global West, there has been decline in the number of people claiming to identify with Anglicanism. The diverse populations across the globe reflect the differences of opinions among its churches regarding the question of homosexuality.

The current position of the Anglican Communion is complex and varied, and the complexity was debated in a conference held by its leaders in 1998, called the Lambeth Conference. The Anglican leaders voted on the issue of human sexuality, and the conclusion of this conference was that homosexuality 'is incompatible with Scripture'. It affirms traditional Christian teaching that marriage is between one man and one woman. Article 1.10 from the Resolutions Archive deals with the issue of human sexuality. The positional statement is that the Anglican Communion:

> b. in view of the teaching of Scripture, upholds faithfulness in marriage between a man and a woman in lifelong union, and believes that abstinence is right for those who are not called to marriage;
> c. recognises that there are among us persons who experience themselves as having a homosexual orientation. Many of these are members of the Church and are seeking the pastoral care, moral direction of the Church, and God's transforming power for

> the living of their lives and the ordering of relationships. We commit ourselves to listen to the experience of homosexual persons, and we wish to assure them that they are loved by God and that all baptised, believing and faithful persons, regardless of sexual orientation, are full members of the Body of Christ;
>
> d. while rejecting homosexual practice as incompatible with Scripture, calls on all our people to minister pastorally and sensitively to all irrespective of sexual orientation and to condemn irrational fear of homosexuals, violence within marriage, and any trivialisation and commercialisation of sex;
>
> e. cannot advise the legitimising or blessing of same sex unions nor ordaining those involved in same gender unions.
>
> (Anglican Communion Office, 1998)

In terms of bisexuality, Church of England episcopal guidance assumes that Christians who are bisexual will align their sexual expression with heterosexual marriage or celibacy:

> if God's overall intention for human activity is that it should take place in the context of marriage with someone of the opposite sex, then clearly the Church needs to encourage bisexual people who are capable of entering into such a relationship to do so.
>
> (House of Bishops, 2003: 283)

The resolution at Lambeth in 1998 is not legally binding for the churches; however, the nature of 'common faith' in baptism is what unites the Anglican Communion. That means there is huge variation in the practices among the churches which form its membership; from churches that do not accept LGBTQ+ individuals, to accepting and inclusive churches that are happy to welcome same-sex partnered people who are not celibate. Of course, lesbian, gay, bisexual, and transgender people comprise some of the church ministers and leaders. The issue and differences of opinion between the churches belonging to the Communion have led to controversial discussions of rifts between the union of churches.

The current position of the churches certainly points to a general perceived hostility towards LGBTQ+ people. There is a risk that the position of the churches becomes the dominant voice in discussions of LGBTQ+ persons and Christianity. I agree with Colby Dickinson and Meghan Toomey who state how queer theologies decentre theology, and 'one way it accomplishes this is by continually shifting focus onto the real persons and lives that exist at the margins of both society and Christianity' (Dickinson & Toomey, 2017: 3). In such a climate, how do LGBTQ+ people live out their Christian faith with their gender and/or sexuality?

LIFE STORIES AS QUEER THEOLOGIES

> There is an embarrassed reluctance to listen to alternative stories about sex ... because of the substantial investment of hetero-patriarchy among powerful parts of church and society.
>
> (Nixon, 2008: 613)

David Nixon foregrounds paying attention to life stories as a source for theology, which moves away from institutions and their embedded heteronormative and patriarchal structures. In this context, this chapter focuses on contextual queer theologies, grounded in the lives, beliefs, and practices of non-normative individuals. By 'non-normative', I refer to people whose self-identifications and/or sexualities do not align with traditional Christian understandings of gender and sex. What are considered 'non-normative' identities are pitted against religious beliefs and doctrines, and there is a perception that Christianity is hostile to non-normative individuals and groups. At one end of the spectrum, there is the extremist homophobic language used by Westboro Baptist Church, which uses banners proclaiming how 'God hates fags'. In the middle are the positions of church authorities, as noted above, which result in continuous, complex, and controversial conversations. Happily, at the other end of the spectrum, many Christians are on the ground, in various denominations and contexts, working towards welcoming and even celebrating LGBTQ+ individuals.

The injunction for life-story research as a source of theology emerges throughout the literature in the sociology of religion and queer theologies. Althaus-Reid states, 'At the bottom line of queer theologies, there are biographies of sexual migrants, testimonies of real lives in rebellions of love, pleasure and suffering' (Althaus-Reid, 2003: 8), and some of that suffering has come at the hands of the churches, as well as widespread prejudice and discrimination. To explore queer theologies further, the testimonies and life stories of queer Christians are an essential source. Of course, life-story research is contextual, as illustrated through queer theologies in global contexts in Chapter 3. In early gay and lesbian theology, the themes of conflict and reconciliation demonstrated tensions between the religious and sexual identities of lesbian and gay people. Institutional forms of religion and the use of the Bible to condemn same-sex relations meant that many lesbian, gay, and bisexual people experienced inner emotional conflict while attempting to wrestle with their religious and sexual identities. The psychological impact and damage done by churches and the misuse of scripture is widespread. Michael Ford notes how 'Christ may have said that the truth sets people free, but for many homosexuals, including those in the church, the fear of their own self-identity keeps them locked in psychological captivity' (Ford, 2004: 11).

In *Undoing Theology: Life Stories from Non-normative Christians,* I examine the rich potential in producing queer theologies from the sharing of life stories and experiences (Greenough, 2018). There are five major outcomes from producing queer theologies from our own sexual and gendered experiences:

> (i) stories are transformative because they are relational; (ii) stories can help individuals make sense of their lives; (iii) stories are messy; (iv) stories disrupt the binary between material and divine; (v) stories have the potential to mark and queer heterosexuality.
>
> (2018: 26)

The act of sharing experiences is evocative; it resonates with others. Stories are punctuated with feelings and emotions, as personal and subjective as they may be. Sharing experiences with others is a relational task, characterised by both vulnerability and affirmation. Human experiences are messy, so the telling of people's stories is something which is also messy, as it is based on memory, selection, and the constant reinterpretation of life experiences. When life experiences become stories of faith, they become testimonies. These stories also complement scripture as sacred stories. Moreover, queer theologies are not something produced solely by LGBTQ+ people, but queer heterosexuals exist, as I discuss in a later section.

In an example of life-story research from *Undoing Theology,* I explore the spiritual and religious journeys of three protagonists, each of whom choses a pseudonym. The aim is to listen to the queer theologies that emerge, and the process of 'undoing' allows people to renegotiate their faith based on their life experiences. Religious identities, like all identities, are not fixed. Life stories are a source for queer theologies as they value the potential of personal, experiential theologies which allow people to transform their understanding of Christianity. These stories offer bottom-up queer theologies from Alyce, an intersex identifying Catholic; Caddyman, a former leader of 'ex-gay' conversion therapy in the USA; and Cath, a heterosexual woman who practises acts of bondage and submission. The aim of 'undoing theology' is therefore to focus on how the protagonists have negotiated traditional theology in light of their experiences. The process of 'undoing' means that an individual's religious and spiritual identities are not static. They evolve and change over the course of a lifetime, as queer theory exposes how identity is not stable in any case. This allows different elements of Christianity to be reconceptualised based on one's self-awareness and self-identifications. Narratives about identity, lived experience, and belief are not fixed but change and evolve over time; therefore, theologies are temporal.

Theologies from individual lives expose how God has been constructed as fixed in traditional theology, whereas the very nature of God is unfixable, uncapturable, and unpredictable. By 'undoing' God, the divine is freed from bondage, which has been repeated through rigid, traditional theological frames. Looking at experience and life stories adds colour and diversity to theology, but it does have its own limitations too. One of the cautions is that humans end up making God in our image, rather than humans being made in the image of God. It is important that non-normative Christians use their own voices to tell of the damage done by Christianity and its policing of gender and sexuality, but also to preserve what is good in Christianity within their lives.

QUEER LIVES AND SOCIOLOGY OF RELIGION

Sociology of religion is the academic area which focuses on how religion functions in society. Aside from work done in theology and religious studies, extensive work on LGBTQ+ Christians – their beliefs and lives – has emerged in sociology. Extensive and ground-breaking research has been conducted in the following areas: Andrew Yip's pioneering work on gay male Christians (Yip,

1997) and further work on sexual identities and spiritualities (Yip, 2000, 2002, 2003); Alex Toft's work on bisexual Christians (Toft, 2009, 2014); and Melissa Wilcox's research with lesbian, gay, bisexual, and transgender Christians (Wilcox, 2002, 2003, 2009).

Research into the lives of gay, lesbian, and bisexual Christians was carried out by sociologist Andrew Yip. He collected data from 565 gay, lesbian, and bisexual Christians who completed a 17-page questionnaire regarding their religious beliefs, and then, he interviewed 61 respondents. The results of the project were widely published. The research project covered a large section of those within mainstream denominations – Church of England (48%), Roman Catholic (26.4%), and Methodist (5.1%) (Yip, 2003: 141). Yip's analysis of the data demonstrates how 'most respondents saw no conflict between their sexualities and their Christian faith' (2003: 137), and concludes that 'the majority of respondents appeared to have developed positive self-identities that harmoniously incorporated their stigmatised sexualities and Christian faith' (2003: 137). Yip's research shows how, at the turn of the millennium, lesbian, gay, and bisexual Christians were able to reconcile faith with their sexualities. As part of his study, Yip asked his participants about sources of authority in their faith, including church and the Bible. He asked respondents to rank, in order of importance, four ideologies considered core elements to Christian faith: personal experiences, the Bible, human reason, and church authority. Overwhelmingly, the majority of non-heterosexual Christians (81.9%) ranked 'personal experience' as the basis of their faith (Yip, 2002: 207). His research demonstrates that non-heterosexual Christians personalise their faith, rather than relying on sources of authority such as the church or the Bible. One of his participants, Kim, states:

> I certainly know why I put church authority at the bottom. That's because of my attitude to the church. The reason I put personal experience on the top is that any Christian will tell you that their relationship is about their personal experience of god. That's the same with me. When people talk to me about Christianity, the only way I can relate it to them is to talk about my own personal experience of god, and how my life has changed as a result of coming into contact with god. That would never have happened by the church authority telling me god existed. Having encountered god, my own reasoning told me that there was god. The

> bible, in a sense also backs up what I have experienced. So yes, it is my reasoning and my reading of the bible, in relation to my experience, not what the church has to say [*sic*].
>
> (Yip, 2002: 206)

In addition to collecting rich data and snippets of interviews throughout his work, Yip places emphasis on the importance of life-story research:

> Accompanying the development of social scientific literature is the emergence of anecdotal narratives and personal biographies [...] The importance of such writings cannot be denied. They often offer moving and powerful stories of courage, resilience, and wisdom. In many ways, they could be more effective than scholarly writings precisely because they are not wrapped in academic language.
>
> (Yip, 2010: 48)

Inclusive church congregations, such as the Metropolitan Community Church (MCC), welcome lesbian, gay, bisexual, and trans Christian worshippers. In a study of these congregations, Wilcox highlights that the vast majority of congregants are male. She asks, 'Where are all the women?' (Wilcox, 2009: 5). Wilcox goes in search of the queer women in order to explore their experiences of spirituality and faith across a wide range of religious institutions, such as mainstream churches, liberal synagogues, LGBT welcoming and affirming congregations, as well as alternative spiritual practices such as contemporary paganism. This shows the variety of religious practices across a broad spectrum of queer women, but Wilcox also explores the motivating factors that lead to the religious practices. She highlights how queer women exercise choice, resulting in a religious individualism which is based on their own experiences, rather than institutional membership. This issue of choice in an open religious market for LGBT individuals was the subject of her sociological inquiry into 72 members of MCC. In terms of theology, the participants' understanding of God was wide and varied; as Wilcox says, 'for some, God is a father; others think of God as "parent" or "mother/father". And some spoke more loosely of an energy, a flow, a life force, the Universe' (Wilcox, 2002: 506).

Bisexual individuals are often under-researched, and particularly so in terms of their religious identities. Bisexual identities are often conflated under lesbian or gay ones, or there is a common misconception that bisexual people can 'pass' as straight. Wilcox notes how it is dangerous to combine the experiences of lesbian, gay, bisexual, and trans as one grouping because the 'challenges faced by members of LGBT communities differ not only because of gender identity or sexual orientation, but also because of biological sex, race, ethnicity' (Wilcox, 2003: 30). The reason they are grouped as a community is that, collectively, each identity challenges traditional concepts of gender and sexuality in society. Alex Toft has produced some much-needed pioneering work to investigate the lives of bisexual Christians. He notes how 'bisexuality becomes invisible because it sits in the middle of both homosexuality and heterosexuality' (Toft, 2014: 551). His study involved 80 participants identifying as bisexual completing questionnaires, with 20 follow-up interviews. Only 40% of his respondents thought that their bisexuality allowed them to fit into both heterosexual and homosexual communities (2014: 560). Toft explores what the churches say about bisexuality, and then, he looks at how his participants challenge this in some way. He notes how the churches view bisexuality simply as sexual activity, rather than a sexual identity with its own capacity for relationships. Examples of theologies formulated by his participants include that of Rose, who looks at how Jesus related to others, and this informs her bisexuality. Rose says:

> It is based on his works, what he did for people, not just sex ... being open with people and not seeing people as just a man or a woman. Just seeing people as people I guess. He would have been bisexual because of how he related to people.
>
> (2014: 558)

Another participant, Phillip, sees God in everyday life. He says:

> You walk down the street and there is God. I don't find that in the programme of the Church. I read the Bible and the gospels and that seems to be what Jesus was about, just wandering around, outside the structure of religion. Actually talking to people about the world.
>
> (Toft, 2009: 80)

The work conducted by the sociologists of religion explores the living experiences, beliefs, and practices of LGBTQ+ Christians. The work attends to previously neglected or muted voices, in order to document and evaluate how their experiences within the churches have led to a negotiation or rejection of institutional forms of religion. By focusing on their own experiences, including their gender and sexual identities, they personalise their own faith and express it in individual ways.

THEOLOGIES OF INTERSEX LIVES

Intersex is used to describe an individual whose physical sex or reproductive anatomy do not align to typical definitions of female or male. Hormones and genitalia in intersex people are various. Biologically, chromosomes attributed to a male are XY and to a female XX, so they exist in a binary. In intersex people, there are multiple combinations and variations, such as XX, XY, XXY, and XX/XY. In many cases, intersex is not identifiable at birth, and, sometimes, it only becomes identifiable during puberty. Intersex people may only be diagnosed during adulthood when there may be problems with fertility, for example. Many intersex people go undiagnosed throughout their lives. There has been a clinical term, 'Disorder in Sex Development' (or DSD for short), but the use of this term, specifically the word 'disorder', is considered unhelpful despite its usage in medicine. It is more appropriate to talk about intersex people. Even more controversial is the use of surgical interventions on babies to attempt to align external genitalia cosmetically to male or female. Intersex activists challenge such interventions as they are harmful, and the young person cannot consent.

In 2019, the Congregation for Catholic Education published a document entitled: '"Male and Female He Created Them": Towards a Path of Dialogue on the Question of Gender Theory in Education'. The document states, 'in cases where a person's sex is not clearly defined, it is medical professionals who can make a therapeutic intervention. In such situations, parents cannot make an arbitrary choice on the issue, let alone society' (2019: 13). Here, the authority resides directly and solely with medical professionals. The document does not discuss adult intersex agency or consent directly, and therefore is silent on individual agency in making a 'choice' in determining their sex.

Susannah Cornwall is a pioneer in the field of intersex lives and Christian theology, undertaking the first full-length examination of intersex and theology in her book entitled *Sex and Uncertainty in the Body of Christ* (Cornwall, 2010). The book explores intersex people in relation to medical interventions and theological perspectives, including the themes of incarnation and the Body of Christ. In placing value on the theologies from intersex lives, Cornwall highlights the importance and value in listening to the theological insights from intersex people:

> Intersex people have their own stories to tell, and ... the Church needs to listen. If the memory and story of Jesus are embodied by those who share in it, then the body of Christ is also an intersex body, constituted and subverted by those intersex Christians whose lives are testimonies of the place faith has held in their journeys.
>
> (Cornwall, 2014: 31)

Cornwall's interviews with ten intersex-identifying people demonstrate a common feeling among her participants that they are made as God intended (Cornwall, 2013). Some participants see their intersex bodies as unique, bringing spiritual gifts. One participant feels this gift gives her the impetus to educate people more about intersex. These accounts reveal how intersex people put their faith, and relationship with God, above other sources of authority such as the Bible or church.

In *Undoing Theology* (Greenough, 2018), Alyce tells her story as an intersex Christian. Assigned male at birth and brought up to present as male throughout her life, Alyce shares her experience at the age of 62, where she is coming to terms with her undiagnosed intersex body. She describes herself as XXY Catholic. Her story narrates childhood trauma described through internal feelings of sin and shame, adolescent anguish, and episodes of bullying. There is a conflict in her presentation, as an assigned male who feels like a woman. Nevertheless, theologically Alyce sees how her body is made in the image of God; as she states:

> As far as God's gender, I was taught that I was made in His image and likeness. Therefore, God is just like me. Of course, everyone can make the same claim. But the bottom line is that God made me as I am, and I must accept that and thank Him. I'm working on it.
>
> (Greenough, 2018: 92)

ASEXUALITY

Asexual people (or, aces) do not experience sexual attraction to others. There are a number of related terms. The opposite term to asexual, that's to say those who experience sexual attraction, is allosexual. Aromantic people experience little or no romantic attraction to others. To be grey-asexual means that sexual attraction is sometimes experienced. An individual identifying as demisexual experiences a personal and emotional connection with someone before sexual attraction. Also, the term autosexual is sometimes used to describe individuals whose primary sexual attraction is directed towards themselves.

Asexuality disturbs or queers the expectation that people will relate to one another sexually. In terms of theologies of sexuality, Elizabeth Stuart observes a general absence of asexual voices in theology, stating how 'asexual people are currently an almost completely silenced group within the theology of sexuality [...] and the asexual person should raise uncomfortable questions for all of us who have valorised sex and sexual desire perhaps at the expense of relationship' (Stuart, 2014: 29). In the Hebrew Bible/ Old Testament, there are numerous references which point to the goodness of sexual relations, especially in terms of reproduction. In Genesis 9:7, God/Yahweh says to Noah, 'as for you, be fruitful and increase in number; multiply on the earth and increase upon it'. Jessica Coblentz (2026) seeks to make visible this 'invisible orientation' and offers strategies for reading the Bible. Coblentz uses the example of one of the Bible's most prominent figures, Jesus, to illuminate this point:

> Read through an affirmative-identifying ace hermeneutic, some of the Bible's nonsexual figures might be seen as positive models for asexual personhood. For example, the canonical gospels present Jesus as an unmarried, celibate Jewish man, and apart from a few detractors, scholarly consensus accepts that Jesus lived a nonsexual lifestyle. Like many aces today, Jesus focused his life on his nonsexual passions – namely, proclaiming and actualizing the reign of God – which he pursued with a community that foregrounded mutual, nonsexual relationships. At times, he positively contrasted this nonsexual community to other more predominant models of family that were defined by sexual relationship.
>
> (Coblentz, 2026: 82)

CELIBACY

Celibacy describes a commitment to refraining from sexual activity. Within Christianity, the promotion of celibacy as an ideal has resulted in language such as virginity, purity, and chastity being used to promote sexual abstinence. Celibacy is also promoted by the churches, as noted earlier, as the path people who feel same-sex attraction are encouraged to take. It is also a requirement within Catholicism for those who undertake religious orders, as giving up sex is considered to enhance a religious person's spiritual gifts. Within the New Testament, celibacy is promoted as an ideal state for Christians, particularly in the letters of Paul. In one example, 1 Corinthians 7, Paul does not say that it is wrong to get married, but that it is better for Christians to stay single. Paul puts forward the idea that, by being married, a man has to focus on his wife, while being single means he can focus on the Lord's work. He states: 'I wish that all of you were [single] as I am. But each of you has your own gift from God; one has this gift, another has that'. Paul's preference for celibacy is traditionally seen as a concession rather than a command. Nonetheless, this and other scriptures are interpreted to promote celibacy as part of spiritual discernment among those who have taken holy orders.

The 'ex-gay' movement is a Christian-organised drive to discourage people from same-sex activity. Based on the idea of so-called conversion therapy, it views same-sex desires as ungodly and sinful. Being gay is incompatible with being Christian in the movement. It considers that people can 'convert' from having same-sex desires to being heterosexual. The 'ex-gay' movement has been a popular practice in evangelical circles in the USA. During the process of so-called conversion, gay-identifying people are encouraged to ignore their sexuality and attempt to change it. Therefore, the gay, lesbian, or bisexual person commits to celibacy or heterosexuality. The full conversion is often seen as complete when an 'ex-gay' individual commits to heterosexual marriage. The movement has been damning and causes intense psychological and emotional damage to the gay-identifying people who undergo the therapy. So-called gay conversion therapy is widely acknowledged as connected to the risk of self-harm and suicide. Those who survived the intense psychological damage caused by the 'ex-gay' movement and the attempt at conversion therapy are known as 'ex-gay survivors'.

STRAIGHT QUEERS

Can a straight identified person do queer theologies? There is an assumption that to engage with queer theologies or queer biblical studies a person has to be LGBTQ+ in some way. In my article, '"Queer Eye" in Theology and Biblical Studies: "Do you have to be queer to do this?"' (2019), I tackle this question head on. I offer four points about the engagement of straight queers in theology and biblical studies:

> i) queer theory reveals how all identities are unstable, including heterosexuality;
> ii) heterosexuality is not the site of disruption for queer studies – it is patriarchy, cisnormativity and heteronormativity which require dismantling;
> iii) queer is about the production of antinormative knowledge, a practice that anyone can engage in;
> iv) where queer studies are also done in conjunction with nonnormative gender and sexualities, researchers must incorporate voices from those individuals or communities.
>
> (Greenough, 2019: 26)

Deryn Guest queries how there may be some justification for writing from the space of one's identity, stating how those 'who choose to self-identify as such, have experiences of looking that derive from that' (Guest, 2012: 152). Guest concludes that heterosexual-identifying people who engage with queer projects 'step aside from, or deliberately disinherit themselves from, the more normative and privileged aspects of their identities' (2012: 159). So, to identify as 'queer' involves a sacrifice of the social privilege which comes with heteronormativity.

Queer disrupts binaries and destabilises identity and authority. An individual does not need a particular set of credentials or to self-identify in a certain way to engage in the task of queering theology. As queer theologies disrupt and interrogate traditional theology, the task of queering theology is political, social and cultural. Althaus-Reid puts it very simply: 'let us remember here that the Genderfucker may also be straight' (Althaus-Reid, 2003: 68). The principle for inclusion is a commitment to justice. Heterosexual queers may be allies to LGBTQ+ people. In this vein, Kwok Pui-lan asserts:

> Sexual theology is not just the specific concern of queer, gay, lesbian, bisexual and transgendered theologians – as it is often assumed to be – but a project that all theologians, whether consciously or unconsciously, participate in.
>
> (Kwok, 2003: 151)

Susannah Cornwall is an example of a self-identifying cisgender, heterosexual woman who has excelled in the field of queer theologies. Cornwall describes herself and her work as 'a non-intersex person who writes about intersex; as a cisgender person who writes about transgender; as an able person who writes about disability; as a straight married person who writes about queer theology' (Cornwall, 2017: 41). She moves beyond categories of identification to highlight the agenda for justice within her work:

> Queer theory, queer theology and queer biblical criticism are increasingly taught in universities and seminaries as postmodern methodologies alongside a range of others, often by scholars who do not call themselves queer. I am one such scholar. I am a heterosexual married cisgender woman, and I do not claim anything very subversive about me or my life. I try to bring into question unjust sexual, gender and economic relations, and to model respectful pedagogies and dynamics with my students.
>
> (Cornwall, 2017: 32)

Of course, Cornwall herself acknowledges that writing from one's position as LGBTQ+ can offer further insights for queer theologies. She states how 'transgender people know things about transgender experience that I do not: of course, that is indubitably true' (Cornwall, 2017: 41). In one example of the commitment to just sexual, gender, and economic relations, Cornwall claims that transgender experience is also human experience and is therefore something all human beings should take an interest in. The responsibilities and ethics of non-trans people formulating trans theologies is discussed further in Chapter 6.

Self-disclosure is an important element to offering one's position in the production of queer theologies. Queer theologians and those working at the intersections of gender, sexuality, race, class, dis/ability, and other positions that inform their writing usually reveal their own self-identifications and positions and how these influence their work. This allows for transparency and demonstrates how the author is aware that their own positional influence may shape, or limit, their work.

KINKY CHRISTIANS

The acronym BDSM is used to represent the practice of bondage, discipline/dominance, submission/sadism, masochism. It is the practice of role-playing and of inflicting pain or receiving pain, depending on whether a participant is dominant or submissive. For those who practise it, engaging in BDSM is often seen as pleasurable, satisfying, and even healing. Within contemporary culture, the practice has become popularised through literature and film, such as *50 Shades of Grey* (James, 2011) and the sequels. In sociology and psychology, studies about participants and acts of BDSM practices help us to understand elements of human desire: how and why humans relate to one another, and about physical needs. On a cultural level, the idea of BDSM can be broadly connected to Christian religious imagery, including crucifixes, crowns of thorns, and whips. Christianity has a long history of self-inflicted pain, from those who took religious orders and discipline themselves through flogging, to the wearing of chastity belts or other torturous instruments to regulate personal sexual desire.

In feminist theology, Mary Daly's *Gyn/Ecology* (1978) describes the 'sadomasochistic gospel that proclaims that female suffering is joy' (Daly, 1978: 93–94). Daly goes on to offer an example of such narratives, including Mary's pregnancy by the Holy Ghost and the torturous scene of the crucifixion. She says how 'torture for "higher causes", religious and secular, has always been legitimised by christian cross-bearers' [*sic*] (1978: 95). It is not too difficult to see how the Christian narrative is connected to ideas of dominance and submission; it is a narrative that has pain and suffering at its core in the crucifixion of Jesus. Daly relates the idea of control and pain to patriarchy.

In BDSM, the person who is dominant is called a 'top' and the submissive partner is 'bottom'. Althaus-Reid relocates the idea of sadomasochism and applies it to the struggle for liberation in Latin America. Althaus-Reid describes God as the 'top' and the Christian as the 'bottom'. She calls this a 'master sketch of Christianity done in a moment' (Althaus-Reid, 2000: 153). Yet, she highlights a significant difference, that 'the desire for a whip in a fetish scenario is not the same as experiencing the whip of the God the Father' (2000: 153). The Father's whip is too close to the dominant ideas of political repression of the poor. The difference highlighted by Althaus-Reid is the subject of consent. In a BDSM scene, the bottom and top negotiate the act beforehand, they consent, and there is usually a code, known as a 'safeword', which may be called as an instruction to stop. The dynamics of top and bottom do not simply show control of the top to the bottom, as the top largely carries out the wishes of the bottom as negotiated beforehand. In an analogy not too far away from Christianity, this negotiated space could be similar to prayer.

A theology of BDSM becomes a source for queer theologies, as it disrupts the sexual codes cherished by Christianity. Sex between a man and woman designated for procreation is turned upside down when the scene is about pain and pleasure. A theology of BDSM is not necessarily about gender or sexuality, as the practice may or may not involve genitalia. It is therefore not unusual for same-sex partners to play together, even where one or both are heterosexual. One detailed account of the theological considerations of a Christian who engages in kink practices is located in the story of Cath, a Christian who engages in BDSM (Greenough, 2018). For Cath, the practice allows her to gain spiritual and emotional freedom. As she engages in rope play through being tied up, she experiences a meditative state which allows her to focus and simply to be. This allows Cath to meditate on God, and she describes how she finds the process healing. She says:

> the act of being spanked or flogged or cropped or such like gives me permission to cry out. It's a safe way of letting all these emotions out, without fear of being judged for them. A sort of cathartic release. Very often I'm left feeling very peaceful afterwards.
>
> (2018: 144)

A discussion of BDSM and Christianity is taboo for many, and some readers of stories and theologies connected to kink activity may feel a little uncomfortable. Queer theologies are about rupture and disruption, so the feeling of being unsettled is part of the project.

QUEER NUNS: SISTERS OF PERPETUAL INDULGENCE

The Sisters of Perpetual Indulgences are an order of drag nuns committed to protest and social justice for LGBTQ+ people. There are orders in the USA, UK, Europe, Canada, Australia, and Latin America. The nuns have a variety of gender and sexual identities, but the majority are gay men. In dragging up as Catholic nuns, they often retain gendered features such as beards, but with heavy makeup applied. The Sisters are an activist organisation, fundraising for charities, especially for HIV/AIDS and cancer care. They are committed to raising awareness of sexual health, and dedicated to the eradication of homophobia, racism, classism, and other prejudiced-based behaviours. They offer outreach and support.

Queer Nuns: Religion, Activism and Serious Parody (Wilcox, 2018) provides an in-depth examination of the Sisters of Perpetual Indulgence. Melissa Wilcox traces the origins of the first San Francisco order (in 1979) and its spread across the globe: Canada (1981), Australia (1983), England and France (1990), and Germany (1991). Of course, the Sisters parody the religious nuns of Roman Catholicism in their dress, yet this parody leads to serious activism. Wilcox demonstrates how 'genderfuck meets religionfuck' (Wilcox, 2018: 129), noting how playing with gender presents itself to conservative audiences as 'whores in virgins' clothing, importing psychological and physical illness and the sinful nature of their sex into the purest possible human space' (2018: 137). Presenting as nuns in this way makes queer religious identities visible. It queers religion as it disrupts normative presentations of religion and the human body. Moreover, the identity of a nun is one which is dedicated to service. The idea of 'religionfuck' raises important questions over cultural assumptions about religious identities, beliefs, and practices. In claiming their identity as nuns, the Sisters believe the following:

> (1) the Sisters do the same work as nuns do, sometimes they do it better, and they are more fun; (2) they have more moral integrity than the

> Roman Catholic Church, especially toward queer communities and toward Roman Catholic nuns; (3) their work is spiritual or even prophetic, like that of vowed women religious; and (4) the Roman Catholic Church has no monopoly on nuns anyway.
>
> (Wilcox, 2018: 88)

The range of religious beliefs and practices among the Sisters varies – from secular Sisters to those who attend Catholic worship. By and large, the majority of the Sisters claim to be spiritual rather than religious, denoting a rejection of the traditional idea of religion with its structures of authority. Often the Sisters blend traditions and beliefs in practising their spirituality. One of the nuns Wilcox interviewed is a former 'ex-gay' man ordained in the Church, known as Sister Krissy Fiction – a parody name on the word 'crucifixion'. Sister Krissy describes herself as a 'spiritual slut' (Wilcox, 2018: 190). She uses a metaphor of religions as language. She adds, 'so I say I'm fluent in Christianity and fluent in neopaganism, I can kind of ask where the bathroom is in Buddhism' (2018: 191). One of the nuns who is Catholic talks about how her ministry in raising awareness of the importance of sexual health is inspired by Jesus. Sister Marie says:

> I look at the example of Jesus, I see that work of accepting people where they are, no matter what. Instead of jumping on the woman caught in adultery, saying, 'Well go and do better. Go do better next time' ... We're trying to do the same thing. 'Here's a condom. Go do better next time. We're here for you'.
>
> (Wilcox, 2018: 193)

Exploring the work of the Sisters offers a fascinating lens into how religious or spiritual beliefs are queered. They are shown to be performative, unstable structures and this is highlighted through their parody. The dragging up as nuns destabilises the idea of solid, firm, religious identities. It demonstrates performative, embodied, and activist living queer theologies.

CONCLUSION

The sharing of life stories from queer Christians can be empowering and transformative. The stories are relational, evocative, and emotional. In the opening to her work on lesbian biblical hermeneutics, Guest writes about how she had never met a lesbian, and the word held connotations of undesirable attributes reserved for those who lived unfulfilled, tragic lives. Her mother had handed her a Christian pamphlet on the trials of being a teenager, which warned against developing crushes on the same sex. Despite her mother's intentions, Guest writes, 'I was glad to hear about these women because it was at least a relief to know that there were other women out there who were attracted to members of their own sex' (Guest, 2005: 3). For LGBTQ+ people working through issues of gender or sexuality alongside their Christian faith, reading and learning from others' experiences can be a source of strength, hope, and nourishment. This is where queer theologies become practical theologies.

In theological terms, the sharing of stories can also be problematic. The construction of theologies from the vantage point of our gender and sexual identities can result in new theologies deemed indecent, sexual, or taboo. Conservative Christians often dismiss such theologies as indulgent, self-serving, and too far removed from recognisable Christianity. Yet, queer theologies expose how Christianity, constructed with blocks of patriarchy and cemented with heteronormativity and cisnormativity, is a performance, sustained and repeated. Queer lives and those who inhabit Christianity differently break through this.

In attending to queer voices, I am sensitive to the numerous voices which have not been included here, or those who are silenced or have yet to speak. Moreover, one voice is not representative of a particular group: the experience of one person is not the same as another's. 'Theology' is God-talk, and it must be open to endless conversations from endless voices. As this chapter has discussed the importance of listening to the experience of queer Christians, attention in Chapter 6 turns to trans people specifically.

FURTHER READING AND RESOURCES

Cornwall, S. (Ed.) (2015) *Intersex, Theology, and the Bible. Troubling Bodies in Church, Text, and Society.* New York: Palgrave Macmillan.

Insightful discussions looking at intersex from a range of perspectives: life stories, biblical studies, and pastoral care.

Greenough, C. (2018) *Undoing Theology: Life Stories from Non-Normative Christians*. London: SCM Press.

This book details the advantages and transformative possibilities of exploring life stories as a source for theology, as readers engage with the biographical and spiritual journeys of three non-normative Christians: an intersex Catholic, an ex-gay minister, and a Christian who engages in fetish practices.

Robinson, B. (Ed.) (2017) *Our Witness: The Unheard Stories of LGBT+ Christians*. London: Darton, Longman and Todd.

This book provides powerful stories of LGBT+ Christians and their witness to the churches. The stories look at the experiences of rejection and marginalisation of LGBTQ+ Christians by the churches, and also at how LGBTQ+ Christians reconcile their faith with their gender or sexuality and the gifts this brings.

Wilcox, M. (2018) *Queer Nuns: Religious Activism and Serious Parody*. New York: New York University Press.

A comprehensive examination of the religious/spiritual lives of the Sisters of Perpetual Indulgence and their commitment to activism for social justice.

REFERENCES

Althaus-Reid, M. (2000) *Indecent Theology*. London: Routledge.

Althaus-Reid, M. (2003) *The Queer God*. London: Routledge.

Anglican Communion Office (1998) 'Resolution I.10 – Human Sexuality'. *Lambeth Conference: Section I.10*. Available at: http://justus.anglican.org/resources/Lambeth1998/LC98res/sec1.html#1.10 (Accessed: January 2026).

BBC News (2013) 'Pope Francis: Who Am I to Judge Gay People?' 29 July. Available at: www.bbc.co.uk/news/world-europe-23489702 (Accessed: January 2026).

Catechism of the Catholic Church (1993) Available at: www.vatican.va/archive/ENG0015/_INDEX.HTM (Accessed: January 2026).

Coblentz, J. (2026) 'Making Visible the 'Invisible Orientation': Strategies for Seeing Asexuality in the Bible and Its Reception'. In Greenough, C. and Blyth, C. (Eds.) *T&T Clark Handbook of Sexualities in the Bible and Its Reception*, pp. 77–94. London: Bloomsbury.

Congregation for Catholic Education (2005) 'Instruction Concerning the Criteria for the Discernment of Vocations with Regard to Persons with Homosexual Tendencies in View of their Admission to the Seminary and to Holy Orders'. Available at: www.vatican.va/roman_curia/congregations/ccatheduc/documents/rc_con_ccatheduc_doc_20051104_istruzione_en.html (Accessed: January 2026).

Congregation for Catholic Education (2019) '"Male and Female He Created Them": Towards a Path of Dialogue on the Question of Gender Theory in Education'. 2 February. Available at: www.vatican.va/roman_curia/congregations/ccatheduc/documents/rc_con_ccatheduc_doc_20190202_maschio-e-femmina_en.pdf (Accessed: January 2026).

Congregation for the Doctrine of the Faith (1986) 'Letter to the Bishops of the Catholic Church on the Pastoral Care of Homosexual Persons'. Available at: www.vatican.va/roman_curia/congregations/cfaith/documents/rc_con_cfaith_doc_19861001_homosexual-persons_en.html (Accessed: January 2026).

Congregation for the Doctrine of the Faith (2003) 'Considerations Regarding Proposals to Give Legal Recognition to Unions between Homosexual Persons'. Available at: www.vatican.va/roman_curia/congregations/cfaith/documents/rc_con_cfaith_doc_20030731_homosexual-unions_en.html (Accessed: January 2026).

Cornwall, S. (2010) *Sex and Uncertainty in the Body of Christ: Intersex Conditions and Christian Theology*. London: Equinox.

Cornwall, S. (2013) 'British Intersex Christians: Accounts of Intersex Identity, Christian Identity and Church Experience'. *Practical Theology*, *6*(2), pp. 220–236.

Cornwall, S. (2014) 'Telling Stories about Intersex and Christianity: Saying Too Much or Not Saying Enough?' *Theology*, *117*(1), pp. 24–33.

Cornwall, S. (2017) 'Home and Hiddenness: Queer Theology, Domestication and Institutions'. *Theology & Sexuality*, *23*(1–2), pp. 31–47.

Daly, M. (1978) *Gyn/Ecology: The Metaethics of Radical Feminism*. Boston: Beacon Press.

Dickinson, C. and Toomey, M. (2017) 'The Continuing Relevance of 'Queer' Theology for the Rest of the Field'. *Theology & Sexuality*, *23*(1–2), pp. 1–16.

Ford, M. (2004) *Disclosures: Conversions Gay and Spiritual*. London: Darton, Longman and Todd.

Greenough, C. (2018) *Undoing Theology: Life Stories from Non-normative Christians*. London: SCM Press.

Greenough, C. (2019) '"Queer Eye" in Theology and Biblical Studies: "Do You Have to Be Queer to Do This?"' *Journal of Interdisciplinary Biblical Studies*, *1*(1), pp. 26–41.

Guest, D. (2005) *When Deborah Met Jael: Lesbian Biblical Hermeneutics*. London: SCM Press.

Guest, D. (2012) *Beyond Feminist Biblical Studies*. Sheffield: Sheffield University Press.

House of Bishops (2003) *Some Issues in Human Sexuality: A Guide to the Debate*. London: Church House Publishing.

James, E. L. (2011) *Fifty Shades of Grey*. London: Arrow.

Kwok, P-L. (2003) 'Theology as a Sexual Act?' *Feminist Theology, 11*(2), pp. 149–156.

Nixon, D. (2008) 'No More Tea, Vicar: An Exploration of the Discourses Which Inform the Current Debates about Sexualities Within the Church of England'. *Sexualities, 11*, pp. 595–620.

Stuart, E. (2014) 'The Theological Study of Sexuality'. In Thatcher, A. (Ed.) *The Oxford Handbook of Theology, Sexuality and Gender*, pp. 18–31. Oxford: Oxford University Press.

Toft, A. (2009) 'Bisexual Christians'. In Hunt, S. (Ed.) *Contemporary Christianities and LGBT Sexualities*, pp. 67–86. Farnham: Ashgate.

Toft, A. (2014) 'Re-imagining Bisexuality and Christianity: The Negotiation of Christianity in the Lives of Bisexual Women and Men'. *Sexualities, 17*(5–6), pp. 546–564.

Wilcox, M. (2002) 'When Sheila's a Lesbian: Religious Individualism among Lesbian, Gay, Bisexual, and Transgender Christians'. *Sociology of Religion, 63*(4), pp. 497–513.

Wilcox, M. (2003) *Coming Out in Christianity: Religion, Identity and Community*. Bloomington: Indiana University Press.

Wilcox, M. (2009) *Queer Women and Religious Individualism*. Bloomington: Indiana University Press.

Wilcox, M. (2018) *Queer Nuns: Religious Activism and Serious Parody*. New York: New York University Press.

Yip, A. K. T. (1997) *Gay Male Christian Couples: Life Stories*. Westport: Praeger.

Yip, A. K. T. (2000) 'Leaving the Church to Keep My Faith: The Lived Experiences of Non-Heterosexual Christians'. In Francis, L. J. and Katz, Y. J. (Eds.) *Joining and Leaving Religion: Research Perspectives*, pp. 129–145. Leominster: Gracewing.

Yip, A. K. T. (2002) 'The Persistence of Faith Among Non-Heterosexual Christians: Evidence for the Neosecularization Thesis of Religious Transformation'. *Journal for the Scientific Study of Religion, 41*(2), pp. 199–212.

Yip, A. K. T. (2003) 'Spirituality and Sexuality: An Exploration of the Religious Beliefs of Non-Heterosexual Christians in Great Britain'. *Theology & Sexuality, 9*(2), pp. 137–154.

Yip, A. K. T. (2010) 'Coming Home from the Wilderness: An Overview of Recent Scholarly Research on LGBTQI Religiosity/Spirituality'. In Browne, K., Munt, S. R. and Yip, A. K. T. (Eds.) *Queer Spiritual Spaces: Sexuality and Sacred Places*, pp. 35–50. Farnham: Ashgate.

TRANS THEOLOGIES

INTRODUCTION

In recent years, trans theologies have emerged as a necessary development within queer, feminist, liberation, and contextual theologies. This chapter considers the similarities and differences between queer and trans theologies. It then attends to trans theologies by asking what theology has done to trans lives, and what trans lives, in turn, do to theology.

Throughout the chapter, three key approaches to trans theologies emerge: corrective, constructive, and ethical. In the first part, attention turns to the impact of mainstream (and cisnormative) theology *on* and *about* trans people. It pays attention to how theology *by*, *for*, and *with* trans Christians offers deeper insights to discourse about God and the interpretation of scripture. Attending and amplifying trans voices serves as a form of *corrective* theology, through challenging harms and raising questions of exclusion. The second section focusses on how attention needs to be given to where trans theologies are *constructive*, through creative reimagining of God, naming as a calling, and a focus on joy. Finally, in the third section, corrective and constructive approaches are brought together in a consideration of how trans readings of the Bible move beyond queer approaches, towards more ethical readings of the text.

DOI: 10.4324/9781003434993-7

AN OVERVIEW OF TRANS THEOLOGIES

Trans is a term used to refer to transgender people as a collective group, but there are some more accurate terms to use. A trans man is someone who was assigned female at birth but transitions to live as a man. A trans woman is someone assigned male at birth but transitions to live as a woman. Trans itself literally means 'beyond' or 'across'. The process of transition may be a social process, in which a trans person presents in their new gender in daily life, or a physical process, which may involve gender reassignment surgery. A trans person is trans whether they have transitioned socially, physically, or both. That's to say, surgery is something which individual trans people may choose for themselves, but it is a personal and private choice. Non-binary is a term for people who do not identify in binary terms as male or female. In this chapter, I largely use the term *trans*. This reflects the fact that many trans people also identify as non-binary, and that non-binary identities are often located within broader trans frameworks because they differ from sex assigned at birth. At the same time, I remain attentive to the fact that not all non-binary people identify as trans. Equally, my use of the term trans occasionally moves beyond its use as an identity label, as it proves to be a useful relational, methodological category (a way of thinking and reading) when doing theology.

Using the correct pronouns to describe trans people is really important. Some may adopt the pronouns of their transitioned gender, and it is common for some trans people to adopt the pronoun 'they' to avoid using 'he' or 'she'. A person may choose to self-identify as 'agender', which means they do not adopt binary gender labels. 'Bigender' refers to someone who identifies as male and female and presents gender according to choice or their setting. There are other terms used by people to reject gender labels and gender identities, including 'non-binary', 'genderqueer', 'genderfluid', and 'gender variant'; they may self-identify and live as women, men, neither, and/or both, again according to choice and to situation.

There is an increased visibility of trans people due to both legal recognition of gender reassignment as a protected characteristic in a number of countries, and because of trans activism.

Therefore, trans theologies are relatively recent. They destabilise traditional binary ideas of gender. Concern from conservative Christians often points to the physicality of a trans person, reinstating biology and resisting the results of surgical procedures, while trans people themselves focus on the question of identity. A number of texts have emerged in which trans Christians speak for themselves, including *Transgendering Faith: Identity, Sexuality and Spirituality* (Dresser, 2004), *Trans/formations* (Althaus-Reid & Isherwood, 2009), *This is My Body: Hearing the Theology of Transgender Christians* (Beardsley & O'Brien, 2016), and *Transfaith* (Dowd, Beardsley & Tanis, 2018).

One significant text on trans theology and ministry is Justin Tanis's *Trans Gendered: Theology, Ministries and Communities of Faith* (Tanis, 2018). Writing as a trans person on trans issues, Tanis explores a range of topics grounded in the real-life experiences of trans people, offering his own life-story narrative and including sections on a search for selfhood and gender variance in the scriptures. Within the volume, Tanis explores the experience of trans people in their faith communities as well as offering guidance for communities of faith that seek to welcome trans people authentically. In the chapter on 'transgendered theological thought', Tanis explores concepts relating to how gender is beyond male and female and how gender is a calling from God. Tanis's work is seen as ground-breaking scholarship in the area of trans theologies.

ARE TRANS THEOLOGIES QUEER THEOLOGIES?

The relationship between queer theologies and trans theologies can be thought of as one of kinship. They can be described as siblings rather than twins. Like siblings, queer and trans theologies have a shared genealogy in LGBTQ+ theologies, so they share an ancestry and have had mutual influence on one other. Here, I deliberately use the term siblings, given the popularity of gendered language in Christian worship, where congregations are often addressed as 'brothers and sisters'. In terms of similarities, both queer and trans theologies are grounded in feminist and liberation theologies and poststructuralist critiques of essentialism (see Chapter 1). They offer resistance to claims about nature, bodies, identities, and God. Indeed, there is a solidarity in their kinship, as they both work to challenge normativity in theology (heteronormativity, cisnormativity, reproductive-normativity) and they open up spaces of resistance that speak back to church and institutional structures whose positional statements often regulate, judge, and discriminate against bodies, relationships, and lives. Therefore, there is genuine overlap in how trans theological voices emerged and operated via and alongside queer theological spaces. Both queer and trans theologies share the same theological tools that emerge from creative challenges to traditional, restrictive, and harmful frameworks. As kin-theologies, queer and trans theologies share political, social, cultural, religious, and activist agendas and commitments; they employ complementary methods of critique, and they both operate as shared sites of struggle against mainstream theology that has been dominant and exclusionary.

The DNA matches highlighted above reveal how queer and trans theologies belong to the same theological family. Yet, it is important to note that queer and trans theologies also pose different theological questions and expose different types of harm. Trans people may or may not identify as queer. Trans theologies intersect with queer theologies but are not subsumed or contained by them. Indeed, trans theologies engage queer theologies as critical partners; yet, trans theologies should not be considered a subfield of queer theologies. Historically, queer theologies have focussed largely on sexuality. This is evident through the corpus of texts that explore desire, sexual ethics, the regulation of intimate relationships, and heteronormativity in Christian theology. By contrast, trans theologies do not hold sexuality as a primary concern. They are concerned with gender and the power dynamics that surround gender performativity: how gender is assigned, how bodies are interpreted, how names are recognised, and how trans people are governed within religious communities. Trans theologies reveal and challenge forms of theological harm that have not always been considered or focussed upon in queer theologies.

PART 1 – WHAT THEOLOGY DOES TO TRANS LIVES: CORRECTIVE APPROACHES

As trans lives have become increasingly visible, they have also become more intensely regulated by religious institutions and theological discourse. Theology has functioned as a site of exclusion, discipline, and harm for trans people. Focussing on harm and violence is a negative position with which to begin an overview of trans theologies, but it is an ethical imperative that actually centres the impact of Christian thought, teaching, and statements on trans people. A focus on the harm, internalised shame, and theological trauma trans people experience serves to ground discussion about trans people in humanity, rather than in abstract thinking or ideology. Theologies about trans and non-binary people are not a neutral site for debate, but they have lived consequences for the people who very often are excluded from the conversations. In such debates, trans people are considered a theological puzzle or problem to be solved, rather than as a site of rich, powerful, lived faith. Therefore, recognising this harm as an act of violence is an unavoidable methodological commitment and shows how at odds Christian practice is from its central belief based on Jesus second commandment 'Love your neighbour as yourself' (Matthew 22:39, Mark 12:31, and Luke 10:27). Trans lives expose theological harm, and theology must be judged ethically by the damage it does.

One primary example of trans-negative abuse is the focus on the divine status of sex assignment at birth. Traditional cisnormative theologies of creation seek to fix sex assigned at birth as an act of God's work and therefore divinely mandated. This produces harm by denying trans people authority over their own lives and by positioning God against their self-knowledge. In the opening to *Transforming: The Bible and the Lives of Transgender Christians* (Hartke, 2018), Justin Sabia-Tanis tackles this question head on by asking, 'Did God make a mistake?' (2025: 1).

The persistence of this question reveals how deeply trans lives are framed as theological problems. Sabia-Tanis responds by refusing the premise altogether: 'I don't think that God made a mistake. I think God made me transgender on purpose' (2018: 2). One interviewee, M, sharpens the critique further: 'If there's a mistake at all, it's that we've created this understanding of gender that is so deeply limiting of God's creation. That's the mistake'

(2018: 4). Being considered a 'mistake' or told that being trans is a rejection of God's design causes irrefutable harm to trans people. Not only that, but it depicts a limited theology that cannot imagine gender beyond rigid binaries.

One participant in Clare-Young's study, Alex, describes the violence of gender assignment at birth in sobering terms: 'Just because as a tiny little baby my genitals were a certain shape and size, I was condemned to a prison of gender that was neither accurate nor chosen' (Clare-Young, 2024: 53). If gender is considered as divinely mandated and therefore should not be changed, traditional theology legitimates misrecognition of trans people and forecloses the possibility of true trans inclusion and acceptance. Austen Hartke writes in *Transforming: The Bible and the Lives of Transgender Christians* (2018) how 'this is where transgender Christians have been forced to live: out on the edges. They walk the fine line between acceptance and rejection, between God's love and the church's judgment' (2018: 20). The violence here is spiritual too, as such pronouncements are sanctified as God's will. It seems the loudest voices are also the most oppressive ones, often speaking on behalf of others (including God!), and muting all others out. In Clare-Young's research, Star puts this spiritual fear and trauma attached to inherited theological symbols very powerfully: 'I'm fucking terrified of the cross right now... it's got so much baggage from my former life and theology' (2024: 143).

To talk about harm or violence may seem drastic to some, but the repercussions are often internalised. Dominant theological narratives shape trans people's inner lives, resulting in experiences of shame, fear, and self-rejection. In one example, Evie recalls years of nightly prayer shaped by the belief that being trans was fundamentally wrong: 'I felt that being trans was a bad thing… I remember for years praying for an hour every night that I would wake up as female' (Clare-Young, 2024: 40). Here, prayer becomes a site where one seeks to deny oneself and to erase oneself, rather than being a Spirit-filled act of affirmation. Traditional theology here can be seen to contribute to self-hatred rather than faithful flourishing. Evie's narrative shows how external structures and influences can create internalised trans-negativity. Evie's prayer to change locates the 'problem' within the individual, rather than the social, cultural, political, and religious ideologies that cause harm to people.

In turn, this reinforces the idea that one's existence must be denied or undone in order to be acceptable to God. In identifying and naming the harm done by Christian theology to trans people, the violence is slow, cumulative, and structural. Harm continues to be perpetrated when ideologies and concern about others' responses and attitudes are prioritised over lived experiences.

Siân Taylder, a Catholic trans woman, describes an experience of prejudice in her chapter in *Trans/formations* (Althaus-Reid & Isherwood, 2009). Taylder experienced employment discrimination in El Salvador at a Catholic institute where she had applied for a post. She was told her personal circumstances (being trans) were not compatible with the ethos of the school. Taylder's response is to return this inhospitality:

> I, in turn, practise a rigid system of discrimination against those who subscribe to racist, homophobic (transphobic?) or sexist points of view. It's a theology of *quid pro quo*, and I don't see why I should be expected to tolerate those who refuse to tolerate me.
>
> (2009: 72)

Taylder later returns to the church next to the school during the celebration of Sunday Mass and looks her discriminators in the eyes. Taylder asks, 'You think my theology's a little too aggressive?' (2009: 73). Rather than aggression, this is an act of resistance that requires courage, bravery, and visibility.

A comprehensive analysis of each Christian teaching on trans people is beyond the scope of this chapter, but below are two case study examples from Roman Catholicism and Anglicanism as prominent global denominations. The following examples show how institutional responses to trans people have emerged unevenly, often attempting to manage harm without actually dismantling the theological frameworks that produced it.

ROMAN CATHOLICISM

While there is explicit condemnation in relation to homosexuality, there is no official positional statement regarding transgender individuals in the Catechism of the Catholic Church. It is clear that doctrinal teachings do equate birth anatomy with gender. Where there is a lack of firm teaching, the pastoral experience of transgender Catholics varies depending on parish communities.

An example of this is that Catholics who take holy orders and enter religious life are often segregated based on sex (monks/nuns). In 2014, a trans woman, Tia Michelle Pesando, was accepted as a nun into the Carmeline Sisters' community in Canada. News broke that she was the world's first trans nun (CTV London, 2014).

Just one year later, in September 2015, the Bishop of Cádiz and Ceuta in Spain wrote to the Vatican's Congregation for the Doctrine of the Faith, responsible for enforcing Catholic doctrine, as he sought advice about a request for a trans man to serve as a godfather. The response conflated sexuality with gender identity and went on to say:

> The result is evident that this person does not possess the requisite of leading a life conformed to the faith and to the position of godfather (CIC, can 874 §1,3), therefore is not able to be admitted to the position of godmother nor godfather. One should not see this as discrimination, but only the recognition of an objective absence of the requisites that by their nature are necessary to assume the ecclesial responsibility of being a godparent.
>
> (Catholic News Agency, 2015)

In 2019, the Congregation for Catholic Education published a document entitled: '"Male and Female He Created Them": Towards a Path of Dialogue on the Question of Gender Theory in Education'. The document is concerned with an 'educational crisis' (2019: 1) and states how 'gender ideology' causes confusion. It advocates that Catholic education should counter this through dialogue, anthropology, and formation.

The document reaffirms existing arguments about 'nature', stating how sex is biologically determined. In doing so, it makes recourse to the Genesis text, one that has often been used against trans people, discussed further below. It states:

> In the Book of Genesis, where we read that 'God created man in his own image [...] male and female he created them' (Gen. 1: 27). These words capture not only the essence of the story of creation but also that of the life-giving relationship between men and women, which brings them into intimate union with God.
>
> (2019: 17)

The document contains a number of normative assumptions about reproduction, family units, and the complementarity of male and female reinforcing an understanding of these as 'traditional' values. Indeed, the emphasis on such values problematises the notion of clerical celibacy when such ideals are upheld as Christian principles!

In 2023, the Vatican sought to provide further guidance on the 'issue'. Bishop José Negri from Brazil wrote to the Church's Dicastery of the Doctrine of the Faith, asking for guidance on LGBTQ+ people and their participation in baptism and matrimony. The response includes the following:

> 1. Can a transgender person be baptised?
> A transgender person – even after undergoing hormone treatment and sex-reassignment surgery – can receive Baptism under the same conditions as other believers if there are no situations in which there is a risk of generating public scandal or disorientation among the faithful. In the case of children or adolescents with problems of a transgender nature, if they are well-prepared and have the right disposition, they also can receive Baptism.
> 2. Can a transgender person serve as a godparent?
> Under certain conditions, an adult transgender person – even after undergoing hormone treatment and sex-reassignment surgery – may be admitted to the function of serving as a godparent. However, since this task does not constitute a right, pastoral prudence demands that it should not be permitted if there is a danger of scandal, undue legitimization, or disorientation in the educational sphere of the ecclesial community.
>
> (Dicastery for the Doctrine of the Faith, 2023)

The response was hailed by news outlets as progressive and welcomed by many LGBTQ+ Christian groups as a step forward. Yet, the language remains discriminatory, describing transness as 'problems' and suggesting that local arrangements can be made depending on perceptions of the pastoral community and any controversy that these inclusive acts may cause.

ANGLICANISM

The Anglican tradition is not monolithic. Across the Anglican Communion, there are autonomous provinces, and each exercises its own autonomy in relation to the production of doctrine, pastoral guidance, and liturgical practice. Consequently, no single definitive position on trans people in Anglicanism exists, and individual experiences can vary depending on geographical location and community. That said, there are some notable explicit statements that have been made pointing to the inclusion of trans people, in the Churches of England and Scotland, the Episcopal Church (USA), and the Anglican Church of Canada.

In 2016, the Church of Scotland General Assembly encouraged church councils to 'promote congregational learning and awareness of the issues transgender and gender non-conforming people experience' (Church of Scotland, 2016), with the aim of ameliorating pastoral care and inclusion of trans people. A resulting publication was *Diverse Gender Identities and Pastoral Care*, a booklet developed in partnership with the Scottish Trans Alliance that shares first-person stories of trans and non-binary people connected to the church and encourages reflective pastoral practice (Church of Scotland, 2016). The Church of Scotland has also engaged with public policy debates, notably in response to the Scottish Government's Gender Recognition Reform Bill. The Faith Impact Forum submitted evidence highlighting the importance of dignity, wellbeing, pastoral care, and service for people with diverse gender identities (Church of Scotland, 2022).

The General Synod in 2017 recognised the need for trans people to be welcomed and affirmed in parishes. In response, the Church of England produced pastoral guidance on welcoming transgender people (Church of England, 2018), stating that: 'The Church of England welcomes and encourages the unconditional affirmation of trans people, equally with all people, within the body of Christ'. The guidance was produced in consultation with trans clergy, including Revd Dr Tina Beardsley, the Revd Sarah Jones, and the Revd Canon Dr Rachel Mann. This includes worship for trans people to mark gender transition through an Affirmation of Baptismal Faith. This is based on an adaptation of existing rites to encourage clergy to respond pastorally.

Since 2017, the Church of England has been engaged in a project entitled 'Living in Love and Faith' (LLF) with the aim of discussing identity, sexuality, relationships, and marriage in the contemporary world and expressing the church's willingness to engage in such conversations.[1] The process included an apology by the House of Bishops for the failure to welcome LGBTQ+

people into the Church, and expressed a commitment to address this lack of welcome and inclusion. LLF uses language of listening, learning, and discernment in relation to these themes, putting themselves in the role of student.

Alex Clare-Young (2021) pays attention to the power dynamics, structures, and processes by which LLF was produced, as a trans man who was involved in the project. They seek to reveal some of the biases that exist in the formulation of the resources. On the composition of the co-ordinating group, they write:

> One member was an out transmasculine non-binary person. One member was an out gay person. In other words, as far as I know, 85% of the Co-ordinating Group was cisgender and heterosexual. There was no out female LGBTQ+ representation... I felt very strongly that the LGBTQ+ representation in the co-ordinating group was tokenistic.
>
> (2021: 118)

Elsewhere, Clare-Young writes, ‘As a trans, non-binary Christian, I have often felt like a ‘resource’ used as an object of pity, education, prayer, or abuse (2024: 16)

Increased visibility of trans people seems to increase hostility. Austen Hartke notes that:

> as more trans people come forward and share their stories and the struggles that they face, those who find trans identities distasteful or morally corrupt feel that they must also come forward with their own opinions, policies, and theological pronouncements.
>
> (2018: 11–12)

In the same way, Clare-Young describe a response from Christian Concern, a conservative Anglican organisation as a ‘contemporary text of terror’ (2021: 124), as they experienced abuse as a direct consequence of their position. Clare-Young writes how these include:

> comments contained threats to my home, my vocation, and my life as well as threats to members of my church. I also received several threatening emails. I have received hate mail before, but some of the extreme language and plausible threats in these emails were deeply concerning.
>
> (2021: 124–125)

The Church of England also applied its influential position in social and political discussions to trans lives. In 2025, a Supreme

Court pivotal judgement in relation to the definition of 'sex' and the status of trans people in the Equalities Act (2010) ruled that 'sex' refers to biological sex, not acquired gender. In response, the Church of England encouraged thoughtful engagement, emphasising dignity and care to all people who are made in the image of God and that 'their status before Christ, remain unimpacted by gender reassignment' (Church of England, 2025).

In the USA, the General Convention of the Episcopal Church (2012) included 'gender identity and expression' in its non-discrimination canons, with the aim of ensuring full acceptance of trans people in the religious life of the organisation. At the General Convention six years later, in 2018, the Episcopal Church adopted Resolution 2018-C054, which lays out 'Guiding Principles for the Inclusion of Transgender and Non-Binary People'. These principles include commitments to: (i) protect the rights and dignity of trans and non-binary persons, (ii) refuse dehumanising language or behaviour, (iii) provide safe environments in parishes, schools, and camps, and (iv) engage the realities of transgender lives rather than ignoring them (The Episcopal Church, 2018).

Anti-trans legislation began to ramp up in 2025. A federal executive order (14168), entitled 'Defending Women from Gender Ideology Extremism and Restoring Biological Truth', directs the US government to treat sex as both biological and binary. This effectively sought to erase gender recognition for trans people. The same month documented a barrage of legislative attacks on trans people including the following executive orders: 14183 – excluding trans people from the military, 14187 – a block on federal funding for gender-affirming care for minors, referring to procedures for gender reassignment as 'chemical and surgical mutilation', and all DEIA (diversity, equity, inclusion, and accessibility) programmes were ended via executive order 14151. Although the 2025 executive orders marked a sharp escalation in federal restrictions on transgender rights, their implementation has been uneven. Multiple legal challenges by states, organisations, and individuals have resulted in injunctions and delays. Several provisions have been paused, partially blocked, or subject to ongoing judicial review, resulting in an uncertain legal environment for trans and non-binary people. Nonetheless, individual political ideologies begin to merge with religious beliefs, which are reactive, defensive, regulatory, and harmful.

In an increasingly hostile public arena since 2025, Episcopal leaders have repeatedly affirmed support for transgender people in public statements. The church's Office of Government Relations released a statement publicly affirming the rights and freedoms of transgender and gender non-conforming people following the sweep of legislative changes in 2025. The Rt. Rev. Bishop Rowe states, 'LGBTQIA+ people are beloved children of God who should be treated with dignity and respect' (The Episcopal Church, 2025).

The Anglican Church of Canada's General Synod authorised 'Pastoral Liturgies for Journeys of Gender Affirmation and Transition' (Anglican Church of Canada, 2023). The church recognises that trans people have always been part of the faithful, as they state:

> we know that gender non-binary and transgender people have been within the church, are baptised full members of the church and have always been present in the church. The assumption behind the provision of these rites, though, is that gender non-binary and transgender people are already with us, as baptised members of worshiping communities. We do not 'welcome' them as newcomers. The care of a supportive community can speak a more profound welcome, however, and be an important witness to those who feel marginalized elsewhere in church and society.
>
> (Anglican Church of Canada, 2023: 3)

The worship material includes prayers and blessings tailored to gender affirmation, guidance for liturgy that explicitly affirms transgender and non-binary people, and reflections on pastoral care and baptismal identity in the context of gender transition. Yet, one very small sentence is revealing, 'These rites are offered to the church for use where permitted by the local Ordinary (the Diocesan Bishop)' (2023: 4), again highlighting how these affirmations rely on localised agreements and are not universal rights.

The relative advancement and support in positional statements and guidance for inclusion of trans and non-binary people are welcome by many LGBTQ+ support organisations. Indeed, many Anglican dioceses hold Transgender Day of Remembrance vigils and services that honour the lives and losses of trans people in the community. Yet, as with all religious groups, locality and context matter. Some trans Episcopalians have highlighted the unevenness of inclusion across the organisation. Rev. Gwen Fry, a former president of the Episcopal LGBTQ+ group Integrity, says, 'We've done an amazing job of beginning the process of inclusion at the churchwide level, but it just isn't translating to the diocesan and parish levels' (Episcopal News Service, 2022). The church's work towards LGBTQ+ inclusion remains a continued project.

Given the continued debates and divisions around questions of sexuality (see Chapter 5), the survey of teachings and guidance from Anglican churches in the Global North, at least, show a willingness to engage in inclusion for trans and non-binary people. Such progress is not uniform, as the guidance is permissive rather than mandatory. As such, clergy have a choice in offering affirmations, but they are not required to. Moreover, such steps towards inclusion and affirmation of trans Christians have equally been met with concern from voices within the Church of England. Groups continue to challenge the guidance publicly, arguing how 'trans ideology' remains at odds with traditional frameworks. Increased visibility of groups that seek to reform their institutions away from exclusion or mere tolerance, but to true radical acceptance, often leads to shifting dynamics in congregations.

The issue at play may seem subtle to some, but there is a significant difference between welcome and recognition. The language of 'welcome' can indeed point to tolerance, rather than a genuine attempt at institutional and theological transformation. Terry Dresser describes their transition and how they grew to hate their body and began self-mutilation as breasts developed on their body during puberty. This also resulted in a rejection from church. However, the difficult journey led to self-acceptance; as they say, 'I've been lucky to have a close relationship with God and to know deep down inside that no matter what others said I knew God loved me and accepted me as the child God created me to be' (Dresser, 2004: 42). In another example, Beth narrates experiences of transphobia in her church community, as she was unable to come out in the parish in which she worked. Beth's supervisor suggested not telling others about her pronouns, and she had to attend multiple meetings in order to be told that this was problematic (Clare-Young, 2024: 85). In such examples, inclusion is conditional, often demanding silence, respectability, or concern about congregational response. The move to inclusion can be transformational, however. Sam asserts that a relocation to an inclusive church has given a sense of belonging:

> Now I'm in an inclusive church... I end up standing at the door greeting people. I love reading the lesson. I love being seen as a trans person without any question in that church. It liberates me hugely and helps undo a lot of the hurt that I suffered in churches when I was young.
>
> (Clare-Young, 2024: 174)

Such narratives highlight the contextual conditions on being accepted when one meets specific preferences or criteria set out via clergy or jurisdiction. This reveals institutional inequity, and a nervousness to demand change across and within the culture entirely. Until such institutional transformation takes place, the inclusion of trans people remains conditional. Equally, it is important to note that the vast majority of the statements of inclusion detailed above are very recent and therefore decades of silence, and the wrongful equation of trans people as a 'sexuality issue' means that many trans and non-binary people experienced and continue to experience discrimination and harm.

Attending to harm is an important starting point for trans theologies, and a necessary intervention to expose the institutional structures that exclude trans and non-binary people. This is a form of corrective theology. The analysis in Part 1 shows how Christian theology has shaped the conditions under which trans people are excluded. Trans theologies go beyond exposing such harm, and the following section considers how theology is enriched when its starting points are located and grounded in trans experiences.

PART 2 – WHAT TRANS LIVES DO TO THEOLOGY: CONSTRUCTIVE APPROACHES

So, what happens when theology starts from trans lives instead of institutions? Marcella Althaus Reid rightly claims that 'the everyday lives of people always provide us with a starting point for a process of doing a contextual theology without exclusions' (2000: 4). In turning attention away from apologetics (explaining or defending trans Christians), constructive, fruitful, and joyful theologies from trans people reach far beyond simple defence and have a lot to teach theology.

It is important to engage with trans Christians when producing trans theologies, so that they are grounded in real-life experiences rather than being speculative or generalised. The production of trans theologies without engagement with trans communities is a concern of Mercia McMahon. She notices the limitations of trans theologies produced by non-trans people and states how this situation is unavoidable, given the low number of trans theologians. To ensure trans voices are included in theologies, she calls for a commitment to working with trans communities, as she says:

> The ideal trans theology is one that is written by members of trans communities, but with so few trans identified theologians this is a long way from becoming reality. Due to this situation those who engage in trans positive theology as outsiders need to be careful that they are fully engaging with the community and not making assumptions about what trans people experience.
>
> (McMahon, 2016: 61)

In addressing such concerns directly, Alex Clare-Young's work (2024) is illuminating for trans theologies, as they ask: what views about God and about being human are held by people who identify as Christian and trans or non-binary? They engage in a detailed ethnographic study with trans and non-binary Christians, revealing rich theological engagement through narratives of endurance and emancipation through faith. Their research is authored exclusively by trans and non-binary people, where authors hold *author*ity, speaking from lived experience. Such authority does not homogenise accounts of trans theologies; however, full diversity and difference in positions are recognised. In dialogue with ten participants, Clare-Young frames the work as 'not a trans-inclusive theology; it is a cis-exclusive theology' (2024: 65). This position seeks to protect and prioritise the inclusion of trans people within trans theologies, encouraging allies and scholarship to engage in constructive dialogue, centring trans experiences in the formation of such theologies rather than ideological speculation. Clare-Young states:

> That does not mean that there should not be any further theological research or writing *about* trans and/or non-binary people and not

> necessarily by us. Rather, this absolutely necessary and valid research should be complemented by wider theological research and writing by trans and non-binary people who can benefit the theological discipline more widely, on an infinite range of topics, rather than only having relevance to trans people and those who wish to discuss the ethical ramifications of our existence.
>
> (2024: 185)

Constructive trans theologies prioritise engagement with trans people as an ethical method that draws on experts by experience, first and foremost, rather than frames trans people's existence as a topic. The distinction is clearly important – as noted previously, when trans people have been reduced to ideological debate and a 'topic' of discussion, harm has been done. Concerns about voice, tokenism, and ventriloquism are paramount when attending to voices from the margins. Rather than 'giving voice', which implies people are voiceless and often results in an act of ventriloquism, trans ally researchers ought to *amplify* voices of trans people. In an intentional act that swerves the notion of ventriloquism, Joseph N. Goh writes, 'I do not speak for transgender people, but with them as a respectful trans ally who continues to learn' (2020: 3).

Joseph N. Goh has examined trans theologies across Asia. His work illuminates the key issues relating to acceptance, tolerance, and inclusion. He explains how 'transgender Christians in the Asia Pacific region often experience conditional acceptance or even blatant rejection from their churches and faith communities' (2020: 1). Focussing specifically on Philippine and Tongan trans women, Goh underscores how the notion of 'affirmation' is much more pertinent than 'acceptance' or 'tolerance' alone. Acceptance does not mean agreement, and tolerance does not even meet the bar of inclusion. The distinction between these terms is significant, as they are not cognates for inclusion. In practice, the Christian community has a problem at its core, where, as Goh writes, 'many gender-nonconforming Christians experience unrequited love from their faith communities' (2020: 1). Goh holds that 'while churches can act as locations that spearhead persecution and even diminishment, they can also become stepping-stones that lead to non-compliance, emancipation, and empowerment' (2020: 4). Goh labels this transformative process as a 'hospitable ecclesiology', noting its legacy at the very foundations of Christianity when early Christians were considered counter normative. Reflecting on her small, grounded community, one of Goh's dialogue partners, Mataele, a Tongan trans Christian woman, refers to her community's Bible-sharing gatherings as a 'little programme' (Goh, 2020: 10). This is a stark example of how trans people can shape theological life. Attending to trans lives contribute not only to critiques of dominant normative power in theology, but they also reveal new, intimate, and grounded ways of doing theology. In seeking to move away from a framework of harm, attention now focusses on trans theologies of joy.

Three examples of the constructive creativity that trans theologies boast are detailed below (i) re-imagining God, (ii) naming and calling, and (iii) joy, euphoria and flourishing.

(I) RE-IMAGINING GOD

As theology is 'God-talk', trans theologies are able to use their insights to release God from rigid gender boundaries, that have resulted in patriarchal, heteronormative, and cisnormative privilege in Christian theology. Trans theology is relational and experiential. Clare-Young write how God is beyond gender binaries, positing that 'God is gender-full and gender-less' (2024: 1). One of their participants, Star, says 'God is becoming – God doesn't sit still – God delights in transformation' (2024: 126).

The Christian notion of *imago Dei*, being created in the image of God, is key to self-acceptance for trans Christians, but it is also essential for trans flourishing. Throughout trans theologies, God has been conceived as non-male, or non-binary, or multi-gendered. The powerful theological concept here produced by trans theologies is that God is beyond rigid, artificial, constructed, categories. The use of these categories in theology simple serves to limit God. The need to fix God as male has resulted in patriarchal privilege. Here, trans theologies expose the power that is held and maintained in theological traditions, and, in doing so, reveal the limitations of the traditions in maintaining such concepts.

In *Undoing Theology* (2018), I write about the fixation of God's gender into the same rigid theological and gender frameworks used for people. I call for an undoing and liberation, as I write:

> We desire an open, inclusive God, who is freeing in their creative abundance. This is why contextual theologies have been so important in allowing Christians to conceptualize a God who is welcoming, affirming and loving... By undoing God, we allow God to be free. Traditional, normative Christian theology has resulted in a God who has been bound tightly in biblical leather and traditional ecclesiology. Yet God's consent was never sought in this fixed image.
>
> (Greenough, 2018: 174)

This deconstruction and rebuilding of theological concepts is a joyful task, which sheds new light on the use, function, and impact of a gendered deity in Christian theology. Diversity, unpredictability, and freedom show vast theological possibilities that remove God from a fixed sameness.

(II) NAMING AND CALLING

Naming is a significant act in Christian theology; it is constitutive of relationship, recognition, and vocation. The act of naming occurs in sacraments of baptism and confirmation, as well as being used in holy orders, matrimony, and anointing of the sick. The correct use and recognition of one's name hold a basis in scripture. In Isaiah, God's act of calling by name signals intimacy, relationship and belonging: 'I have called you by your name, you are mine' (Isaiah 43:1).

Theology has long recognised that God's call is personal before it is doctrinal; all the sacraments begin with a calling by name before the act of vocation. Naming is therefore an affirmation of a person before God and before community. Trans theologies rejoice in making this theological structure visible by insisting that naming is not only something God does to people, but something people do in response to God. As Clare-Young articulates, 'our names are a calling, given to us by God' (2024: 38). For trans Christians, the process of choosing one's name can be an act of self-identification as well as a process of discernment in response to faith and God.

Conversely, deadnaming – the use of an individual's name assigned at birth rather than their chosen name – exposes the violence of misrecognition. It is an act which denies an individual their truth, by repositioning them in a past that no longer corresponds to their self-understanding and lived reality. Recognition, therefore, is a theological act. To recognise a trans person's name is to bless their becoming and being, to acknowledge their place within the body of Christ, and to affirm their belonging. This is why being seen and named rightly within church life through a number of blessings and rites, highlighted in the survey of Christian positions on trans people discussed previously, matters so much.

More significantly, biblical traditions of renaming to mark new becomings make this logic explicit. As God transforms and becomes closer to people, renaming marks this new transformation, mission, and faithfulness. Abram and Sarai become Abraham and Sarah as their calling is re-spoken and expanded (Genesis 17:5, 15–16). Likewise, Saul's renaming as Paul in Acts marks a decisive shift in vocation and identity within the early church (Acts 13:9). In these moments, naming signals a calling, a new becoming and identity in response to God.

Not all bodies are granted the privilege of renaming within scripture. Alongside traditions of renaming that mark covenantal belonging, there are figures whose very bodies exclude them from participation in the assembly. Eunuchs are one such group (discussed further below in relation to trans readings of the Bible). Under Mosaic law, eunuchs are explicitly barred from full inclusion 'No one whose testicles are crushed or whose male organ is cut off shall enter the assembly of the Lord' (Deuteronomy 23:1). In Isaiah 56:5, the Lord gives them 'a name better than sons and daughters', 'an everlasting name'. In this light, naming practices are central to Christian theology, bound to calling, recognition, and true acceptance by God. This very same argument signals that to refuse a name or to deadname deliberately is more than a microaggression, it is a pastoral failure.

(III) JOY, EUPHORIA, AND FLOURISHING

In contrast to the harm and suffering narratives that have formed part of a dominant discussion in trans theologies noted above, trans theologies also demonstrate a resistance to suffering-only narratives. Resilience, playfulness, creativity, and joy become theological tools in order to engage with aspects of Christian theology as a site of flourishing, rather than suffering. While 'gender dysphoria' has been used as a medical term for trans diagnosis,

Mike plays with this idea and seeks to focus on euphoria rather than dysphoria (Clare-Young, 2024: 103).

In *Transgendering Faith: Identity, Sexuality and Spirituality* (2004), one of the authors describes the difficulties faced following the decision to transition. Dzintra Alksnitis talks about the gifts received from the Holy Spirit during the most challenging and scary period of their life:

> The gifts I received as I had cried out to the Spirit were peace, understanding, love, courage, faith, and wisdom. Little did I know that I was going to need every one of these in order to survive and grow.
>
> (Alksnitis, 2004: 31)

Trans joy is *pneumatological*: a demonstrable fruit of the Holy Spirit – rather than being a form of naïve optimism or false positivity. It is Spirit produced.

Mary Elise Lowe (2017) discusses the gifts that trans Christians have that actively reshape Christian theology and practice. She identifies four interrelated theological gifts offered by trans Christians to the church: co-creativity with God, steadfast self-love (*hesed*), an integrated understanding of body-mind, and a Spirit-led embrace of plurality, freedom, and becoming. Trans theologies highlight how God's creation is not a past event, but a gift of the present. Lowe shows how trans lives witness to God's ongoing work of creation, as people participate as 'created co-creators' in forming congruent identities and embodiments. Rather than holding a dichotomy between mind/body that has been popular throughout early and contemporary Christian thought, trans theologies affirm a coherence and unity of body and mind.

Importantly, such theologies are not solely beneficial to queer or trans theologies, but they invite the whole church to re-imagine God, embodiment and community beyond binary, static, and exclusionary norms. According to Lowe, trans Christians do not sit and await to be a passive recipient of welcome, or an act of ecclesial hospitality. Rather, they are active bearers of theological gifts that destabilise dominant theologies about God, human embodiment, love, and relationships. Lowe writes how trans Christians bring gifts of 'plurality, newness, unity, unpredictability, and freedom' (2017: 34). Joy manifests as an example of God's ongoing creative work and relationship with humanity. This is not a performative joy, but a product of theological transformation.

For trans Christians, this fruitful joy surfaces through difficulty and hardship, not after the removal. Romans 5:3-5 names this pattern directly as rejoicing in suffering, because suffering produces endurance. Endurance is a pathway to transformation and abundance. This notion of joy is an imperative from Christ, as Jesus says in Matthew 5:11–12, 'Blessed are you when others revile you and persecute you… Rejoice and be glad, for your reward is great in heaven'. For Jesus, joy is *eschatological* in that it is a faithful response that refuses to allow suffering to be the final word. Such expressions of joy can be found in trans biblical interpretation where methods prioritise play, imagination, re-reading, and expansion, as discussed in the next section.

PART 3 – TRANS INTERPRETATIONS OF SCRIPTURE: ETHICAL APPROACHES

One contemporary volume that attends to transgender biblical hermeneutics is *Transgender, Intersex, and Biblical Interpretation* (2016), co-authored by Teresa Hornsby and Deryn Guest. Guest details a way of reading using a 'transgender gaze' that consists of the following four areas: (1) locating gaze in trans experience; (2) exposing constructedness of gender; (3) confronting heteronormativity with alternative visions of gender; (4) calling for political and religious engagement challenging the negative effects of biblical interpretation on trans people (2016: 50–51). These approaches bring together both elements of correction and construction detailed in parts 1 and 2 of this chapter, as well as maintaining a focus on trans experiences.

For trans people, there are texts of terror which are used to bolster arguments against gender identity and surgery. For example, in addition to Deuteronomy 23:1 noted above, Deuteronomy 22:5 prohibits cross-dressing: 'A woman must not wear men's clothing, nor a man wear women's clothing, for the Lord your God detests anyone who does this'. These readings can be seen as another example where one of the 613 Hebrew laws are selected as important in Christian contexts while others are discarded. It is also an example where the verse can be counter-balanced by another scripture elsewhere in the Bible. For instance, in the New Testament there is a promise within the Bible that offers

Christians a heavenly embodiment which defies binary gender. In Galatians 3:28, Paul writes, 'There is neither Jew nor Gentile, neither slave nor free, nor is there male and female, for you are all one in Christ Jesus'.

Gender variance has always existed, as Marchal et al. write, 'gender variation is as ancient as stories about creation' (2025: 1). The creation story itself is often used as a 'proof-text' for binary gender, and Genesis 1:27 has been weaponised against trans and non-binary people: 'So God created man in his own image, in the image of God he created him; male and female he created them'.

Star pushes back against such an interpretation, noting a possibility 'I could live in the 'and' of male and female' (Clare-Young, 2024: 101–102). What is quite interesting from the story of the Fall is that binary gender roles are created as a punishment from God – Adam's dominance of Eve, her woes in childbirth (Genesis 3:16) and Adam's instruction to toil the land (Genesis 3:17–19). Greenough (2023) notes how this account does not sanction or sanctify cisnormativity and heteronormativity. Neither is prioritised in this account, and cisnormativity and heteronormativity are actually the result of an undesirable punishment, and therefore not God's original intention for humanity.

Trans readings of scripture share many of the tools of queer hermeneutics (see Chapter 4), including disruption, play, re-reading, and refusal of fixed interpretations. There is therefore overlap in methodology, yet it is imperative to highlight that trans hermeneutics emerge from different epistemic pressures, ethical questions, and sites of interpretation. As they share similar tools of interpretation, trans and queer readings both become allies in the disruption of normative readings and the resistance of normative claims relating to gender, sexuality, bodies, identities, and desire.

It is important to note that there are different starting points and locations from where queer and trans hermeneutics begin. Queer hermeneutics historically emerged from questions and experiences around sexuality, eroticism, heteronormativity, and reproductivity. In contrast, trans hermeneutics emerge from trans experiences of gender reassignment, embodiment, naming, misrecognition, agency, identity, and diversity. Both approaches disrupt norms, using their specific contexts to set the agenda.

This matches what Marchal et al. insist as they state 'trans forms of figures within biblical interpretation should not be located solely within queer hermeneutics' (2025: 23). Simply put, not all trans readings are queer, and, certainly, most queer readings are not trans. Sexuality has informed and dominated queer theory, and a normativity of its own has been produced with many trans issues sidelined or underrepresented. While a queer framework holds a space of possibility for trans hermeneutics, trans interpretations are richer when examined through their own agenda. Indeed, as will become clear, trans hermeneutics can *unqueer* queer readings by offering more ethical interpretations of texts, as is detailed in the case study of eunuchs below.

EUNUCHS

The figure of the eunuch has been popularised in trans readings. Quite simply because the Bible does not contain modern categories of gender identity and no one in the text self-identifies as trans or non-binary, eunuchs become a site of possibility through which readers can think about non-normative embodiment without inventing characters or categories. Eunuchs are read as figures who are explicitly gender-nonconforming in the text, and their bodies and social roles are noted for their distinction from dominant gender and reproductive norms.

As discussed in Chapter 4, eunuchs are banned from inclusion in Deuteronomy 23:1, yet texts such as Isaiah 56:4 affirm acceptance and inclusion of eunuchs: 'For this is what the Lord says: I will bless those eunuchs who keep my Sabbath days holy and who choose to do what pleases me and commit their lives to me'. In Acts 8, Phillip baptises the Ethiopian eunuch.

In Matthew's gospel (19:12), Jesus addresses such questions directly:

> For there are eunuchs who have been so from birth, and there are eunuchs who have been made eunuchs by others, and there are eunuchs who have made themselves eunuchs for the sake of the kingdom of heaven. Let anyone accept this who can.

On a simple yet literal level, the use of this biblical text can be used as a proof-text for trans acceptance.

Anachronism is a charge often levelled at readings of contemporary identities onto biblical characters or historical figures. It is considered problematic in biblical studies, under the pretext that it adds ideologies and social and cultural lenses to a text that were not in existence at the time of biblical writers. In formulating trans ways of reading, Max Strassfeld boldly reveals his aim is 'to practice deliberate anachronism' (2025: 32). Strassfeld continues, 'I'm skeptical as to whether the tools developed to study histories of sexuality are sufficient to address the study of androgynes and eunuchs in antiquity' (2025: 41). Rather than retroactively labelling eunuchs or other biblical figures as trans, Shannon Kearns observes how 'writing about eunuchs is complicated because their experiences come from a very different time and place. It's dangerous to try to read twenty-first-century identities back onto ancient people, especially when the eunuchs' identities were often a result of trauma' (2022: 18).

McMahon expresses caution about the place of the eunuch in trans readings. She notes how there are no direct resources for transgender people within the Bible. They are able to look at texts – for example, the biblical eunuchs – and see elements that offer some evidence of gender variance, but she warns that these texts 'are rich virgins' as 'they do not fully equate to the experience of trans people' (McMahon, 2016: 66).

A text about eunuchs may resonate for a trans reader, and that resonance can be powerful, yet there is a further ethical step to take. Unlike idealised or heroic figures, eunuchs often come into being through coercion, violence, or imperial power. This individual history makes them useful for readings that want to acknowledge bodily trauma, marginalisation, and loss. These histories also raise ethical questions. Such readings can move away from identity-based concerns and interrogate the systems by which texts are read more fully.

Yet, at the same time, a text compiled thousands of years ago can only reveal fragments about the social and cultural lenses in existence in ancient contexts. Trans may be a modern word, but the blurring of gender categories is not. More importantly, the lenses readers have in the contemporary world are located in the social and cultural worlds of today. There is no neutral process of interpretation where the reader abandons the modern world when reading the ancient text. An attempt to set these lenses aside would equally signify that the ancient text has no relevance for today's world. In fact, a more ethical reading is to be had when both are considered in dialogue with one another.

Accordingly, one act of reading is when interpreters sometimes read transgender or non-binary identities *onto* biblical characters. The function of such readings may be to assert and claim that a character was specifically trans or non-binary, or that there is sufficient evidence for gender ambiguity. Examples exist such as Aysha W. Musa's reading of Jael (2020) and Jo Henderson-Merrygold's reading of Sarah/Sarai (2020). Henderson-Merrygold encourages readers to be suspicious of the assumed cisnormativity of biblical characters, and uses the term 'cispicion' to describe this trans-informed method (2020: 502n24).

The potential for reading gender difference in the biblical text is plentiful, and such realisations are able to resonate with trans readers, juxtaposing scripture and teachings with their own identities. Justin Sabia-Tanis sees the benefits for trans inclusion as 'reading with an eye towards these "trans-cestors" yields some of the richest stories of inclusion in the Bible' (2025: 105). However, Marchal et al. write how 'trans interpretation can do more than look for biblical figures who can function as trans-cestors' (2025: 22). An example of how trans readers can go beyond such strategies is found in the work of Jo Ladin (2025). Ladin gives a warning that highlights an ethical tension within trans biblical interpretation. Ladin argues that efforts to resist cisnormativity can unintentionally reproduce the very harm it seeks to undo, because it assigns gender identities to characters who never name themselves. In fact, assigning gender to others is precisely the violence being resisted in trans readings. Ladin writes:

> But since no biblical character tells us how they identify in terms of gender, we cannot assign them to either side of the trans/cis binary without violating the principle that gender is a matter of self-identification. Efforts to overcome cisnormativity in biblical tradition by reading transgender and non-binary identities into the text paradoxically mirror the cisnormative practices of projecting anachronistic categories onto ancient texts and of treating gender as something that is assigned to others rather than determined by individuals themselves.
>
> (2025: 52)

Since trans ethics insist that gender is determined by self-identification, projecting modern identity categories onto biblical figures risks violating that principle. In this sense, trans hermeneutics can often take a step back from some queer interpretive habits in order to remain ethically consistent. What specifically is being 'un-queered' here is less to do with the creative and imaginative approach to reading, but the practice of assigning identities to others without consent. Trans readings can provide a useful benchmark to investigate the ethics of queer, playful readings.

Trans readings of biblical texts place emphasis on *how* reading happens, rather than on the texts themselves. The prioritisation of method over material allows readers to examine how a text may reproduce or resist harm. Because trans people often read under conditions of vulnerability, interpretation becomes an ethical act with real consequences, rather than a neutral academic exercise.

The Bible continues to hold cultural and social value today outside of religious spheres. It is often invoked in 'controversial' debates and answers are sought from within its pages to address many of the contemporary issues today that did not occur or bother the biblical writers at the time of its production. Trans hermeneutics move beyond static and literal readings and embrace multiple readings of a text, rather than one single authoritative reading. This does not mean that the Bible does not hold authority in the lives of trans Christians – it does. But trans readings pay testament to how such readings are never neutral, given the role of the biblical text in the production and perpetuation of harm, and the process of healing. As well as noting sites of gender variance, trans hermeneutics pay close attention to method, ethics, and responsibility, thereby resisting readings that fix identity or reproduce violence.

CONCLUSION

This chapter has shown that trans theologies are at work in two ways. First, they operate as a necessary and constructive theological response to harm, exclusion, and misrecognition. Yet, through this process of attending both to what theology has done to trans lives and to what trans lives do to theology, it becomes clear that trans theologies are more than corrective; they are creatively constructive. They expose the limits of cisnormative frameworks, re-open questions of creation, naming, embodiment, and joy, and insist that theology must remain accountable to lived faith. This ethical dimension is unique: trans theologies are presented here as one of the most important contemporary sites in which queer theology is tested. In doing so, trans theologies are not located entirely outside or inside of the Christian tradition, but create abundant space using the tools of both lived experience and Christianity itself to invite new transformation of centuries-old teachings and traditions.

FURTHER READING AND RESOURCES

Althaus-Reid, M. and Isherwood, L. (2009) (Eds.) *Trans/formations*. London: SCM Press.

A range of essays discussing trans theologies.

Beardsley, C. and O'Brien, M. (Eds.) (2016) *This Is My Body: Hearing the Theology of Transgender Christians*. London: Darton, Longman and Todd.

This book, written by trans people, explores individual trans experiences with faith. It serves to redress the balance to allow those who identify as trans to produce their own theologies.

Clare-Young, A. (2024) *Trans Formations: Grounding Theology in Trans and Non-Binary Lives*. London: SCM Press.

Rich ethnographic accounts of trans theologies produced through research with, by and for trans and non-binary people.

Tanis, J. (2018) *Trans-Gendered: Theology, Ministry, and Communities of Faith*. Cleveland: Pilgrim Press.

A Second Edition of Tanis's comprehensive consideration of trans theologies, first printed in 2003. Tanis covers a wealth of topics, including trans body theologies and how churches can offer genuine affirmation and welcome to trans people.

Journal of Interdisciplinary Biblical Studies. Special Edition on Transgender and Genderqueer Perspectives, edited by Caroline Blyth. Available at: https://jibs.hcommons.org/archive/volume-1/ (Accessed: January 2025).

Free, open-access academic texts exploring trans biblical hermeneutics.

NOTE

1 For resources and to access the Learning Hub, see the Church of England, *Living in Love and Faith*: www.churchofengland.org/resources/living-love-and-faith/about-living-love-and-faith (Accessed: January 2026).

REFERENCES

Alksnitis, D. (2004) 'Living in the Palm of God'. In McCall Tigert, L. and Tirabassi, M.C. (Eds.) *Transgendering Faith: Identity, Sexuality and Spirituality*, pp. 29–30. Cleveland: Pilgrim Press.

Althaus-Reid. M. (2000) *Indecent Theology*. London: Routledge.

Althaus-Reid, M. and Isherwood, L. (Eds.) (2009) *Trans/formations*. London: SCM Press.

Anglican Church of Canada (2023) *Pastoral Liturgies for Journeys of Gender Affirmation and Transition*. Toronto: Anglican Church of Canada. Available at: www.anglican.ca/wp-content/uploads/liturgies-gender-transition-affirmation.pdf (Accessed: January 2026).

Catholic News Agency (2015) 'Vatican Says "No" to Transsexual Godparents Amid Spain Controversy'. 2 September. Available at: www.catholicnewsagency.com/news/32559/vatican-says-no-to-transsexual-godparents-amid-spain-controversy (Accessed: January 2026).

Church of England (2018) *Pastoral Guidance on the Affirmation of Baptismal Faith in the Context of Gender Transition*. London: Church of England, December. Available at: www.churchofengland.org/sites/default/files/2018-12/pastoral-guidance-affirmation-baptismal-faith.pdf (Accessed: January 2026).

Church of England (2025) *Pastoral Response to Supreme Court Ruling: Replacement*. London: Church of England, June. Available at: www.churchofengland.org/sites/default/files/2025-06/pastoral-response-to-supreme-court-ruling-replacement.pdf (Accessed: January 2026).

Church of Scotland (2016) *Diverse Gender Identities and Pastoral Care*. Edinburgh: Church of Scotland. Available at: www.churchofscotland.org.uk/__data/assets/pdf_file/0005/48866/Web_PDF_Diverse_Gender_Identities_and_Pastoral_Care.pdf (Accessed: January 2026).

Church of Scotland (2022) *Response to the Gender Recognition Reform (Scotland) Bill*. Edinburgh: Church of Scotland. Available at: www.churchofscotland.org.uk/__data/assets/pdf_file/0011/95564/gender-recognition-reform-scotland-bill-response.pdf (Accessed: January 2026).

Clare-Young, A. (2021) 'Living in Love and Faith? The Construction of Contemporary Texts of Terror'. *Theology & Sexuality*, *27*(2–3), pp. 115–136.

Clare-Young, A. (2024) *Trans Formations: Grounding Theology in Trans and Non-Binary Lives*. London: SCM Press.

Congregation for Catholic Education (2019) *'Male and Female He Created Them': Towards a Path of Dialogue on the Question of Gender Theory in Education*. Vatican City: Vatican Press. Available at: www.vatican.va/roman_curia/congregations/ccatheduc/documents/rc_con_ccatheduc_doc_20190202_maschio-e-femmina_en.pdf (Accessed: January 2026).

CTV News London (2014) 'Call to Religious Life Strong for Transgender Londoner'. Available at: www.ctvnews.ca/london/article/call-to-religious-life-strong-for-transgender-londoner//#ixzz37B0Avz3g (Accessed: January 2026).

Dicastery for the Doctrine of the Faith (2023) *Answers to Several Questions Regarding Participation in the Sacraments of Baptism and Matrimony by Transgender Persons and Homosexual Persons*. Vatican City: Vatican Press. Available at: www.vatican.va/roman_curia/congregations/cfaith/documents/rc_ddf_20231031-documento-mons-negri_en.html (Accessed: January 2026).

Dowd, C., Beardsley, C. and Tanis, J. (2018) *Transfaith*. London: Darton, Longman and Todd.

Dresser, T. (2004) 'Terry's Journey'. In McCall Tigert, L. and Tirabassi, M.C. (Eds.) *Transgendering Faith: Identity, Sexuality and Spirituality*, pp. 40–42. Cleveland: Pilgrim Press.

Episcopal News Service (2022) 'Transgender Priests Ask Church to Live Fully into LGBTQ+ InclusionDuring Executive Council Plenary Session". 26 January. Available at: https://episcopalnewsservice.org/2022/01/26/transgender-priests-ask-church-to-live-fully-into-lgbtq-inclusion-during-executive-council-plenary-session/ (Accessed: January 2026).

Goh, J. N. (2020) 'Trans/Forming Church in the Asia Pacific Region: Narratives of Hospitable Ecclesiology by Philippine and Tongan Transgender Women'. *QUEST: Studies on Religion & Culture in Asia, 4*. Available at: www.theology.cuhk.edu.hk/quest/index.php/quest/article/view/75 (Accessed: January 2026).

Greenough, C. (2018) *Undoing Theology: Life Stories from Non-Normative Christians*. London: SCM Press.

Greenough, C. (2023) 'Eve and the Punishment of Heterosexuality'. In Blyth, C. and Colgan, E. (Eds.) *The Routledge Companion to Eve*, pp. 398–410. Abingdon: Routledge.

Guest, D. (2016) 'Modelling the Transgender Gaze: Performances of Masculinities in 2 Kings 9–10'. In Hornsby, T. and Guest, D. (Eds.) *Transgender, Intersex, and Biblical Interpretation*, pp. 45–80. Atlanta: SBL Press.

Hartke, A. (2018) *Transforming: The Bible and the Lives of Transgender Christians*. Louisville: Westminster John Knox Press.

Henderson-Merrygold, J. (2020) 'Gendering Sarai: Reading Beyond Cisnormativity in Genesis 11:29–12:20 and 20:1–18'. *Open Theology*, *6*(1), pp. 496–509.

Hornsby, T. and Guest, D. (Eds.) (2016) *Transgender, Intersex, and Biblical Interpretation*. Atlanta: SBL Press.

Kearns, S. T. L. (2022) *In the Margins: A Transgender Man's Journey with Scripture*. Grand Rapids: Eerdmans.

Ladin, J. (2025) 'Beyond the Trans/Cis Binary: An Experience-Centered Approach to Teaching and Practicing Trans Hermeneutics'. In Marchal, J. A., Sellew, M. H. and Valentine, K. E. (Eds.) *Trans Biblical: New Approaches to Interpretation and Embodiment in Scripture*, pp. 47–64. Louisville: Westminster John Knox Press.

Lowe, M. E. (2017) 'From the Same Spirit: Receiving the Theological Gifts of Transgender Christians'. *Dialog: A Journal of Theology*, *56*(1), pp. 28–37.

Marchal, J. A., Sellew, M. H. and Valentine, K. E. (2025) 'Introduction: Variations on Interpretation and Embodiment: Contextualizing Trans Approaches to Scripture'. In Marchal, J. A., Sellew, M. H. and Valentine, K. E. (Eds.) *Trans Biblical: New Approaches to Interpretation and Embodiment in Scripture*, pp. 1–29. Louisville: Westminster John Knox Press.

McCall Tigert, L. and Tirabassi, M. C. (Eds.) (2004) *Transgendering Faith: Identity, Sexuality and Spirituality*. Cleveland: Pilgrim Press.

McMahon, M. (2016) 'Trans Liberating Feminist and Queer Theologies'. In Beardsley, C. and O'Brien, M. (Eds.) *This Is My Body: Hearing the Theology of Transgender Christians*, pp. 59–68. London: Darton, Longman and Todd.

Musa, A. W. (2020) 'Jael Is Non-Binary; Jael Is Not a Woman'. *Journal for Interdisciplinary Biblical Studies*, *1*(2), pp. 97–120.

Sabia-Tanis, J. (2025) 'Walking While Trans on the Jericho Road'. In Marchal, J. A. et al. (Eds.) *Trans Biblical: New Approaches to Interpretation and Embodiment in Scripture*, pp. 99–116. Louisville: Westminster John Knox Press.

Strassfeld, M. (2025) 'Androgynes, Hybrid Animals, and the Project of Trans History'. In Marchal, J. A. et al. (Eds.) *Trans Biblical: New Approaches to Interpretation and Embodiment in Scripture*, pp. 31–46. Louisville: Westminster John Knox Press.

Tanis, J. (2018) *Trans-Gendered: Theology, Ministry, and Communities of Faith*. Cleveland: Pilgrim Press.

Taylder, S. (2009) 'Shot from Both Sides: Theology and the Woman Who Isn't Quite What She Seems'. In Althaus-Reid, M. and Isherwood, L. (Eds.) *Trans/formations*, pp. 70–91. London: SCM Press.

The Episcopal Church (2012) *Journal of the 77th General Convention*. Available at: https://extranet.generalconvention.org/staff/files/download/9899.pdf (Accessed: January 2026).

The Episcopal Church (2018) *Resolution 2018-C054: Guiding Principles for the Inclusion of Transgender and Non-Binary People*. Available at: https://digitalarchives.episcopalarchives.org/cgi-bin/acts/acts_resolution-complete.pl?resolution=2018-C054 (Accessed: January 2026).

The Episcopal Church (2025) *Affirming Our Values: Affirming Transgender and Non-Binary People*. Available at: www.episcopalchurch.org/ogr/affirming-our-values/ (Accessed: January 2026).

AFTERWORD
Beyond the basics

This short concluding section considers the impact and issues of queer theologies in the public sphere, noting that engaging with queer theologies is a political and practical task. Suggestions for further reading in the area are also given, including advice for those who wish to go beyond the basics.

> Queer theology throws open the shutters, allowing the sun to stream in, and showing up just how dusty and threadbare some of those theological rugs really are.
>
> (Cornwall, 2011: 252)

Some dusty and threadbare theological rugs are cherished as heirlooms, handed down with sentimentality having served a purpose for Christian thought throughout the ages. What is trash to one person is treasure to another. This means that there are tensions between queer theologies and mainstream theologies. Deryn Guest describes queer as 'the critical undo-er … an approach that squatted everywhere but refused to be defined or packaged, it managed to upset everyone' (Guest, 2012: 43). Within queer theologies, the upset extends beyond the academy, as church and state hold stakes in theological conversations. Public institutions are interwoven with long histories of religious influence. While queer theologies resist and interrogate mainstream theologies, mainstream theologies may resist the queer project. Sara Ahmed notes how, 'when we speak about what we come up against, we come up against what we speak about. Another way of saying: walls come up when we talk about walls' (Ahmed, 2017: 148).

Christian theology is over 2,000 years old, yet queer Christian theologies are still breaking their teeth, as queer theory was first coined by Teresa de Lauretis in 1990. Trans theologies are even more recent. Within the academy, there is much rich, intellectual attention given to queer theologies; the basics of such work are presented throughout the pages of this book. As has been discussed, across churches there are ongoing heated and muddled conversations around the issues of LGBTQ+ inclusion. In society, there are debates and repercussions for those who subvert normative gender and sexuality, and this is further compacted in contexts where legislative measures do not exist in order to protect individual characteristics or where legislative gains are reversed.

Even in countries with such legal positions, prejudice and discrimination still exist. Gender, sexuality, and religion are core identity categories in law and society, but sometimes they collide. In the public sphere, this can be seen in media reports of customer service assistants who refuse to serve same-sex couples, grounding their refusal in their religious beliefs. Where there are tensions, there is still much work to be done. The triad of academy, church, and state mean that queer theologies disrupt different systems and are taken up in different ways. Whether they are considered self-indulgent, too personal, too intellectual, or too theoretical, future queer theologies must pay attention to Isherwood and Althaus-Reid's injunction that 'queering theology is not a rhetorical pastime but a political duty' (Isherwood & Althaus-Reid, 2004: 3). Or, as Jeff Hood states, 'theology without the practical is dead, and dead theologies do not bring about the resurrection. I seek theology that speaks life into death' (Hood, 2015: 1).

Queer theologies disrupt the stability of identity and tackle the power structures at play in identity construction. Queer has also been used as a catch-all collective term for LGBTQ+ identities, although as a theory, it was never intended to function in this way. Given these two functions – disruption of identities and critical analysis of theology in light of identities – queer theologies are always plural. They speak in different languages and cover a range of issues and methods. Queer theologies do not even agree with one another. One of the delights in researching this area of study is to explore the range of topics and approaches on offer.

In suggesting helpful ways for the motivated reader to move beyond the basics, it is recommended to engage with the suggested reading, resources, and references in each chapter. To offer one important piece of advice: these texts can be challenging and complex, offering ideas which delight and confuse within the pages.

A final reminder: queer theologies cannot be captured; they are fluid, dynamic, and ever evolving. This book is not the final word on the topic, but simply is offered as part of an ongoing conversation and evolution.

REFERENCES

Ahmed, S. (2017) *Living a Feminist Life*. Durham: Duke University Press.

Cornwall, S. (2011) *Controversies in Queer Theology*. London: SCM Press.

Guest, D. (2012) *Beyond Feminist Biblical Studies*. Sheffield: Sheffield Phoenix Press.

Hood, J. (2015) *The Courage to Be Queer*. Eugene: Wipf and Stock.

Isherwood, L. and Althaus-Reid, M. (2004) 'Queering Theology'. In Althaus-Reid, M. and Isherwood, L. (Eds.) *The Sexual Theologian*, pp. 1–15. London: Continuum.

GLOSSARY

ABSTINENCE	The act of restraining oneself from something, including sex.
AGENDER	A person who self-identifies as without a gender identity.
ALLOSEXUAL	Someone who experiences sexual attraction; the opposite of asexual.
ALLY	A person who actively supports and advocates for a marginalised group to which they do not belong.
ANGLICAN COMMUNION	A group of worldwide churches historically based on the Church of England.
ANOINTING OF THE SICK	A sacrament in the Roman Catholic Church to bless the sick.
APOLOGETICS	The defence of Christian religious doctrine through reasoned arguments.

AROMANTIC	A person who experiences little or no romantic attraction to others.
ASEXUALITY	A lack of sexual attraction to others.
AUTOSEXUAL	A person who experiences sexual attraction primarily or exclusively toward themselves.
BAPTISM	A rite of admission to the Christian Church, through sprinkling of water or full immersion in water.
BDSM	Bondage, discipline/dominance, submission/sadism, masochism.
BIBLIOLATRY	Worship of the Bible.
BIGENDER	A person who experiences two gender identities, either simultaneously or at different times.
BINARY	Two opposites.
BISEXUALITY	Experience of sexual attraction to more than one gender.
BODY OF CHRIST	Two definitions in Christianity. (i) Jesus's words at the Last Supper: 'This is my body', in Luke 22:19–20; (ii) used to refer to the Christian Church.
CAMINATA	A walk (Spanish). Based on the theology of Marcella Althaus-Reid, this is the act of practical theology, of walking with one's community.
CAPITALISM	An economic system of private ownership used to generate profits.
CATHOLIC CHURCH	Branch of the Christian Church which accepts the Pope as its leader and is based in Rome.
CELIBACY	Deliberate choice to abstain from sexual relations.
CHASTITY	The practice of expressing sexuality according to a moral or religious code.

CHICANA	A girl or woman of Mexican origin and descent.
CHRISTOLOGY	The study of the person, nature, and role of Christ in Christian theology.
CISNORMATIVITY	The assumption that everyone identifies with the sex they were assigned at birth.
COMING OUT	A metaphor relating to the self-disclosure of one's sexual orientation or gender identity.
CONFIRMATION	The rite in which a baptised person affirms their Christian belief as a full member of the Church.
CONSENT	To give permission (in a sexual context, freely given and informed).
CRUISING	To search for a sexual partner.
DEADNAMING	Calling a trans or non-binary person by the name assigned to them at birth, rather than their current name. It is offensive and harmful.
DECONSTRUCTION	A method of critical analysis that examines how meaning is constructed and how texts may have multiple interpretations.
DEMISEXUAL	Considered half-way between sexual and asexual; a person who does not feel a sexual connection without an emotional connection.
DIASPORA	A group of people who spread from one original country to others.
DOCTRINAL	Concerned with a set of beliefs traditionally held and taught by the Church.
DOGMA	A system of principles/beliefs set out as undeniably true.

ECCLESIASTIC	Relating to the church and/or its clergy.
EUCHARIST	A sacrament commemorating the Last Supper in Christian services.
EUNUCH	Generally used in ancient times to denote a man who has been castrated.
EUROCENTRIC	Focused on European culture, history or philosophy.
EX-GAY	A controversial term used to describe someone who claims to have changed their homosexual orientation, often associated with conversion therapy, which is widely criticised and considered harmful.
FEMINISM	The advocacy of women's rights, examining how inequalities between men and women should be challenged.
FIRST-WAVE FEMINISM	A period of feminist activity in the 19th and early 20th centuries which focused on legal rights for women, particularly the right to vote.
GENDER-FLUID	A person whose gender identity changes over time.
GENDERQUEER	A person who does not identify with a particular gender but may identify as neither male nor female, both, or a combination of binary genders.
GREY-ASEXUAL	Between sexuality and asexuality; someone identifying as grey-asexual may only experience sexual attraction occasionally.
HEGEMONIC	Ruling or dominant.

HERMENEUTICS	The area of study that deals with the interpretation of the Bible.
HETERONORMATIVITY	The idea that heterosexuality is the normal sexual orientation.
HETEROSEXISM	Discrimination against homosexuality on the grounds that one considers heterosexuality to be the normal sexual orientation.
HETEROSEXUALITY	Attraction to the opposite sex or people of a different gender.
HETERO-SUSPICION	A method of removing the presumption that all people are heterosexual.
HISTORICAL-CRITICISM	The study of the worlds and origins of ancient texts.
HOLY ORDERS	A rite of passage to religious orders; ordination as a member of the clergy.
HOMOSEXUALITY	Sexual attraction to people of the same sex or gender.
INCARNATION	When a deity takes human form. In Christian theology, the person of Jesus Christ, God as human incarnate.
INTERSECTIONALITY	A framework that shows how systems of oppression and discrimination are multiple. The most marginalised people therefore fall under multiple minority groups.
INTERSEX	A person born with sex characteristics that do not fit typical definitions of male or female bodies.
JUBILEES	An event celebrated by African American communities to mark the end of slavery, based on Leviticus 25:9–10.

KINKY	Non-normative sexual interests or practices.
LATINX	A gender-neutral term for a person of Latin American origin, used instead of Latino/Latina.
LGBTQ+	Lesbian, gay, bisexual, trans, and queer (+ other non-normative expressions of gender and identity).
LITERARY CRITICISM	In religious studies, the practice of viewing the Bible as a suitable object for literary study rather than as an exclusively sacred text.
LITURGY	A particular form of worship.
MESTIZA	In Latin America, a woman of mixed race.
MISOGYNY	Dislike or contempt for women.
MONOGAMY	Having a romantic or marital relationship with one person at a time.
MONOLITHIC	Something that is large, united, and difficult to change.
NON-BINARY	Someone whose gender identity is neither male nor female.
NON-NORMATIVE	Not conforming to normative expectations of gender and/or sexuality.
NORMATIVITY	Relating to a standard expectation.
PAGANISM	A range of spiritual beliefs and practices, including nature worship, different from those in mainstream world religions.
PANSEXUALITY	A form of sexuality where preference is not limited by gender identity.
PATRIARCHY	A society or community in which men hold power and women are largely excluded.

PNEUMATOLOGY	The study of the Holy Spirit in Christian theology.
POLARI	A form of gay slang, formerly used by gay people.
POLYSEXUALITY	Sexual attraction to more than one gender.
POST-CHRISTIAN	Someone who chooses to distance themselves from the language and assumptions of traditional Christianity, including sexism.
POSTCOLONIALISM	The study or examination of the lasting impact of colonialism, including the cultural legacy of control and exploitation.
POSTMODERNISM	The theory that there is no absolute truth, that in the postmodern world everything is shaped by the cultural context of a particular time, place and community.
POST-STRUCTURALISM	A critical theory that rejects framework and structure as methods of analysis.
PRO-FEMINIST	A commitment to challenge sexism and gender injustice; someone in favour of supporting feminism.
PURITY	The belief that not having sex is morally good.
QUEER	(i) (verb) to disturb, disrupt, spoil or ruin; (ii) (noun) someone who is non-normative.
QUEER THEORY	A critical theory which works to disrupt normative ways of thinking.
QUESTIONING	Someone who is questioning their sexual identity.

RECEPTION CRITICISM (READER-RESPONSE)	How a text, such as the Bible, has been received by the reader and how their position informs their reading of the text.
RECLAMATION	The act of claiming something back.
RECONCILIATION	A sacrament in Roman Catholicism where an individual acknowledges their sins to a priest and is absolved of them.
RE-ENGAGEMENT	An act of engaging with something again.
RESISTANCE	The refusal to accept or comply with something.
RUPTURE	The act of breaking away from something.
SECOND-WAVE FEMINISM	A period of feminist activities from the 1960s which lasted approximately two decades, including activist activity relating to the workplace, sexuality, and reproductive rights for women.
SLAVE SPIRITUALS	A Christian song which describes the hard and difficult oppressions experienced under slavery.
STRAIGHT	Heterosexual.
SYSTEMATIC THEOLOGY	In theology, systematic theology formulates ordered and reasoned accounts of Christian doctrines, looking at what the Bible teaches or what is known and true about God.

TRANS/TRANSGENDER	A person whose gender identity does not correspond to their sex assigned at birth.
TRANS MAN	Someone who was assigned female at birth but transitions to live as a man.
TRANSSEXUAL	An older term referring to a person who seeks medical transition; in contemporary language, many prefer the term transgender.
TRANS WOMAN	Someone assigned male at birth but transitions to live as a woman.
VIRGINITY	The state of never having experienced sexual intercourse.
WESTERN	Relating to the countries of Europe and North America.
WOMANIST	A feminist of colour.

BIBLICAL REFERENCES INDEX

Genesis
1 121
1:27 108, 109, 167, 182
3:16 182
3:17–19 182
9:7 148
17:5 179
17:17—19 182
19 106
19:5–8 105

Exodus 116, 118, 120, 129
20:4 49

Leviticus
18:22 104, 106, 124
20:13 104
25:9–10 198

Deuteronomy
22:5 181
23:1 109, 179, 181, 183

Ruth 114, 116
1:16–17 113–114

1 Samuel
16:18 112
18:1–5 112

2 Samuel
1:26 113
6:20 113
6:21–23 113

Proverbs
13:20 126

Isaiah
43:1 178
56:4 110, 183
56:5 110, 179

Lamentations 119

Matthew
5:11–12 181
19:12 110, 183
22:39 164

Mark 127
10:46–52 128
12:31 164

Luke
10:27 164
22:19–20 195

John 61, 124–5
3:16 124

Acts of the Apostles
8 183
8:36–39 110
13:9 179

Romans 91
1:26–27 104–6
5:3–5 181

1 Corinthians
6:9 105, 106
6:9–10 111
7 149

2 Corinthians
3:6 102

Galatians 57, 122–3
3:28 182

1 Timothy
1:10 105, 106

AUTHOR INDEX

Ahmed, Sara 69, 192
Alksnitis, Dzintra 180
Althaus-Reid, Marcella 33, 38–46, 48, 51, 56. 58, 60, 71, 80–1, 94, 127–8, 135, 140, 150–3, 162, 166, 187, 192, 195
Anzaldúa, Gloria 70, 73, 82, 93

Bailey, Derrick Sherwin 103
Baldwin, James 86
Barker, Meg-John 34
Beardsley, Christina 162, 187
Boer, Roland 120
Bohache, Thomas 130
Bong, Sharon 69–70, 73, 75, 93
Braunston, Andy 53
Buechel, Andy 58
Burrus, Virginia 48
Butler, Judith 24, 28–9, 31

Cabrera, Oscar 128
Carrette, Jeremy 47
Carvalhaes, Claudio 81
Cervantes Ortiz, Leopoldo 42
Chan, Pui-man 74
Cheng, Patrick 8, 46, 62, 64, 72–4, 93, 95, 122–3
Cherry, Kittredge 49–50
Chitando, Ezra 77
Clare-Young, Alex 165, 170, 173–5, 177, 178, 180, 182, 187
Coblentz, Jessica 148
Comstock, Gary David 18
Cone, James 83
Cooper, Brittney 86
Cooper, Thia 64
Córdova Quero, Martin Hugo 47–8, 75
Cornwall, Susannah 18, 34, 40, 41, 60–1, 69, 89–90, 93–4, 110, 147, 151, 156, 191
Cox, Jillian 91–2
Crenshaw, Kimberlé 27

da Silva, Fernando Candino 127
Daly, Mary 14, 152
de Beauvoir, Simone 22
De Gruchy, Steve 77

De La Torre, Miguel 82
de Lauretis, Teresa 29, 192
de Saussure, Ferdinand 21–2
Derrida, Jacques 22
Dickinson, Colby 94, 139–40
Dinham, Adam 9
Donis, Alex 49
Douglas, Kelly Brown 84, 96, 128
Dowd, Chris 162
Dresser, Terry 162, 173

Edward, Mark 9

Finley, Stephen 85
Ford, Michael 141
Foucault, Michel 23–4, 28, 31, 68
Francis, Matthew 9

Garrigan, Siobhan 54
Germond, Paul 77
Gill, Sean 19
Glaser, Chris 62–3
Goh, Joseph 74, 75, 95, 123–4, 176–7
González Ortuño, Gabriela 80
Goss, Robert 19, 20, 34, 59, 61–2, 68, 87–8, 104, 107, 130
Greenough, Chris 9, 51, 130, 141, 147, 150, 153, 157, 178, 182
Gross, Sallie 109
Guest, Deryn 33, 56, 102, 114–19, 130, 150, 156, 181, 191
Gunda, Masiiwa Ragies 126
Gutiérrez, Gustavo 12

Halperin, David 30
Hampson, Daphne 16
Harrelson, Becki Jane 49
Hartke, Austen 164, 165, 170
Henderson-Espinoza, Robyn 82
Henderson-Merrygold, Jo 185
Hinkle, Christopher 49
Hirano, Kunisuke 75
Hollywood, Amy 48
Hood, Jeff 192
hooks, bell 24, 27
Horie, Yuri 75
Hornsby, Teresa 114, 181

Isherwood, Lisa 41, 44, 94, 162, 166, 197, 192

Jagose, Annamarie 31
Jordan, Mark 89

Kapya, John Kaoma 77
Kelly, Michael Bernard 191
Kinsey, Alfred 16
Koch, Timothy 103, 115
Kornegay, EL 85–5
Kuruvilla, Philip 76
Kwok, Pui-lan 68, 75, 124, 151

Ladin, Joy 185
Larrimore, Mark 51–2
Liew, Tat-siong Benny 124–5
Lightsey, Pamela 84, 86–7, 96, 129
Lim, You-Leng Lroy 123
Lorde, Audre 24, 27
Loughlin, Gerard 7, 39, 46, 47, 61, 64, 69, 89
Lowe, Mary 180
Lyon, Phyllis 18

Marchal, Joseph 182, 183, 185
Martin, Del 18
Martin, James 121
McFague, Sallie 15–16
McMahon, Mercia 175, 184
Meyerhoff, Miriam 28
Musa, Aysha W. 185

Nelson, James 88
Nickoloff, James 81–2
Nixon, David 140

Obadare, Ebenezer 95
O'Brien, Michelle 162, 187
Ohlson Wallin, Elisabeth 49

Panotto, Nicolas 81, 96
Petrella, Ivan 12
Phiri, Lilly 76, 78–9, 94
Punt, Jeremy 69

Rajkumar, Vincent 76
Rangiwai, Byron 93
Rich, Adrienne 24–5, 29, 76
Robinson, Brandan 157
Robinson, Margaret 90–1
Rubin, Gayle 24–6, 29
Ruether, Rosemary Radford 14–15

Sabia-Tanis, Justin 117, 162, 164, 185
Sander, David 92
Scheele, Julia 34
Sedgwick, Eve Kosofsky 29–30
Sneed, Roger 84–5
Spelman, Elizabeth 31
Strassfeld, Max 184
Stringer, Martin 53–4
Stuart, Elizabeth 19–20, 34, 38–41, 46, 47, 51–3, 56–60, 64, 102–3, 121, 148
Sugirtharajah, Rasiah 70, 73
Sweasey, Peter 89

Taylder, Siân 166
Thatcher, Adrian 88–9, 102, 123, 131
Thomas, Calvin 30
Thoreson, Ryan 79
Toft, Alex 108, 143, 145
Tolbert, Mary Ann 72, 120–1
Tonstad, Linn 38, 50, 64
Toomey, Meghan 94, 139–40
Toy, Michael Jonathan 92

van der Walt, Charlene 77
van Klinken, Adriaan 94, 95, 76–80, 126

Walker, Alice 27
Warner, Michael 29
West, Gerald 77–8
West, Mona 107, 118, 130
Wilcox, Melissa 108, 143–5, 154–5, 157
Williams, Delores 83–4
Wilson, Jan 92
Wilson, Nancy 106–7, 114
Wittig, Monique 24, 26

Yip, Andrew 108, 142–4
Yip, Lai-shan 74

Zachariah, George 76

For Product Safety Concerns and Information please contact our EU representative GPSR@taylorandfrancis.com
Taylor & Francis Verlag GmbH, Kaufingerstraße 24, 80331 München, Germany

www.ingramcontent.com/pod-product-compliance
Ingram Content Group UK Ltd.
Pitfield, Milton Keynes, MK11 3LW, UK
UKHW021425020726
472852UK00004B/65

* 9 7 8 1 0 3 2 5 6 3 3 5 0 *